Contents

Preface to the English Edition   ix

The Background

The collapse of western Europe: out of
   Egypt into the desert   1
The relics of classical education   7
The educational reforms of Charlemagne   12
The monasteries and civilization   13
The seven liberal arts   15
Theology in the footsteps of the Fathers   24
'Dionysius' and the hierarchical vision of
   the world   26
The fourfold sense of the Scriptures   28
Worldly wisdom and the wisdom of God   31
The literature of the monasteries   35
A world of tangible concepts   38
Platonism and humanism in the Middle
   Ages   40
A day at Chartres   42
Medical and humane learning   44
The cathedral schools transcend the
   monasteries   49

The New Learning

Pierre Abélard, the first 'academic'   53
The 'old' logic   55
Porphyry and the universals   58
The *Categories*   61
Propositions and oppositions   62
Definition: capturing the essence of things   64

The beginnings of judicial scholasticism 65

The glossators of Bologna 67

Canon law and the beginnings of historical
  criticism 73

The *Decree* of Gratian 76

The logic of revelation 78

Abélard: reason takes precedence over faith 81

Bernhard of Clairvaux the
  antidialectician 83

The form of the lecture is established 85

Lombard – 'the master of the Sentence' 87

The 'new' logic 92

'Dialectical' scholarship: the art of
  convincing 95

Sophistry: the art of deceiving 97

The beginnings of the academic approach I:
  syllogisms 99

The beginnings of the academic approach
  II: the universal proposition 103

The new professionalism 106

The new physics 108

The Aristotelian picture of the world 110

Aristotelian psychology 112

Aristotelian metaphysics 117

Arabic philosophy: Aristotle meets Allah 121

The University: Form and Contents

The origin of the University of Paris – a
  social invention 125

Freedom within limits 129

Resistance and submission 133

Privileges, the organization of faculties and
  the office of rector 135

Bologna – student democracy and the
  nations 138

The World of
Medieval Learning

Anders Piltz

The World of Medieval Learning

translated into English by David Jones

Basil Blackwell · Oxford

English translation © Basil Blackwell 1981

First published as *Medeltidens lärda värld*, 1978, by
Bokförlaget Carmina, Stockholm

First published (revised edition) in Great Britain in 1981 by
Basil Blackwell Publisher
108 Cowley Road
Oxford OX4 1JF
England

British Library Cataloguing in Publication Data
Piltz, Anders
The world of medieval learning
1. Universities and colleges – Europe – History
I. Title   II. Jones, David
378.4   LA267

ISBN 0-631-12712-7

1003792026

Typeset in Monotype Plantin
by Cotswold Typesetting Ltd, Gloucester
and printed in Great Britain by
The Camelot Press, Southampton

Lectures and degrees   143
Theology challenged by Aristotle   145
Lectio and disputation   148
Medical theory . . .   150
. . . and practice   153

Scholasticism: the Masters and their
    Schools

The mendicant orders reach Paris   159
The seraphic doctor: knowledge and
    wisdom   163
Research with awe   168
Oxford – experiment and experience   170
Albertus Magnus the Encyclopaedist   174
The complete Aristotle direct from the
    Greek   178
Aristotle's *Ethics*   179
Aristotle's *Politics*   183
Thomas and the scholastic synthesis   185
Theology – the study of the meaning of life   187
The language of mystery   189
Authority and common sense   193
Grace perfects nature   196
Dazzled by the obvious   198
The creation, the existence of God and the
    problem of evil   201
The senses, instinct, imagination, thought
    and the memory   204
Reason and nature as the highest norms   209
The Garden of Eden and the distortion of
    natural order   211
Self-fulfilment in this world and the next   214
The state, democracy and 'the rational
    distinction'   216

The art of memory I: grammar, conduct
and the essence of the true schoolboy   219

The art of memory II: the abbot and the
wild boar   223

The double-truth theory and intelligence as
a source of enjoyment   227

Scepticism, delusion and the absence of free
will   230

'Sortes' and sophistry   233
The modists and Occam's razor   238
Duns Scotus and the 'formalities'   240
The primacy of will over intellect   243
Occam: the universals as labels   245
A capricious God and a frail universe   247
Via antiqua and via moderna   251
A freshman's handbook about the 'ways'   258
Epilogue   261

Texts   265
Notes and References   283
Chronology   289
Index   293

Preface to the English Edition

For three centuries, from the thirteenth century until the revolutionary changes that took place at the beginning of the sixteenth century, all the people in Europe with any claim to education at all could make themselves understood to each other. This was not only because they shared a common language in Latin. What is even more remarkable is that they shared a common world picture and uniform terminology for describing it. Anyone taking part in a discussion or an argument knew the exact meaning of the terms he used, and so did his adversaries. Profound disagreement might exist about the issue under debate, but this disagreement was not the result of using the same terms to mean different things. During this period scholars were using in their thought processes what were literally the same categories: they referred to the same interior landscape.

This work is an attempt to present an alien world so that its main features at least are reasonably comprehensible for anyone who takes pleasure in confronting his own intellectual habits, his ways of thinking and his attitudes, with those of cultures which are remote from his own in time or in space. If it succeeds in arousing interest in only a few aspects of medieval culture, its modest aim will have been achieved.

For this reason the book concentrates on just those features of medieval culture that are dismissed in standard surveys of literary history as quaint examples of scholasticism. This is an undertaking that can be criticized as being as foolhardy as the proposal (which has probably never been seriously considered) to publish Kant's *Critique of Pure Reason* as a book-of-the-month selection. Whether such an objection is a fair one can best be judged by the reader. However, in writing this book I have had to guard against two different temptations: over-simplification and over-elaboration. No single volume can do justice to the complexity of the medieval world of learning. Today when medieval intellectual concepts are becoming increasingly remote, not least because of the decline in the study of Latin, there may, nevertheless, be some justification for a book such as this which has the limited aim of presenting some of the most important elements in the educational ideals of the period and the terminology that was used to deal with them. The standard textbooks on medieval philosophy tend to deter any reader who has no specialized knowledge of the history of ideas and some acquaintance with Latin because they are apt to go into immense detail and presume a fair degree of familiarity with the jargon of the schoolmen.

In selecting the individual thinkers dealt with in this book the main criterion has been the influence they have had on their contemporaries and on posterity. This has meant that several interesting figures have been ignored. A major proportion of the book is devoted to Thomas Aquinas, at the expense of other important scholars. This does not mean that other works of the period should be regarded as interesting only insofar as they help to elucidate the text of his *Summa*.

Good textbooks on medieval literary history can be found in more or less every public library and for this reason the book does not go into the literature of the period in any detail. The development of the natural sciences in the Middle Ages has only been described in the broadest outlines. The primary concern of the book is to enable the reader to understand some fundamental elements in the common stock of knowledge that was available to every medieval student. Many of these concepts and lines of thought have survived the Middle Ages, either in their original form or in an adulterated variant. A surprisingly large number of the international words used in everyday speech stem from the Middle Ages. For this reason the key terms have been printed in the margin of the text.

Some Latin texts are provided at the end of the book. This has not been done to frighten off readers who cannot read Latin but to give those who can a chance to gain an idea of the atmosphere of the academic world in the Middle Ages.

Uppsala, January 1980   **Anders Piltz**

The Background

The collapse of western Europe: out of Egypt into the desert

Try the following experiment.

Imagine that a series of sudden wars and catastrophes has left our society unable to function. Trade and commerce break down completely and the specialization that they have given rise to has to be replaced by self-supporting villages and communities. The international trade routes are no longer used and only very seldom do travellers appear who are able to give any news about life outside the immediate horizon. News is nearly always bad news: a gang of wandering bandits has attacked a neighbouring village killing and raping the inhabitants and burning the buildings. If one is lucky, one can, for a generous fee, purchase the protection of some hardy and enterprising gangster. The central authorities, once so well-organized and respected, have faded into an abstract concept that only the old can say anything about. The most complex and best-maintained administrative system that the world has yet seen has, quite simply, ceased to exist. Cultural activities do not even cross one's mind: the immediate needs of everyday living leave no time to worry about books or their fate. The literature and systems of thought that have been created up to now can at best survive in random collections of fragments where some parts of individual libraries have, by some accident of fate, escaped being burnt or destroyed in some other way. Anyone who, for some extraordinary reason, in the generation following the great catastrophe, can still read would gain his impression of the philosophy and poetry of the past from what other people could tell him and the few written remnants he might come across: an anthology for instance, a few portions of a historical treatise, or some pages of advice on husbandry.

rtes oratio
nis quot suut
Octo . Que .
Nomen . pro
nomé . verbũ
aduerbium .
participium .
coniuntio . pr
epositio . inter
iectio . Nomé
quid é . Pars
orationis . cum casu . corpus
aut rem proprie conmuniter ue
significás . Propzie ut roma ty b
eris . Cõmuniter ut urbis . Nume
Nominum quot accidũt . sex . Que
Qualitas . cõparatio . genus . nu

Most people today have, at some time, toyed with the idea that our incredibly complicated civilization could destroy itself and end up in the same position as the one described here, the position of the Roman Empire after the convulsions caused by the migrations of the Germanic tribes. This collapse would no doubt occur more quickly nowadays as specialization has been carried very much further today and the technology which controls every moment of our life is very vulnerable. But the barbarization that began in western Europe in the fifth century AD was a surprisingly fast process. By the seventh century the principal countries of the continent had been enveloped by the great silence.

It is however easy to exaggerate. It is by no means correct to maintain, as so many have done, that all intellectual activity became extinct for several centuries. There are signs suggesting that the school system of antiquity – and before the catastrophe every self-respecting town had its own school – continued to exist in some form in the towns of northern Italy.

What is more important is that one organization survived that did preserve elements of the old system of civil administration: that was the catholic Church. On the whole the bishoprics corresponded to the administrative units of the Roman Empire. Latin, the literary language of Rome, lived on in the liturgy of the Church and was used in its administration. International contacts continued to take place within the Church. This state of affairs meant that as priests-to-be were forced to learn the official language of the Church as a foreign language – and this was true for

Fig. 1. The beginning of Donatus' grammar (*The Donet*), which was the obligatory basic textbook in the schools of the Middle Ages. The elaborately decorated capital P has been chosen by the printer for aesthetic reasons and not because it has anything to do with the contents of the text. This combination illustrates the fact that the Church was responsible for almost all schooling in the Middle Ages, cf. p. 19. *Donatus,* printed by Lienhart Ysenhut in Basle around 1500.

3

Germans, Irishmen and Englishmen – they were to an ever-increasing extent brought into some contact, however modest, with the secular culture, literature and learning of antiquity. The Church had no generally agreed attitude to secular knowledge and was therefore forced to adopt a standpoint to the pagan culture it had inherited. The Church had no philosophy of its own which could provide an alternative attractive to the seeker after intellectually acceptable truth; its commandments were not in the first place based on rational concepts. The Church lived, breathed and had its being in a world of Semitic images with parables and symbols pointing towards a higher and invisible reality. The Church's favourite image of itself was as the new, true Israel which had escaped from captivity in Egypt, which was taken to mean a world obsessed by itself and its blind greed, to be rescued from the tyranny of the Pharaoh – the devil – by the miraculous crossing of the Red Sea – baptism – and was now on its trek through the desert – life on earth – towards the Promised Land – the heavenly Jerusalem. During this difficult and perilous march through the desert its people were sustained by heavenly manna – the Eucharist. From such a perspective as this, secular wisdom would rather be seen as deceptive distractions, tempting mirages in the desert intended to divert attention from the only necessities, sacrifices to the golden calf, paths leading away from the road laid down by the second Moses, Christ Himself.

Attitudes to the blessings of civilization were therefore ambiguous during the first centuries of the Church's existence. But a succession of very gifted men were gradually to succeed in reconciling the apparently irreconcilable to such a point that they became impossible to sunder: the Church was to end up as the final refuge and surety for education.

Since Paul the Apostle no single person has meant so much for the intellectual features of western Europe as Augustine (354–430), the bishop and philosopher. After a large number of deviations from the true path in his youth, he became a devoted Christian and struggled with the problem of how the splendours of heathen civilization – splendours he had studied closely – should be judged in relation to the supreme revelation of truth, the manifestation of God Himself in the

4

Word made flesh. Augustine came to the following conclusion and it was used right through the Middle Ages to gag the anti-intellectual tendencies of Christian 'radicals'.

Fig. 2. Before fleeing from captivity in Egypt, the children of Israel had claimed jewels of gold and silver and raiment. 'And the Lord gave the people favour in the sight of the Egyptians, so that they lent unto them such things as they required. And they spoiled the Egyptians.' (Exodus 12:35–6). Then they went out into the desert and sacrificed the paschal lamb. For Augustine and for medieval man this account had obvious significance. The spoils taken from the Egyptians – the vessels of gold and the clothes – symbolize heathen philosophy and social institutions. The Christian Church, journeying through the deserts of time towards the promised land, feeds off the true Paschal Lamb, Jesus Christ. It is God's intention that the spoils that have been taken shall be used in the true service of God. This reading of the narrative made the study of the culture of antiquity a legitimate part of the educational activities of the Church. Illustration from a German Bible printed by Heinrich Quentell in Cologne around 1479.

The Egyptians did not only have images of goods and heavy burdens that the Israelites hated and fled from. They also had vessels and ornaments of gold and silver and clothes and the Israelites secretly laid claim to them when they left Egypt so that they could make better use of them, not on their own authority but because the Egyptians without knowing what they were doing gave away, at God's command, the possessions they themselves abused. In the same way the teachings of the pagan writers not only contain products of their imagination and superstitious misconceptions, a heavy ballast of wasted effort, which each and every one of us must hate and avoid when we leave pagan society but also the liberal sciences which are very suitable for the new life in freedom. In them can be found invaluable ethical rules and many truths about the worship of the one God. What the Israelites claimed was the gold and silver that the Egyptians had not themselves produced. The providence of God had sealed it into the veins of ore which can be discovered everywhere. In their blindness the Egyptians abused these gifts in the worship of images. When the Christian inwardly flees from such miserable fellowship he should also take what riches he can so that they may serve their true purpose: the preaching of the gospel. Clothing, that is to say human institutions which are necessary for this life, prerequisites for society's functioning, may be taken over and used after they have first been Christianized.[1]

Civilization and all its products have for Augustine value in preparing people for Christianity; they enable Christians to reach the true riches. The treasure of Egypt would be found in Jerusalem, the goal of the long journey, refined and ennobled.

The relics of classical education

The flight out of Egypt took place in haste, however, and it was chance that decided what possessions each of the Israelites took with him into the desert. What knowledge was to become common property in the Middle Ages often depended upon the fates of individual men.

Cassiodorus was a well-educated official who died of old age towards the end of the sixth century. He interpreted contemporary trends correctly and understood that if anything was to be preserved it must be reduced to a manageable size. He retired from public office and founded the monastery of Vivarium in Calabria so that he could gather together the remnants of classical learning and systematize them. He also wrote a handbook on what Augustine had called the liberal arts and tried to establish rules for the orthography of Latin to remedy the confusion that was developing. *artes liberales*

Fate could, however, be no crueller than it was with the greatest of the encylopaedists, Boethius (who died in 524). He was 'last of the Romans and the first schoolman'. He was one of the last people in western Europe who knew Greek and had resolved to translate the whole of Plato and Aristotle into Latin. Had his plans been realized the Middle Ages would have been quite different. Boethius was unfortunate enough to be suspected, for very vague reasons, of being implicated in a conspiracy against Theodoric, king of the Ostrogoths. In prison, awaiting torture and execution, Boethius wrote his book *De consolatione philosophiae* (The consolations of philosophy) in prose and verse without access to any reference works. It is a synthesis of the philosophies of antiquity and bears witness to the author's identification with his subject. Although we may owe Theodoric thanks for providing the indirect impulse for one of the greatest works of literature, it is regrettable that his despotic nervousness deprived posterity of the opportunity of getting to know the most important of Plato's and Aristotle's writings. Boethius succeeded only in translating part of Aristotle's elementary logic and the Introduction (to the *Categories*) written by Porphyry, a commentator on Aristotle, the works that were *De consolatione philosophiae* *Isagoge*

7

to become known in the twelfth century as 'the old logic' (cf. p. 55). For learned history in its real meaning these works on logic, supplemented by some shorter works by Boethius on related subjects, were to be of decisive importance: it could be justifiably maintained that the Aristotelian system for the interpretation of information provided by the five senses must have been imprinted in the very cortex of the students who, in the eleventh century, after the renaissance of Boethius, maintained that logic provided the answers to every mystery of human existence.

The ideas of Boethius will, however, be referred to repeatedly in the rest of this book.

By far the most popular of the compilers was the Spanish Bishop Isidore of Seville (who died in 636). His aim was to collect a digest of all human learning in one single volume

Fig. 3. Arithmetic, presented by her two theoreticians, Pythagoras on the right and Boethius on the left. Arithmetic was the first subject studied in the *quadrivium*. The teaching of mathematics in Carolingian schools was based on the works of Martianus Capella and Boethius. It was the need to establish accurate figures for the working-out of the date of Easter that gave rise to the new science *computus ecclesiasticus* (ecclesiastical computation) in which the basic textbook was *De temporum ratione* by the Venerable Bede (written in 727). Major advances in mathematics did not come until the twelfth century (as was true in many other disciplines as well) and were based on translations from Arabic, principally of the algebra of Al-Khwarizmi (which was called in the Middle Ages *Algorismus* after its originator). In the thirteenth century calculations were made considerably easier with the introduction of Arabic numerals, among them the zero. The standard work in mathematics was *Algorismus Vulgaris* by John of Holywood (Johannes de Sacrobosco), which was written in Paris around 1250. From this period the following terms were used in Latin; *cyfra* (an Arabic word), *additio, subtractio, multiplicatio, divisio, radix, productum*, etc., terms that have also become indispensable in modern languages. In this illustration Boethius is shown anachronistically using arabic numerals. Gregorius Reisch, *Margarita philosophica* (first printed in 1469), printed in Basle in 1583 by Sebastian Henricpetri.

(roughly as large as a fairly long novel). The book was called *Etymologies* because great attention was paid to what were often quite fantastic explanations of the derivations of terms and names. Few writers can have been as successful as this encyclopaedist. A thousand or so copies of the book are still in existence and indeed it was almost certainly to be found in every library of any importance right through the Middle Ages. The titles of the chapters it contains give some idea of its varying contents, squeezed from the many sources that happened to be available in Isidore's own library.

I   Grammar and its parts.
II   Rhetoric and dialectic.
III   Mathematics and its subsections: arithmetic, music, geometry and astronomy.
IV   Medicine.
V   Laws and legal records. Chronology.
VI   The contents of the Bible. The Easter Cycle. Decisions of the Councils of the Church. Saints' Days and the liturgy.
VII   God and the angels. The names of the prophets. The names of the Holy Fathers. Martyrs, priests and monks. Other names.
VIII The Church and the synagogue. Religion and faith. Heresies. Philosophers, poets, fortune tellers, wizards, pagans. Pagan gods.
IX   The languages of the world. Terms for kings, warriors and burghers. Designations of kinship.
X   Derivations of words, in alphabetic order.
XI   The human being and parts of the body. The ages of man. Omens and portents, deformity.
XII   Four-footed animals, reptiles, fish and birds.
XIII The elements: heaven and air, water, the sea, rivers and floods.
XIV   The earth, paradise, regions of the world. Islands, mountains and other geographical concepts.
XV   Cities. Buildings in cities and in the country. Surveying. Travel and communications.
XVI   Types of soil and minerals. Stones and gems. Ivory discovered in marble. Glass. The metals. Weights and measures.

XVII   Agriculture. Different kinds of fruit. On the growing of
        vines and fruit. Herbs and vegetables.
XVIII   Wars and victories. Weapons. Courts of law. Plays. Dice
        and ball games.
  XIX   Ships, ropes, nets, casting and masonry, building-tools.
        Spinning, clothes and decorations.
   XX   Tables. Food and drink. Vessels for drinking. Vessels for
        wine, water and oil, food and flour. Lamps. Beds, chairs,
        carriages.   Farming   and   gardening   implements.
        Harness.[2]

What remained of the philosophy of antiquity was very
limited indeed and often its meaning was misunderstood.
The interest in etymology was accompanied by a belief that
the names of things had some essential relationship to their
nature. Reading Isidore stimulates the imagination to a very
high degree and for people who had no other source of
information available it must have aroused insatiable
curiosity about the vague relationship between reality and
the language that describes it.

The educational reforms of Charlemagne

When, some time around the year 800, Charlemagne managed to establish centralized political power among the people who have nowadays become the Germans, the French and the Italians, the civilization of antiquity was something that had to be recovered after the centuries of violence and isolation that had dominated the continent. Charlemagne nursed a vision of re-establishing the Roman Empire based on Christian principles. The relationship of Church and State was to be like that of body and soul. Education must be raised once more to its former status and the people who were to do this were, according to Charlemagne, the priests. The first binding duty was therefore that the servants of the Church be given a thorough basic education and so it became vital that the language of Cicero and Augustine, the only medium for more abstract reasoning that there then was, should be rescued from its obscurity and restored to its former glory.

Charlemagne was no idle dreamer. He therefore gathered at his court in Aix the intellectual elite of England, Ireland, Italy and Spain, where civilization had led a more protected existence than it had in the ravaged countries at the heart of the continent. From York came the brilliant Alcuin, who was to become Charlemagne's personal teacher and close friend and in many ways the minister of education in the new empire. He was at the same time poet, grammarian, logician, mathematician and astronomer and had a much greater ability than most scholars to stimulate the curiosity of his pupils. In England the preeminent scholar had been Bede (the Venerable Bede, *Beda Venerabilis*), who had written commentaries on the Bible, and works on philology, history and astronomy. Under Alcuin's leadership, therefore, representatives of the leading cultural institutions of the early Middle Ages were gathered together and they were to provide the basis for a systematic educational programme.

The monasteries and civilization

Admiration for the important contributions made by different individuals must not, however, lead to an undervaluation of a collective force which provided the sustenance which was to keep the flickering flame of learning alive. This was monasticism. Cassiodorus had founded a monastery and had established that one form of spiritual struggle against the devil should consist of the copying of texts. He even sang the praises of the craft of producing books:

What blissful exertion, what precious pains in preaching to men with one's own hands, in opening their lips with one's own fingers, in providing mortals with a silent salvation and in opposing the evil wiles of the devil with pen and ink![3]

Cassiodorus enjoined on his monks the sacred duty of tracing and preserving vanished works of literature and many of the manuscripts that he collected or had copied later found their way to the monastery of Bobbio in northern Italy and from there to the Papal library in the Lateran, or to Ireland or to the Venerable Bede's monastery of Jarrow in England.

The rule of St Benedict (who died around 547), which became the basis of western European monasticism, contains nothing that indicates that the founder had any intention of making monasteries the bulwarks of civilization. His only intention was to create 'a school in the service of God'. Not even in their heyday as patrons and practitioners of the arts did the Benedictines regard their contributions to civilization, education, literature, music and architecture as anything but the worship of God in artistic expression. The rule of the order did lay down, however, that certain hours each day must be set aside for 'holy reading', that is reading *lectio divina* from the Bible or the Holy Fathers. At the beginning of Lent every year each brother was to collect a codex from the library and during the year he was to read it from beginning to end. Where there is a library, however, there must be scribes as well, and education must be provided in reading and writing, especially as the monasteries recruited new members among boys who had, for various reasons, been confided to their care by their parents. In remoter parts of the empire this education had to start from the beginning with elementary teaching of Latin. Some of the monks in the monastery must, in other words, have had assigned to them as more or less their main duty the responsibility for this schooling. These monastery schools were the embryos from which the European educational systems developed.

Even though culture was never dignified with the status of an aim in itself, because of the monasteries the Church nevertheless became the principal authority for almost every form of education. Initially this was the result of immediate needs, the necessity of being able to understand the Scriptures and celebrate the sacraments, but it was to lead to a development that was to gain its own momentum.

The seven liberal arts

Alcuin hoped that the Imperial court would become the home of a re-established academy: an academy that would equal Plato's in eminence but which would also be consecrated by the knowledge of Christ's truth:

If many participate in the studies you have planned, Athens could rise once again in France, an Athens even more lustrous than the first one. Ennobled by the teachings of Our Lord Jesus Christ, our college will outshine all the endeavours of the academy, which occupied itself with the teachings of Plato and won fame for its pursuit of the seven liberal arts. Here all secular wisdom would be surpassed by the new Athens, which, in addition, would have been endowed with the seven-fold gift of the Holy Ghost in all its plenitude.[4]

This is an extract from a letter he wrote to his Emperor. Old manuscripts were copied with renewed enthusiasm. A new and more legible form of script was developed. This script was known as Carolingian miniscule and it is the model on which the typefaces used in modern printing are still based. The Carolingian educational programme was based on the existing monastery schools. In addition a school was to be established at every cathedral to guarantee a supply of young men to be recruited to the priesthood. Parish priests were asked to keep their eyes open for gifted young boys and to teach them to read free of charge. A minimum standard of education was laid down for priests. The intention was to standardize education to some extent so that it could provide ideological uniformity and unity to prop up the rather shaky structure of the new Empire.

The teaching in the 'Carolingian' monastery and cathedral schools was divided up into three levels. The first dealt with elementary knowledge such as writing, reading, singing, a little grammar and knowledge of the calendar. Then came the seven liberal arts, which were divided into the *trivium*, i.e. grammar, rhetoric and dialectic, and the *quadrivium*, consisting of arithmetic, geometry, astronomy and music. The last stage involved actual preparation for the tasks of the

septem artes liberales
trivium
quadrivium

priesthood such as reading and interpreting the Scriptures, preaching, the liturgy and teaching the catechism.

The seven liberal arts had been described so in antiquity because they were regarded as proper pursuits for all free men, although one can argue whether 'free' referred mainly to people born into freedom or people with free time. Now the contents of study of these arts was decided by the books which were available. Apart from Cassiodorus' and Boethius' compilations, a turgid volume by Martianus Capella existed. It had been written in Carthage at some during the fifth century and it was to be an immensely popular textbook of the Middle Ages. Its title was *On the Marriage of Mercury and Philology* and it was written in a mixture of verse and prose in a style that very few people today would find enjoyable. The mythological framework – in it Mercury is about to enter marriage with scholarship (*philologia*) – enabled the writer to give a short account of the content of each of the seven liberal arts, by personifying them as female figures who make speeches on their own behalf.

De nuptiis Mercurii et Philologiae

Fig. 4. All scholarship starts with familiarity with grammar, shown here as a fine lady who in her right hand is showing a young schoolboy a tablet with the alphabet written on it. In her left hand she holds the key to the temple of knowledge. The ground floor is occupied with people doing grammar exercises in *congruitas*, the art of combining words in the right cases. At the very bottom sits Donatus, on the floor above him Priscian. The lowest floor of the tower is occupied by Aristotle with logic, Cicero with rhetoric (which includes poetry) and Boethius with mathematics. Above them is Pythagoras with music, Euclid with geometry, and Ptolemy with astronomy. The two figures on the next floor are Aristotle once again, but now with physics, and Seneca with ethics. At the top Peter Lombard sits in solitary state with his theology and his metaphysics. The study of the ultimate principles was called 'metaphysics', so long as it confined itself to areas covered by natural reason, and 'theology' when it assumed divine revelation. Gregorius Reisch, *Margarita philosophica*, printed by Sebastian Henricpetri in Basle in 1583.

trivium:
grammatica

dialectica

rhetorica

quadrivium
geometria

arithmetica

astronomia

harmonia

Grammar is dreadful to behold and bears bitter medicines ready to remedy all forms of linguistic abuse. She teaches how to write and speak in a learned way, a survey of phonetics, the parts of speech and accidence. Dialectic, or 'logic' to use a more modern term, is a pale lady with a penetrating glance, wandering eyes and tightly curled hair in Capella's fanciful description. The hook that has replaced her right hand is concealed, in her left hand is a snake. She teaches us to divide perceived reality into genus and species and what a definition is. She describes ambiguity, types of propositions and syllogisms. Rhetoric is tall and radiant and carries a shield and she teaches us Cicero's tricks for finding the right words to persuade our listeners effectively. The four ladies who together form the *quadrivium* are concerned with things rather than with words. Geometry, with a ray of light and a globe in one hand, can measure the earth and divide it into longitude and latitude and also has knowledge of all the countries of the world. Arithmetic is clad in complex vestments of artfully interwoven rays of light which imply the complex structure of nature. She introduces us to the significance of numbers and reveals the secrets of monads, dyads and so on up to decades, each of them with their own individual characteristics. Astronomy, her brow adorned with stars and with glittering hair, describes how the world, composed of the four elements, is immoveably fixed at the centre of the revolving spheres of stars. Finally Harmony, whose refined dress of thin metal chimes gently, teaches us the skills of experienced musicians.

The teaching in Alcuin's schools also involved practical application of theoretical knowledge. Children began by learning the most important prayers and the Book of Psalms by heart. They were taught how to write on tables of wax, and how to work out the date of Easter every year with the aid of the astronomical tables. Exercises in rhetoric were carried out with the help of collections of examples. The classical writers of different genres were studied carefully, and more or less every word or construction was studied and noted so that they could be memorized and used later in the scholar's own work. Learning by rote was a favourite aid and many of the elementary textbooks were written in the same way as the catechism with questions and answers that were to be learnt by heart (and it should be added that the reward for failure was corporal punishment). Here, in a way that no longer exists today, advantage was taken of the capacity for memorization which small children have but which they inevitably lose in their early teens. There can be no question that the monotonous dialogues in Donatus' elementary grammar were etched eternally in the memories of the pupils: Donatus

— How many are the parts of speech?
— Eight.
— What are they?
— Noun, pronoun, verb, adverb, participle, conjunction, proposition, interjection.

— What is a verb?
— A part of speech which refers to time, person (without case) in the active, passive or in neither.[5]

It is not difficult to imagine these soulless dialogues being chorused aloud by a whole class to the beat of the teacher's cane. Here were to be found the answers to most questions, not only those about the parts of speech but also about solecisms, different kinds of stylistic devices, every example being illustrated by a quotation from one of the Latin authors:

— What is irony?

The whole class should immediately respond with this refrain:

— Irony is the trope which uses the opposite of what is being referred to, for example
'Fame everlasting and spoils of great value you gain by your actions, You and your son and heir . . . '[6]

In the study of oratory, rhetoric, the purpose of which is to persuade, there were five different elements: how to word a question and an argument, how to dispose material, how to

find the right words and effective stylistic devices, how to commit everything to memory – for to speak from notes or from a manuscript was to make oneself ridiculous – and finally how to find the right intonation and suitable gestures, voice control and mime. In the Carolingian schools rhetoric became the study of how to draw up official and private letters and public records.

ars dictaminis

The content of the *quadrivium*, the subjects with more immediate practical applications, was less substantial. In arithmetic the use of the abacus was taught, in music how to play the monochord, an instrument which was played by plucking a single string, and how to sing the musical parts of the liturgy. The study of music was believed to foster noble

Fig. 5. Music played an important role in the Carolingian schools. In both the monastery schools and the cathedral schools, one of the duties of the pupils was to provide the choral singing for the different services. The singing consisted of Psalms and hymns, which were chanted (Gregorian plainsong) in the eight keys used by the Church. Guido d'Arezzo, the Benedictine monk and musical theorist (who died around 1050), invented a method of learning the notes which was typical of the methods used in the monastery schools. He started with the first verse of a hymn which is sung at vespers for the celebration of St John the Baptist (23 and 24 June) and he gave the notes in the scale the names *ut, re, mi, fa, so, la*:

> *Ut* queant laxis *re*sonare fibris
> *mi*ra gestorum *fa*muli tuorum,
> *so*lve polluti *la*bii reatum,
>   sancte Oannes.

('Holy John, remove the sin from our unclean lips so that we, thy servants, can give free expression to our innermost feelings and praise thy wondrous actions.') The melody of the hymn went up one tone on each of the syllables marked here. Later the name *si* or *ti* was added for the seventh tone, and in Italy *ut* has been replaced by *do*. This method is called solmization and was used up until the seventeenth century and was reintroduced into music teaching at the beginning of the twentieth century. Gregorius Reisch, *Margarita philosophica*, Basle 1583.

feelings. In a short essay on harmony which was to be one of the basic texts for the serious study of music until well into the eighteenth century, Boethius had observed that the performance of music sharpened the ability to think and perceptions of reality, a characteristic he ascribed to the mathematical relationship the different notes had to each other.

Alcuin was a born teacher and in his own textbooks he tried to make the rather boring subject matter a little more appetizing. He was able to express even the most abstract relationships in pictorial and comprehensible terms. He collected fifty-three riddles together to encourage people learning to count to use their wits. One of them presents the problem of how three men, each accompanied by his own sister, are going to be able to cross a river. The only boat available will hold two people at the most and there are good reasons to believe that none of the girls can safely trust her virtue to any custody other than her brother's. How is the crossing to be arranged if the demands of virtue and the limitations of the boat must be taken into account?

He also managed to endow the dialogue technique with a little life. In the following dialogue the model pupil is no less a personage than the Emperor Charlemagne himself. His interest in learning is confirmed by evidence in other sources as well.

Charlemagne: Tell me how 'philosophy' may be defined.
Alcuin: Philosophy is enquiry into the nature of things, and such knowledge about both the human and the divine as is granted to mortal man. Philosophy is also an honourable life, the desire to live well, contemplation of death and contempt for the world.
C: Of what does it consist?
A: Of knowledge and opinion.
C: What is knowledge?
A: Knowledge is knowing the certain reasons for things, such as that an eclipse of the sun is caused by the moon shadowing the surface of the sun.
C: What is opinion?
A: Opinions are held of things that are hidden and which cannot be defined with certainty, for example the extent of the heavens or the depth of the world.

C: Who dares to speak derogatively of philosophy?

A: No wise man.

C: Indeed no. But let us continue with logic. Tell me first what logic is.

A: Logic is the science of reason. It is able to ask questions, define, and enquire and even to distinguish truth from falsehood.

C: What distinguishes logic from rhetoric?

A: As the fist can be distinguished from the palm of the hand. Logic combines reasoning in as few words as possible. Rhetoric, rich in words, is allowed free reign in the sphere of oratory. One compresses words, the other extends them.[7]

Theology in the footsteps of the Fathers

Even though it was in no way laid down that study of the liberal sciences would culminate in the study of theology, all this teaching was, nevertheless, considered as preparation for the study of the Bible. As we have seen, even mathematics placed great emphasis on the interpretation of numbers which, according to the unanimous testimony of the writers of the early Church, was indispensable if the Holy Scripture was to be elucidated correctly. Logic and training in rhetoric was also necessary to understand texts that were often obscure. Augustine, who had himself been a professor of rhetoric, had made this clear. At this period theology was substantially the same as careful reading of the Scriptures. Interpretation was not made easier by the fact that these were a collection of translated texts, and that it was impossible to find anybody with a knowledge of the original languages of the Bible, Hebrew and Greek. To be able to understand what was obscure, one had to turn to traditional interpretations from the Fathers of the Church, and in *doctores ecclesiae* particular to the four Doctors of the Church: Jerome (who died in 420), the translator of the Bible; Ambrose the Bishop of Milan (who died in 397); Augustine his son in God, and Pope Gregory the Great (died 604), who was a crucial figure in the transition between antiquity and the Middle Ages. Theologians looked upon themselves as custodians of an onerous inheritance from past giants such as these, and the only requirement made of a custodian is that he should be faithful. The very nature of the monastic way of life was traditionalism and receptivity: to receive, to assimilate, and to hand on neither having added nor removed a iota, are characteristic of the theology practised within the monasteries. Devotion and loyalty to the Holy Fathers, of whom many also had been the founders of monasteries, was part of the humility of the monks, the highest monastic ideal.

On today's festival, the Assumption of the Blessed Virgin Mary, it is difficult to find a suitable text for a sermon. We are encompassed by the limits laid down by the Fathers and forbidden to transgress

24

them. We dare not therefore say more than that on this day she . . . was received into the highest heaven of heavens.[8]

Loyalty, however, does not preclude reflection. If the Bible was obscure, it could hardly be the result of coincidence. If it did contain the revelation of God, there must be a purpose even in its incomprehensibility.

According to *Glossa ordinaria* (cf. pp. 28 and 54) this incomprehensibility can be related to the passage in the gospels in which Jesus warns the disciples not to throw sacred matter to dogs, and it also met a need in the constitution of human beings. It was, to use a modern term, a psychological requirement if the mystery of the revelation was to be respected sufficiently, and this was yet another expression of divine order. Transparent simplicity would result in contempt:

Anyone who takes the bread from children and gives it to dogs is not a custodian but a ruthless looter. He has not realized that what is hidden is sought after more keenly, what is obscured is regarded with greater worship, what has been long in finding is guarded with greater affection. Nothing taken in moderation can lead to surfeit.[9]

'Dionysius' and the hierarchical vision of the world

Rarely has any literary fiction – many people would describe it as a forgery – had as great an influence as had *Dionysius Areopagita*. All that is known with certainty about its author is that he was a monk and that he was writing around the year 500. In his writing he described himself as one of the officials at the Athenian court of law called the Areopagus and one of Paul the Apostle's first Greek disciples (Acts 17:34). His works in Greek, *Mystical Theology*, *On the Divine Names*, *The Hierarchy of Heaven* and *The Hierarchy of the Church* became available in the Latin West in the ninth century and his medieval readers took him at his word and ascribed to him almost apostolic authority. Dionysius was a neo-Platonist: To him God was like the One, the Good, the eternal and unchanging Light, which communicates some of his Oneness, his Goodness, his light to all created things. ('It is of the essence of good that it should propagate itself.') These emanations from God can, however, only be received to the extent that an object's receptivity allows. All immaterial and material things are in fact part of a hierarchical system in which they can be placed according to their degree of perfection: at the peak, and closest to God, are the creatures of pure spirit, the angels (who are, however, themselves arranged in three hierarchies, within each of which there are three classes); just below them come human beings, who are composed of both spirit and matter and therefore occupy an intermediate position between angels and animals, and at the very bottom can be found organic and dead matter.

The heavenly hierarchy of the angels has a counterpart on earth in the hierarchy of the Church – bishops, priests, deacons, monks, laymen, catechumens and penitents – and the function of both hierarchies is to convey divine life to human beings, to make them as like God as possible. The individual's route to God consists of three stages: the road of purification, the road of illumination and the road of union. Evil, according to neo-Platonic philosophy has no in-

De theologia mystica
De divinis nominibus
De hierarchia caelesti
De hierarchia ecclesiastica

bonum est diffusivum sui

perfectio

via purgativa,
via illuminativa
via unitiva

26

dependent existence; it is merely the absence of the good that ought to exist, the lack of order. privatio boni debiti

Natural language is completely inadequate to describe the real nature of God. All that can be meaningfully said about God is what He is *not*. God is above all attempts to describe him, and the greatest knowledge a human being can acquire about God is the mystic's Cloud of Unknowing; God is a blinding shadow. theologia negativa

Not only philosophers and theologians such as Anselm, Albertus Magnus, Thomas Aquinas and Bonaventura were to have their vision of the world determined by Dionysius, whoever he may have been, but also, naturally enough, the great Christian mystics, and chief among them St John of the Cross (who died in 1591).

The fourfold sense of the Scriptures

In one and the same text the words of the Bible contained many layers of meaning, like crystals they reflected light of a different colour when approached from a different direction. This opinion was not the result of idle speculation but had been proposed most strongly by the Evangelists and the Apostle Paul. The system of interpretation established by

Fig. 6.   The new Jerusalem according to the vision described by the Prophet Ezekiel (Chapters 40–8). Medieval Bible commentary ascribed to the Bible not only its literal meaning but also an allegorical meaning, a moral meaning and an eschatological meaning (referring to the final end of the world). The promises of the Old Covenant are fulfilled in the New and everything recounted in the Old Testament has a counterpart in the New Testament. The unity of content of the two testaments has been described with admirable brevity in a couplet by Hugo of Orleans (it was his contribution to a competition in summarizing the contents of the Bible as briefly as possible)

> Quos anguis tristi virus mulcedine pavit,
> Hos sangui Christi mirus dulcedine lavit.

(They who were so tragically seduced into tasting the poison of the serpent were joyfully washed clean by the saving blood of Christ.) The temple in Jerusalem has its allegorical counterpart in the body of Christ, the Holy Church. Morally it can be interpreted to mean that its individual stones, Christians, will in enduring the sufferings of life be so shaped that they can in loving fellowship be united each with the other. The eschatological reference is to the heavenly Jerusalem. These interpretations, which are more or less obviously suggested in the New Testament itself, are presented systematically in *Glossa ordinaria* (cf. p. 54), the continuous commentary in the margin of the Bible compiled by Anselm of Laon, who was Abélard's teacher. In Ezekiel's vision the city had twelve gates, one for each and every one of the twelve tribes of Israel. The same symbol is used in the Book of Revelation but the number twelve is there associated with the twelve apostles, the twelve foundation stones of the heavenly city. Nikolaus of Lyra, *Postille*, printed by Ulrich Zell in Cologne in 1485.

the 'Carolingian' theologians ascribed four forms of meaning to the words of the Bible: the literal 'historical' meaning and in addition to this three spiritual dimensions of meaning: allegory, tropology and anagogy:

historia

The 'historical' meaning embodies knowledge about a series of tangible events in the past. The Apostle describes it thus: 'It is written that Abraham begat two sons, one by a servant woman and one by his free wife. The son of the servant woman was born of the flesh, but the son of his free wife, on the other hand, was born by virtue of a promise.' It is what is to follow that contains the

allegoria

allegorical meaning. The apparent sequence of events can be described as portent of a mystery yet to come. 'For the two women represent two covenants. One of them comes from Mount Sinai and bears its children in slavery, and the model for this is in Agar. Mount Sinai is called Agar in Arabia and it corresponds to the present Jerusalem, which exists with its offspring in slavery.' The

anagogia

'anagogic' meaning takes us upwards from spiritual mysteries to the highest and most holy secrets of Heaven. And the Apostle adds, 'But the Jerusalem which is above it is free, and she is our

tropologia

mother' . . . The 'tropological' meaning is the moral application, which is displayed in an improved life and in external actions. These four meanings can, if it is desired, combine with each other and the same Jerusalem can be understood in four different ways: historically as the city of the Jews, allegorically as the Church of Christ, anagogically as God's heavenly city, a mother for all of us, and tropologically as the soul of each individual, which is often reproached or praised in the Scriptures under this appellation.[10]

With a key like this in his hand, the Bible commentator found it possible to enter a multitude of rooms which had appeared to be sealed. More or less every word in the Bible could be examined for more than its literal meaning. Our existence had already been explained and all wisdom already summarized and sealed into the Holy Scriptures.

Worldly wisdom and the wisdom of God

Everything that had ever been said that was good or true or beautiful belonged to the Christians according to Augustine's example of the despoiling of the Egyptians. In the monastery and cathedral schools therefore the 'classical' auctores writers (and the term classical included a greater number of writers than it would today since 'post classical' writers like Quintilian, Lucan, Statius and Persius as well as Christian poets such as Juvencus, Prudentius and Sedulius were also listed among the *auctores*) were read with the same earnest attention as the Bible was. These studies also necessitated the extensive copying of manuscripts and it is thanks to the interest shown for classical Latin literature in the Carolingian renaissance that these texts were preserved for posterity. If you look into it carefully, you will soon find that the oldest existing copy of most of the classical authors was made in a monastery at some time after the beginning of the ninth century.

The teaching methods used in the monastery schools hardly changed at all between the eighth and twelfth centuries. Commentaries on both the language and the content (known as *scholia*) of texts were necessary because of the cultural and historical distance from the original environment. Shorter comments on individual words and phrases (known as glosses) were usually written in by hand glossae between the lines or in the margin. Those writers who from the period of Charlemagne's reform and afterwards were regarded as good examples of style were, purely because of this fact, granted what amounted almost to canonization: they could never be accused of any immoral thoughts or actions, even though on many occasions their works gave grounds for such accusations. One need not have read extensively to realize that certain poets do not impress us primarily as examples of impeccable behaviour. Once they had been established in the 'canon', however, they were accepted in their entirety. The commentary techniques used in interpreting the Bible were also used and the texts were seen as allegorical. The literal meaning of a text need not be its real meaning. After all Virgil, the greatest of all the poets, had made the Sibyl prophesy, indirectly, that a virgin should give birth to Jesus Christ.

Time in its path soon will change the unvarying order of ages.
Now as a virgin appears she can herald an age that is golden,
New-born her child will descend from the full height of heaven.[11]

Generations of pupils from the monastery schools, brought up to admire and imitate the heathen poets, faced with words like these could hardly deny the accepted belief that the revelation of Christ shone forth even where it could least be expected. No enormous intellectual effort was needed to see other aspects of meaning, moral and eschatological readings, in the same works. If a writer slipped into obscenity, it was to warn us against immorality.

The allegorical interpretation was added to by Hrabanus Maurus who adduced yet another disarming argument. He referred to the heathen woman mentioned in Deuteronomy (21:10ff.) who has been captured in war and who captivates her captor with her beauty. According to the Bible she may only be taken as a wife after she has shaved the hair from her head and pared her nails.

Taken literally, this is merely comic. It is when reading the heathen poets that we should act like this, when we have books full of worldly wisdom in our hands. If we find anything in them which is useful, we should make it part of our teaching. All that is superfluous, about graven images, sexual love or the considerations of the world, should be excised.[12]

This was an optimistic point of view, tolerant of ancient civilization. Three centuries later Konrad of Hirsau (who died around 1150) had to go to some lengths to defend the value of profane literature. In a dialogue on the school authors (*Dialogus super auctores*) the pupil places the burden of proving his case on the teacher by asking if there really are no risks in allowing students to become familiar with the outspoken poets.

Pupil: But what is there to be said about the other writers, Terence, Juvenal, Statius, the elder and the younger, Persius,

32

Fig. 7. Virgil was one of the most extensively read writers in the Middle Ages. His poems were read as prophecies, and they were interpreted in much the same way as the Scriptures were. The section that best lent itself to allegorical interpretation was in the fourth Eclogue, lines 5–7. In them Virgil makes the Sibyl at Cumae fortell a turning point in the history of the world and the direct intervention of God from Heaven. For the Middle Ages it was obvious that this could refer only to the birth of Jesus Christ, which took place some few decades after the lines had been written. The Sibyl at Tibur was also credited with prophesies of the birth of Christ. According to the *Legenda aurea* she and Octavian (later to be the Emperor Augustus) saw the Virgin and child in a circle in the heavens from the place where the *Ara caeli* church now stands in Rome. Hartmann Schedel, *Liber chronicarum*, printed by Anton Koberger in Nuremberg in 1493.

33

Homer and Virgil, to whom so much attention is paid by secular scholars? Here youth in its folly can seek and find that which for a time can satisfy its own vacuity.

Teacher: The people who have had no objections to long extracts from these works being included in the Church's teaching are best equipped to judge the value that young students can find in such poets' words and the important ideas they express.

P: If you manage in some way or other to prove what you say, I shall believe it completely. The fact is that I find it difficult to convince myself that Bible will not lose some of its lustre or even perhaps become quite featureless if, for no good reason, the testimony of pagan writers is confused with it.

T: Would you reject the writings of Moses and the Prophets because in places they borrow words and expressions from pagan writers? Have I not already told you that all that is true that has ever been said by any human beings or all that is correct that has ever been thought has come from Him who created us?

P: I was not hitherto aware that such things could be found in the Scriptures.

T: That is because you have been misled in some of the following ways; either because you have never set foot in a library which contains the Greek writers, or you have never realized that the Bible has been translated in a special and particular way. The effectiveness that metre gave to the expressions of the poets has been lost in the literal translation into prose. Many of the things that were memorable in the original language have been blunted in the translation. Where do you think Paul got 'Evil communications corrupt good manners' from if not from Menander, the classical poet? Where did the proverb he quotes in the letter to his disciple Titus, 'The Cretans are always liars, evil beasts and slow bellies' come from, if not from Epimenides the pagan poet? How many times does Paul, who was not unfamiliar with the methods of dialectic, state theses, make assumptions, adduce evidence and reach conclusions? If I went into everything in order to untangle you from the web you have got yourself into we would range too far and wide, especially as in your own Rule there is a proverb from Terence: 'Everything in reason!'[13]

34

The literature of the monasteries

Monastic civilization also, of course, encouraged its own literary activity. In this field as well the highest ideal was fidelity to the models that were used. Sister Hrotswit wrote uplifting plays which borrowed the structure if not the message of Terence's works. The speciality of the monasteries was and remained, however, the writing of history, which agreed most happily with their natural traditionalism. It was important that people should be able to see God's great design in the Bible and in profane history so that they could learn from the fates of peoples and princes and see how vices and virtues had been personified upon the stage of history. The preeminent example of a history writer was the classical chronicler Sallust (died in 35 BC), who described the Roman campaign against the African king Jugurtha and the Cataline conspiracy (during the year when Cicero himself was consul) without once missing a chance to present the events of history as lessons in ethics and psychology.

Adam of Bremen was the principal of a monastery school and when, some time around 1075, he wrote a diocesan chronicle about the fate of the archbishopric of Hamburg, which is now the most important source of information about Scandinavia in the tenth and eleventh centuries, he borrowed whole sentences from Sallust, which could at a pinch be used in this new context. One example of this will suffice: When Adam relates how Archbishop Adalbert is accused by Duke Bernhard of being an Imperial spy he adds: 'These words struck deeper into his soul than anyone could have suspected and henceforth he was a prey to wrath and fear and he planned and contrived ways of injuring the Duke.'[14] This brief psychological description has been taken word for word from Sallust's description of the feelings of King Jugurtha and the plans he made when his rival Hiempsal suggests that Jugurtha's right to the throne came not through birth but through adoption. The chronicler's eagerness to produce faultless Latin periods by borrowing in this way must, of course, always be remembered when assessing the value of the chronicle as historical source material.

Secular knowledge could, however, never be an end in itself. All knowledge had to be seen in a higher perspective. One of the seven liberal arts was rhetoric. Its purpose was to persuade, to mould the feelings of listeners, and even to amuse them. This was in itself praiseworthy. If, in addition, it could be used to set the affections of men on things above, to arouse a desire for virtue and a detestation of sin; if, in other words, this valuable vessel taken from the Egyptians could be used in spiritual service in the true temple of God, the giver of all good things, then rhetoric could not be nobler. She would become divine eloquence.

The preaching that developed in the monasteries should, of course, also be regarded as part of their literary history. The most brilliant preacher of them all was Bernard of Clairvaux (who died in 1153). In the true Augustinian tradition, but without acknowledging his own arduous years of study, he attempts to persuade the listener that all that has value, especially the thirst for intellectual knowledge, pales in comparison with the only important thing, which is spiritual experience. Those who have this experience do not need to be convinced by a profusion of quotations from the Fathers, which is a method that might possibly serve to convince a congregation of doubting novices. To provide reasons based on common sense would be to use unnecessary crutches, little better than to blaspheme directly. In his sermon on the Song of Solomon he explains the innermost meaning, the allegorical, tropological and anagogical layers, in this erotic poem, which he and the tradition he belonged to read as the ardent moment of union for the Church or the individual Christian soul with Jesus – the Bridegroom waiting for the final heavenly wedding:

It is a song which in its unique dignity and sweetness surpasses all other songs, and it is with every justification that I call it the song of songs. It is the fruit of all other songs. Only with the unction of the Holy Ghost and experience can an individual learn this song. Those who know what I am talking about will recognize this, those who do not should in their hearts feel yearning, not for

36

knowledge but for experience. This song is not concerned with the empty noises made by the mouth, it is an inward cry of joy from the heart, it is not the mumble of the lips but a movement of gladness, it is the harmonious combination not of voices but of wills. It is not heard by the ears, it does not echo in the streets: only they who sing it can hear it, and He for whom it is sung, the bride and bridegroom. It is a nuptial song. It describes the chaste and ecstatic embrace of the senses, the harmony of customs, emotions in unison and mutual love.[15]

It was no coincidence that the man who wrote such sermons was to be a vehement opponent of the new way of approaching theological problems that was to be embodied by Abélard.

A world of tangible concepts

Another typical product of the literary activity of the monasteries were the florilegia ('bouquets of flowers'), anthologies of memorable sentences arranged according to the authors or to some inner theme. They were not produced for any intellectual purpose, such as being able to find out quickly who said what. They were to be an aid to meditation. They were to be read and read again, concealed and pondered in the heart, or, to use an expression often used in the period, they were to be ruminated on. In this way the thoughts of the Fathers of the Church were ground into the personalities of the monks from the inside. The outward resemblance with the theological, in its technical meaning, collections of sentences (*Sententiae*, cf. p. 87ff.) may be striking. But the purpose of the florilegia was not to establish correspondences or to illustrate and reconcile apparent contradictions. To use a figure of speech belonging to the monasteries themselves, these flowers contained a honey which was to be sucked from various places in the wide field of the writings of the Bible and the Holy Fathers. Mixed with the saliva of one's own contemplation, it would provide sustenance and strength for the continued journey.

The Holy Scriptures draw the reader's senses to his heavenly home, converts his heart so that its longing turns from earthly to heavenly things, sharpens his understanding with its obscure expressions, and entertains the uneducated with its simple language. Diligent reading dispels boredom. The Holy Scripture helps us with direct words and elevates us with exalted ones. It grows in some way with the reader: the novice cannot lose himself in it, yet for the more experienced it is always new. It was said unto the prophet Ezekiel 'Child of Man, eat all that you find here.' Likewise, all that can be found in the Holy Scriptures should be eaten, because its artlessness tempts us to a life of simplicity, its exaltation provides the basis of sharpened understanding.[16]

The frame of reference of the monks consisted principally of pictures and their 'tangibility' appealed to all their senses. The Bible was a never-ending forest, wonderful but almost impenetrable, and he was to learn to feel at home in it. His life had to be a sacrifice of frankincense, a sweet-smelling savour of Christ, he was to be shaped by the Holy Spirit as molten wax takes the print of a seal, his thoughts were in the palpable and tangible language of the Psalms. This has to be remembered if the straightforwardness and abstract universality of the civilization that was to emerge is to be understood against its background.

Platonism and humanism in the Middle Ages

In the twelfth century the schools in Paris became the centre of Europe's intellectual life. In one of them, a school that existed in the monastery of St Victor just outside the city walls, a philosophy strongly influenced by Plato in the tradition of Augustine was fostered. The 'Victorines' represent a tendency that was not followed up in the later phases of the Middle Ages, largely because the only work by Plato available in a Latin translation was the dialogue *Timaeus* and therefore the major characteristics of Plato's thinking remained unknown. But at St Victor's it was unmistakeably Plato's voice that was listened to. The purpose of scholarly study according to the school's most eminent representative, Hugo of St Victor (who died in 1141) was 'wisdom': the eternal and unchanging truths concealed by the myriad deceptions and alterations of perception. The soul of man is composed of every part of nature, and man himself is a microcosm but has forgotten his own origin. When in study he examines the hidden connections of nature, he is involved in nothing so much as slowly remedying his own loss of memory and rediscovering and recognizing what has been forgotten but which has been intuitively understood in the subconscious all the time. In discovering Nature he discovers himself.

homo minor mundus

The mind has been dulled by the emotions of the body and has been lured away from its knowledge by palpable beliefs. It has forgotten what it once was, and as it has forgotten that it has ever been different, it believes that nothing exists apart from what it can see. Through learning balance can be restored so that we can recognize our own nature and learn not to seek elsewhere what can be found within ourselves. The search for wisdom is therefore the highest solace life can offer. He who finds wisdom is fortunate. He who can possess her is blessed.[17]

Studying is in other words following the injunction: 'Know thyself'. The same attitude was embraced in the famous cathedral school at Chartres, not far away from Paris.

Often it is presented as a typical example of genuine medieval humanism, which was open for the inheritance from antiquity, for Arabic sources, for the sciences and philosophy and the Platonic concept of wholeness, but always with emphasis on the fact that a learned man should not be a walking encyclopaedia but also and above all someone who had become one with his knowledge and who could see the difference between entirety and details. The school at Chartres looked to the future: it had greater ambitions than merely to transmit loyally what had once been given. There was also awareness that antiquity was owed thanks for the fact that they had progressed further than antiquity. Self-awareness becomes evident for the first time in the often-quoted words of Bernard of Chartres:

We are dwarves sitting on the shoulders of giants. We can see more than they can and further, not because our eyes are clearer or our bodies taller, but because they arose and lifted us up into the heights.[18]

A day at Chartres

As far as we know Bernard of Chartres wrote nothing that
has been preserved, but the school's best pupil, John of
Salisbury (who died in 1180), himself tangible proof that the
educational ideals of the school could be realized, described
the teaching methods and the teacher he admired extremely
thoroughly. His description of how the *trivium*, the
language-based subjects, was taught carries its readers
directly into the classroom:

Bernard of Chartres, one of the most copious fountains of
knowledge in France, used this method. He demonstrated with
unsullied examples the school authors' correct use of language:
figures of grammar, rhetorical devices and the pitfalls of sophistry.
He also made it clear how each lesson was related to other subjects.
But he did not always go into detail but adapted his teaching to the
level of his pupils. . . . Each of them was obliged each day to give an
account of what he had learnt the day before, some more, some
less. Each day was the preceding day's pupil. The evening lessons,
which were called declination, were so full of grammar that every
pupil, however slow on the uptake, had after one year of study the
ability to read and speak at his fingertips and could not possibly be
ignorant of the meaning of the most commonly used expressions.
Nevertheless, because no schoolday should be without savour of
Godliness, he associated everything with subjects which were
edifying both for faith and conduct, so that it was as it were an
admonition encouraging those who heard him to the good. The
last item in these grammar lessons – or rather philosophical
exhortations – was an expression of his piety. He commended the
souls of the departed to our Saviour by piously repeating the sixth
penitential psalm and the Lord's Prayer as a spiritual sacrifice for
them.
   The lads who took part in the preparatory teaching were made
to read the poets and the orators to learn how to imitate their
poetry and prose. He taught them to follow faithfully in their
footsteps, he showed them how expressions were constructed and
how elegant rhythm could be achieved in prose. If somebody tried
to ornament his work by plagiarism, he would point this out and
rebuke the theft but rarely did he punish anyone. . . . But the first
thing he taught them and fixed in their minds was to be sparing in
their use of language, what could be permitted in the way of

decoration of the content or the expression, when language should be laconic or even ascetic, when they could expatiate or even luxuriate in language. He encouraged them to read historical accounts and poetry carefully and not to feel compelled to get through them as quickly as possible. But he also demanded that each one of them must learn something by heart every day. He taught them to avoid the unnecessary and to confine themselves to the great authors. Remembering every insignificant character who has uttered a few words makes us unhappy and is a foolish waste of time; it occupies and masters our mind, which would be better if kept receptive and open for new and better things. . . . It is for this reason that the classical writers described it as a virtue for the learned to be ignorant in certain areas.[19]

John of Salisbury is the advocate of Christian humanism. It was not only the acquisition of knowledge but also personal assimilation of knowledge that was necessary for maturity or if one wanted to reach further than what was immediately apparent:

Four things are principally necessary for the man who wishes to practise philosophy and virtue: reading, learning, meditation, diligence. Reading presents the subject to one's eyes, learning draws from written sources at times and at times from unwritten ones in the hidden recesses of the memory or the complete awareness of the here and now. Meditation reaches beyond these things, often soaring up to the inscrutable, and it discovers and examines both what is obvious and what is concealed. Diligence finally has its origin in the fact that despite the knowledge which we have we long for more and it paves the way to greater understanding. . . . Grammar, the root and source of all this, sows its seeds as it were in the furrows of nature. But grace comes first. If we are only aided by the presence of grace, the seed grows into the sure strength of virtue and multiplies and brings forth as fruit the good actions for which we are known as, and really are, good men. For only grace gives rise to good endeavours and good works. It is grace alone that makes men good and which grants to those that are so favoured the ability to express themselves in speech and writing and all other good gifts.[20]

Grace does not nullify nature but fulfils it, was how Thomas Aquinas was to summarize the relationship between Christian faith and secular learning a century later.

Medical and humane learning

At some of the cathedral schools established as the result of Charlemagne's transformation, medicine was one of the subjects studied. Any attempt to elevate the art of healing above the level of the saws and adages handed down by word of mouth in folk medicine was forced to turn to the written classical sources that had for some reason escaped the ravages of time. It can be shown that in the ninth and tenth centuries there were already in some monasteries collections of medical textbooks written in the form of dialogues. It can therefore be demonstrated that at that moment when the learning of antiquity was being collected and meted out again, some of the methods of classical medicine that had been developed in Greece in antiquity were once again incorporated into the modest body of theoretical medical knowledge available in the West. In a manuscript from the ninth century can be found a collection of questions and answers which reflect the important principles established by the medical writer and philosopher Galen (who died in AD 199) for inductive analogy, or, in other words, the method of using observation of obvious causes of sickness to deduce unknown reasons. In the same source we are also told that medical theories must be confirmed by experience and by experiment. What is of particular interest is the importance assigned to the general knowledge needed by trainee doctors. They must know grammar, at least enough to be able to understand and comment on the writings of the medical authors. They must be good enough at rhetoric to be able to teach others in their native languages. Elementary facts in geometry and astronomy must be known. No less important demands, however, were the ethical rules of the Hippocratic tradition:

Let us examine the characteristics needed of a doctor. He should have gentle habits, be humble and honest, pious and modest. He must treat the poor and the rich, slaves and free men with the same thoroughness. The art of medicine is the same for all men. If a fee is paid he must accept it and not appear to refuse, if no fee is offered he must not demand one. The size of a fee cannot be related to the benefits of the medical treatment. In making house calls only the needs of the patient should be taken into account. He must also remember the Hippocratic oath so that he can refrain from every criminal act, and especially from taking economic or sexual advantage of his patients. Everything said or done in the home is to be kept absolutely secret. In this way he will increase both his own reputation and the reputation of medicine. He should have sensitive and well-kept hands so that he makes a good impression on everybody and he must have a polished manner when making palpations, as Hippocrates himself emphasized. He should be able to take part in refined conversation and should not be ignorant of philosophy. His behaviour should be unassuming so that professional skill and impeccable conduct should be united in his person.[21]

The same manuscript also gives us an impression of the teaching of medicine at the period when it can be assumed that it had reached its highest level in the monasteries on the continent. The form of the teaching is the familiar one used by Donatus and Alcuin. For every question there is an exact answer. The efficacity of this method should be obvious, especially as the trainee doctors were obliged to learn a large number of foreign (mainly Greek) terms just as they are today:

— What is orexis?
— The appetite for food and drink.
— What is pepsis?
— The digestion, a process in which food and drink consumed is converted into liquid by the effect of the warmth of the blood. From this liquid the other bodily liquids are formed.

— What is the pulse?
— The expansion and contraction of the arteries, proceeding from the heart and the brain through its membrane and not affected by the influence of the will.
— What is epilepsy?
— A sudden attack, which returns at shorter or longer periods. Between the attacks the patient feels nothing but falls suddenly with his body contracted, making inarticulate noises in the throat. The patient experiences noises in his ears and sees lights before his eyes. Parts of the body

tremble. Some patients can, however, feel attacks approaching and warn those around them. Finally they foam at the mouth and have difficulty in retaining consciousness.

— What is hydrocephalus?
— Watery or bloodlike liquid or an accumulation of liquid and pus under the skin of part of the head or the whole head.
— How does one operate on hydrocephalus or other accumulations of pus?
— An incision is made between the skin and the bones of the skull, the pus is vented and the wound given the necessary treatment. If the complaint affects the whole of the head, the incisions are made at regular intervals around the whole of the skull so that the liquid can be discharged. We make one or two incisions horizontally and then treat the wound without bandaging it. We let the liquid discharge and do not use bandages until the wound has stopped oozing. If the accumulation is beneath muscles, we sever the muscles at one side (the muscles run down to the spine) and release the sinews in the direction in which they are attached, and then with an incision of the scalpel allow the liquid to vent. Then we fill the wound with linen cloths and treat it so that the edges knit again. We also make sure that all the connections are reunited and heal. We use a bandage called 'an earless rabbit'.[22]

Fig. 8.   A figure known as 'the man of sores'. The picture is not meant to describe a complicated medical emergency but to illustrate a list of medical theories and methods of treatment described in the accompanying text. The man of sores is an example of a didactic illustration. He is presented together with 'the bloodletting man' and 'the Zodiac man', the first showing where in the body the veins should be opened and the latter what consideration should be paid to the position of the heavenly bodies when carrying out such operations. It was wrong to touch the parts of the body 'governed' by the sign of the Zodiac which the moon had entered at the time. This 'man of sores' comes from Hieronymus Braunschwig's *Buch der Cirurgia, Handwirckung der wundartzny*, printed by J. Grüninger in Strasbourg in 1497. The illustration is reminiscent of a grotesque variant of a motif familiar in ecclesiastical art, namely that of St Sebastian riddled with arrows. The major interest of this picture in the history of medicine is however that it is the oldest printed depiction of an opened abdominal cavity.

Nothing is said about whether these operations really took place or if so, what effect they had.

In the city of Salerno south of Naples, an ancient health resort, a bishopric and the home of a monastery, several doctors formed a guild to undertake some form of organized teaching of doctors. This school was to become the most celebrated medical school of the Middle Ages and prototype of the medical faculties at the universities. It existed until

1812. To begin with the 'scientific' level of the teaching was modest but it pioneered one area of medical knowledge: here began systematic study of the anatomy of the human body. In some sources detailed descriptions of complicated surgical operations can be found. The literary style reveals the importance attached to the personal relationship between teacher and pupil. Learning to become a doctor was not so much a question of being able to read but of being able to listen. Great demands were therefore made on the ability to remember. Detailed rules were laid down on how one would be able to keep the most complicated knowledge in one's mind: the simplest example of this technique is tying a knot in one's handerkerchief. In the later Middle Ages this was to be developed into a science of its own, *ars memorativa* (cf. p. 223ff.).

The leading figure among the physicians of Salerno was Constantine, called the African (Constantinus Africanus), who died in 1087. Long journeys undertaken in the East for study had given him thorough knowledge of the most advanced medical learning of the time, that of the Arabs. His translations of Hippocrates and the writings of the great Arab doctors were to begin a process that was to waken the West from its intellectual isolation and traditionalism and for ever change its appearance. The heritage in the natural sciences from Greek and Arab culture began to be incorporated into the European way of perceiving reality.

The cathedral schools transcend the monasteries

The monastery schools reached their heyday in the eleventh century. The reformist movement in the Church which aimed at snatching the administration of the Church from the hands of secular princes was inclined to regard preoccupation with worldly knowledge as a distraction from the task in hand. At Cluny, which was the centre of the movement, classical studies were not encouraged, and at Cîtaux, the Benedictine order's latest offshoot where the true spirit of St Benedict was to be revived in all its original severity, the library contained only the Bible, the works of the Fathers of the Church, the Missals and a very few classical authors. This newly awakened enthusiasm for the Church, the Bride of Christ, immaculate and untarnished, seems at the time to have left little zeal over for the pursuit of worldly knowledge. There are even numerous examples of teachers at the schools in Paris who had had their fill of intellectual gymnastics and retired to the monastery to devote themselves completely to the service of God.

In this situation the cathedral schools outstripped the monasteries as centres of learning. One of the reforms of Charlemagne had been to enjoin the priests of a cathedral to live collectively with regular hours of worship, in other words to live a life not unlike that of a monastery. This new way of living was governed by a number of regulations (*canones* from which 'canon, is derived). The dean functioned on behalf of the bishop as the head of this family of priests, and one of the canons was to have responsibility for the further education of the priests. He was called *scholasticus*. In certain of the cathedral towns in northern France the bishop and his chapter, which often consisted of highly educated men, became the intellectual pioneers of the time. The school at Chartres, which has already been mentioned, was the most eminent of these centres of learning.

These cathedral schools acquired increased importance as well because they played an important role in the recruitment of priests. This was the responsibility of the archdeacon. It was he, with very little interference from the

canones
canonicus

scholasticus

49

bishop, who supervised the development of the trainee priests and who was called upon to guarantee their suitability for their vocation. Often the task of scholasticus at the cathedral school was combined with the post of chancellor to the chapter, the task of looking after and improving the cathedral's archives and library.

At some time around the year 1100 the population of Europe suddenly began to increase and at the same time its social life slowly began to become more cultivated. Trade and handicrafts which had been dormant since the classical period began to develop again. New cities were founded, old trade routes taken into use again and new ones established. This expansion of urban life led once again to increased occupational specialization. In addition a new class of 'intellectuals' began to be distinguishable. Such stability and security had not been experienced for 700 years.

This new situation also affected ecclesiastical education. The numbers of candidates for the priesthood increased and this meant that at the cathedral schools the scholasticus had to employ assistants in order to cope with the teaching. The educational activity of the cathedral had already become relatively independent of the diocesan bishop and in conditions like these became even more so. As the number of candidates for the priesthood increased constantly, one result was that not all of the pupils could be ordained as priests and naturally the education itself became a powerful attraction for many students. Moreover the job of teaching became relatively lucrative. It was however the scholasticus of the diocese alone who could give people the right to teach and he defended this profitable privilege jealously. In the course of time it was extended to include not only the cathedral school but all the schools in the diocese. The cathedral scholasticus, who was usually also its chancellor, became after a time a minister of education with exclusive privileges. In the 1170s the higher ecclesiastical authorities were obliged to intervene with a formal prohibition against licentia docendi   selling for money the right to teach: any suitable educated man at all who was willing to take on the responsibility of teaching was to be allowed to do so without any obstacles such as having to pay fees being placed in his way. Otherwise

50

there was a danger that knowledge 'which should be granted without payment to everybody would in future become a commodity which could be bought and sold' (Pope Alexander III).

The transfer of culture to the cathedral schools also marked the beginning of its path towards secularization. The teaching could be carried out by people who did not have as their primary purpose the worship of God and prayer. The aim of education was not necessarily seen as a better understanding of the mysteries of the Holy Scripture. Learning became a human activity in its own right.

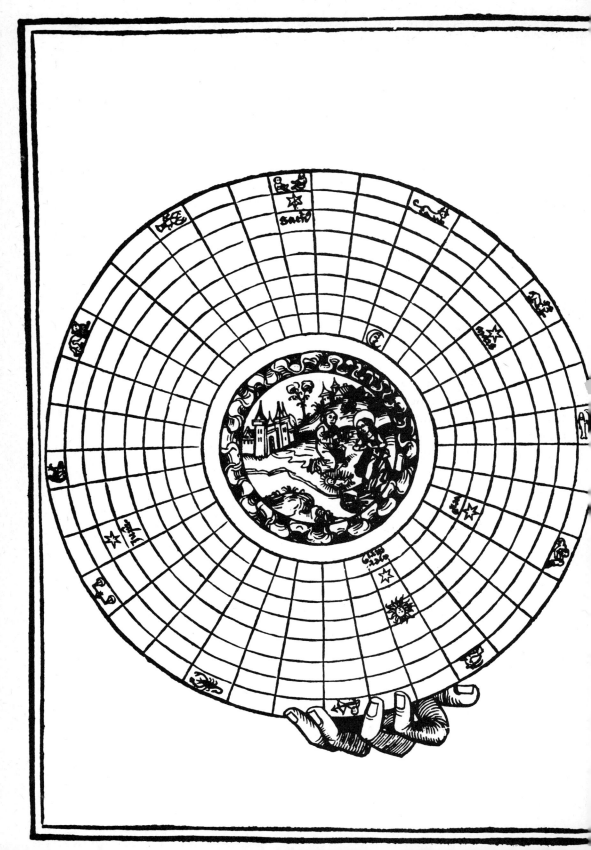

The New Learning

Pierre Abélard, the first 'academic'

In the history of ideas there are some people in whom a whole epoch is incarnate. Pierre Abélard (who died in 1142), nowadays better known for his amorous private lessons with the beautiful niece of an unpardonably naive canon and the tragic consequences they had for his virility, stands out with his restless intelligence, his intellectual vanity, his colossal appetite for rationalistic solutions to the mysteries of reason and faith as the prototype of the contentious academic, the very opposite of the humble traditionalism of monastic learning. He was fascinated by the possibilities of logic; he sought out conflict and threw himself into it with un-shakeable consciousness of his own brilliance.

Abélard had studied in Paris at Notre-Dame for the scholasticus of the cathedral, William of Champeaux. The two became irreconcilable enemies after Abélard had ridi-culed his teacher by showing the impossible consequences that his ultra-realistic conception of universals (which will be dealt with later) would lead to. This is probably the first example of a bitter academic feud about the appoint-ment of a teacher: William did not miss an opportunity to use his position in the diocese to prevent his disrespectful

Fig. 9. This illustration can be taken as a symbol of 'the medieval feeling of life'. In it we see the heavenly spheres in a stylized form with the signs of the Zodiac and the planets. Everything rests in God's all-powerful hand and at the very centre of the world God is born in the form of man, adored by Joseph and Mary. God supports the universe from outside and from within. Stephan Fridolin, *Schatzbehalter*, printed by Anton Koberger in Nuremberg in 1491.

pupil from being able to establish himself as a teacher. In Abélard's autobiographical *The Story of My Misfortunes* he leaves out none of the circumstances that usually attend the careers of misunderstood geniuses, nor is he sparing of sarcasms against the less gifted figures who envied his successes with the students. When he had established his position as an unrivalled logician he plunged into theology. He turned to the preeminent theologian of the period, the venerable Anselm of Laon:

Historia calamitatum

I went therefore to this old man whose reputation depended more on devastating routine than on intelligence or memory. If you were unsure about any question and went to him to discuss it, you left feeling even more unsure. When he lectured he seemed to be a phenomenon, but all the air went out of him if anyone asked him a question. He had a fantastic vocabulary, but his presentation was ridiculously pointless and irrational. When his flame burned it filled the room with smoke but gave no illumination.[23]

It was the fact that no logical rules had been used on the contents of the Bible that occasioned Abélard's contempt for the famous authors of commentaries that had supplied the norms for medieval interpretation of the Bible, *glossa ordinaria* and *glossa interlinearis* (cf. Fig. 6), which were concise summaries of the philological and theological traditions of explaining the running text of the Bible.

glossa ordinaria
glossa interlinearis

The 'old' logic

It may seem remarkable that one of the most formal of all of the branches of scholarship – logic – can arouse any passion at all. The rediscovery of Boethius' translations of Aristotle, however, which, even though they had admittedly been accessible in different places throughout the period, were studied systematically for the first time in the eleventh century, changed the intellectual conception of the world. The teachers and students who penetrated Aristotle's techniques believed that they had discovered in them tools that would enable them to organize reality. It provided a framework that could make nature less elusive, and language could be analysed exactly and its ambiguity removed. One knew where one had things. It was like a revelation.

The books which were later to be called 'the old art' or 'the old logic' were the sections of Aristotle's logic that Boethius had been able to translate, the *Categories* (the ten principal types of linguistic judgement), *On Interpretation* (a survey of types of propositions) and an *Introduction* to the *Categories* by the Greek commentator Porphyry. Boethius did not aim merely to translate them, he also wanted to create a manageable, uniform and exact terminology in Latin, which had not existed up to then. Philosophers using Latin should not, in his opinion, have to use less precise instruments than those which had been provided by Greek. It was, however, not until Abélard that this limited knowledge found a fertile place to grow. He elevated the old logic to a science.

vetus ars logica vetus

Praedicamenta Perihermeneias Isagoge

55

Fig. 10. If one is looking for one single illustration that can sum up the referential system of the medieval scholar, this would be it: 'Porphyry's Tree' (*arbor Porphyriana*). Everything that exists in the universe can with the help of this system be classified in

universals (*universalia*) in hierarchies that are similar to the system of classification used in botany. The example that has been chosen in Porphyry's Tree is the universal *homo*, Man, the universal concept for all individual human beings, here represented by 'Sortes' (the short form of Socrates) on the left and Plato on the right, and between them Johannes, Henricus, Nicolas and Petrus. The individuals form the root of the tree and are, in reality, outside the system; individuals cannot be defined. *Homo* is a *species*. Together with another species, Beast, the species of Man forms a *genus* called 'Living creatures' (*animal*). What distinguishes the species in a genus are certain 'specific characteristics' (*differentia specifica*). In the example here these are 'reason' and 'lack of reason' respectively. These specific characteristics are indicated in the picture on the lowest pair of branches. The genus of 'Living creatures' is in its turn a species in a higher genus, namely 'Organism' (*corpus animatum*), and its specific characteristic in this genus is 'possessing senses'. The other species in this genus, 'Plant', lacks senses. 'Possessing senses' and 'lacking senses' form the next pair of branches. 'Organism' forms in its turn a species in a higher genus, 'Body', which includes the two species 'Organism' and 'Non-organism', and so on. The highest genus (*genus generalissimum*) at the crown of the tree is 'Substance' (*Substantia*), and this is a heading that includes everything that can have an independent existence. Substance is the most important of the ten categories. *Species*, *genus* and *differentia specifica* constitute together with *proprium*, 'property' (for the universal concept of Man the property is 'ability to laugh') and *accidens*, 'accident' meaning fortuitous circumstance (for example, 'having blue eyes' or 'sitting'), the five predicables (*praedicabilia*), which are a system of labels for the universals. The predicables were therefore called reflex universals (*secundae intentiones*), second-level universals 'which do not exist in the nature of things but are the result of cogitation' (Thomas Aquinas). The argument over universals was about whether first-level universals (*primae intentiones*), such as Man, Living creature, Organism, Body and Substance, were entities that 'exist' in reality independent of human thought. The extreme realists such as Anselm of Canterbury insisted that this was the case. Moderate realists like Thomas Aquinas maintained that they had at least 'a basis in reality', whereas the nominalists, William of Occam prominent among them, claimed that they were mainly concepts of the brain. Petrus Hispanus, *Tractatus duodecim*, printed by Johannes Knob in Strasbourg in 1514.

Porphyry and the universals

Porphyry's introduction contains a number of concepts that were so fundamental in every context in the Middle Ages and the late Middle Ages that there is hardly any area of learning that has not been moulded to their requirements. The deepest controversies of medieval philosophy originate ultimately from a few apparently unobjectionable lines at the very beginning:

As regards 'families' and 'species' I will refrain from saying whether they have any independent reality or exist as mere notions and if that is the case if they are corporeal or incorporeal, if they exist independent of the senses or require them, or if they are merely the products of thought. This is a question I will not pursue here as it is a difficult question to fathom and demands a more penetrating discussion.[24]

Porphyry's restraint was taken as a challenge by the later philosophers and every thinker of any note sooner or later had to take a stand on the question. Every systematic description of reality in the later centuries of the Middle Ages was based on a foundation shaped by its architect's attitude to this bone of contention. What at first sight would appear to be a matter of philosophical taste was in fact to reveal the abyss that existed between different ways of describing the fabric of reality and how to acquire knowledge about it – if this is at all possible.

What was the argument about?

Imagine all the chairs in one house. Some of them would be called kitchen chairs, some stools, and some desk chairs. There may also be armchairs, deck chairs and other types as well. Nobody would protest, however, if I called each and every one of the objects a 'chair'. There is some quality in all of them which means that we can use the same designation for them without having to think twice about doing so.

If one has a bent for speculation one might follow the argument a step further: is it possible to combine the group of chairs with other groups of objects in the house and find a common name for all of them? It does not demand a great deal of deliberation to work out that all objects that can be called 'beds' and all that can be called 'tables' could be grouped together with chairs and be given the collective designation of 'furniture', and that each of the objects so far described can be called 'a piece of furniture'.

Given the time and the inclination, this speculative game can be extended until the whole of the universe has been included and neat, tidy labels have been given to all newly discovered groups that are added. But the process must stop somewhere: sooner or later you will end up with the largest class, a designation that fits everything that exists.

If we return to the point of departure, chairs, we can ponder for some time on what quality it is that enables us without any real problems to call a class of objects 'chairs'. What is the smallest common denominator for all chairs? How could one describe a 'chair' as concisely as possible so that the description fits every chair in the world and no other object? If I examine all the chairs in my home, I discover that I can sit on all of them, they have four or at least three legs, some of them have a backrest, some are painted green and some are painted white. Obviously what counts for all chairs is that people can sit on them and that they have at least three legs. On the other hand the concept of 'chair' does not include the fact that they are green or white or even that they have been painted any colour at all.

The most concise and universal description of a 'chair' seems therefore to be 'designed for sitting on'. This description starts with the class above it, in other words 'a piece of furniture' and adds the characteristic that singles out chairs from the other classes which along with chairs are included under the designation 'furniture', namely 'designed for sitting on', and in this way chairs are distinguished from beds and tables.

Porphyry is concerned with these concepts, called *universals*, that are the common designations for individual objects of the same kind (chairs, furniture and so on). The primary collective term for a class of individual objects (*individua*, i.e. indivisible things, 'that chair') he calls *species* (e.g. the species 'chair'). Several species can be united under the common designation *genus*, 'family' (e.g. the family

universalia

individua
species

genus

59

differentia
specifica

'furniture'). For the distinguishing characteristic that can single one species from another within the same genus he uses the term *differentia specifica* (e.g. 'designed for sitting on').

proprium

Most species have almost certainly some quality that they alone possess. Porphyry calls this kind of quality *proprium*, 'property' (for instance the individual nature of a chair, in contrast to a bed or a table, is that it can only be used by one person at a time). In addition within each species there may of course also exist any number of characteristics which are in no way necessary elements of its nature. This type of characteristic which 'just happens to exist' he calls *accidens*, 'fortuitous circumstance' (for instance the chair may very well be green but this is not part of the definition of a chair).

accidens

The argument about these terms, the universals controversy, was in fact about whether genus and species referred to something which existed independently of the individual objects themselves. Is there for instance any objective 'chair concept' some illusive chair-ness that exists independent of whether there are any chairs or not? Do all chairs form part of the same existence which already exists before we conceive of the idea of chair? Or is it rather that the only thing that links one chair to another is the concept of chair that we create in our mind? Perhaps one could go so far as to say that the only thing that chairs have in common is that in every language they are referred to by a certain series of sounds ('empty noise', *flatus vocis*), which is what the most radical opponents of the objective reality of the universals maintained.

flatus vocis

The philosophical contention between the group known as the realists and nominalists only really became heated from the fourteenth century onwards. But what Porphyry called the five predicables – *genus, species, differentia, proprium* and *accidens* – permeated everything from the time of Abélard and they were to crop up not only where they could be expected to but also in many unexpected places as well.

praedicabilia

The Categories

Another network that could be used to map reality and with the help of which new triangulation points could be found from which to survey its structure was Aristotle's *Categories*, or *Praedicamenta* as they were called in the Latin translation.

Praedicamenta

The text of the *Categories* is based on the thesis that everything that can be said using language can ultimately be reduced to ten main types of assertion, the ten categories ('judgements'). All meaningful assertions in language express one or several of the following ten things:

substance (human being, horse, etc.)	substantia
quantity (two cubits in length)	quantitas
quality (fair-skinned, a talent for languages)	qualitas
relationship (double, half, larger)	relatio, ad quid
place (in the Lyceum, in the square)	ubi
time (yesterday, last year)	quando
position (lying, sitting)	situs, situatio
equipment (with shoes on)	habitus
activity (cuts, burns)	actio
passivity (is cut, is burnt)	passio

The first category, *substance* (that which 'stands under', the supporter) is the only one which exists on its own and does not require any of the other categories. The remaining nine on the other hand must belong to one or more than one substance; they have to be supported by something else, the substances, and they were therefore called *accidents*, 'things which are added' to the substances and which cannot endure if the substance ceases to exist. (This use of *accident* has to be kept separate from the meaning of the term when used in referring to the universals.) Accidents can however be altered or cease to exist without this affecting their supporter, the substance.

accidentia

Propositions and oppositions

Perihermeneias (the closest translation of this almost un-translateable word would be roughly 'On propositions') contains a number of definitions of elementary terms in logic. Every expression consisting of two elements which each have a meaning of their own is a sentence (*oratio*).

oratio
enuntiatio
propositio

Sentences do not however become propositions (*enuntiatio* or *propositio*) until they assert or deny something about some subject ('Man is mortal'). Only propositions have the capacity to be true or false. Propositions that assert something positive are called affirmative; propositions that deny something are called negative. Propositions can also be

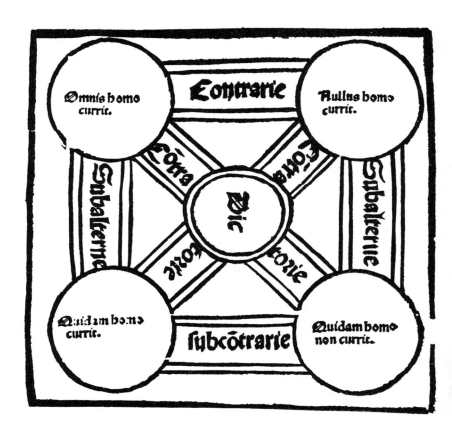

divided into universal propositions, which contain the words 'all' or 'every' (in negative propositions 'no' or 'none'), or particular propositions, which contain the word 'some' ('some . . . not' in negative propositions). These propositions can be in opposition to each other in different ways and rules can be established to show which of the pairs of opposites can be true or false at the same time and which cannot be.

At the end of *Perihermeneias* Aristotle establishes a rule about statements about the future. Assertions about future circumstances which are not the necessary result of something, which can, in other words, be one thing or the other, cannot be absolutely true or false but only probably true or probably false. This thesis gave rise to ingenious theological speculation: did it imply that not even God, the all-knowing could be certain about such non-necessary ('contingent') *futura contingentia* events in the future?

Fig. 11. This was called the square of opposition and it illustrates the different types of categorical propositions and their relationship to each other. At the top left is proposition type A (universal affirmative: 'All men run'); at the top right is type E (universal negative: 'No men run'). In the bottom left-hand corner is type I (particular affirmative: 'Some men run') and bottom right is type O (particular negative: 'Some men do not run'). The relationship of A to O and E to I is *contradictory*: they cannot both be true or both be false at the same time. A and E are *contraries* of each other: they cannot both be true at the same time but they can, on the other hand, both be false. I and O are *sub-contrary* to each other: while both can be at the same time true, they cannot both be false. I and O are *sub-alternately* subordinate to A and E respectively: I can be directly deduced from A and E from O. Contradiction is an either-or relationship (either A or not A) which precludes any third possibility (*tertium non datur*). Contraries are the extreme points on a scale or continuum (black–white for instance) and intermediate points can exist (such as grey). Petrus Hispanus, *Tractatus duodecim*, printed by Johannes Knob in Strasbourg in 1514. Cf. p. 265ff.

Definition: capturing the essence of things

definitio
definiendum

Part of the 'old logic' also consisted of some of Boethius' own shorter texts, and one of the things he did was to summarize Aristotle's teachings about correct definition. The thing to be defined (*definiendum*) must be designated by the genus immediately above it and its specific characteristics (*per genus proximum et differentiam specificam*). For instance if you want to define the concept of 'human being' you start with the genus above it which is 'living creatures'. The specific characteristics of this genus are 'reason' or 'lack of reason' and the species that possesses the specific characteristic of 'reason' is 'human beings'. The correct definition of 'human being' reads therefore as 'a living creature possessing reason', and its validity can be tested by making sure that the content of the definition ('a living creature

definiens

possessing reason', called *definiens*) covers only what was to be defined ('human beings', *definiendum*). If the one matches

definitio adaequata

the other precisely, the definition is adequate ('ground smooth').

essentia

It was thought that a definition of this kind stated the *essence* or nature of the *definiendum*, the fixed and unchanging nature that a given class (a species) was regarded as possessing. To use another term, the definition expressed an

quidditas

object's *quidditas*, it was the answer to the question: 'What (*quid*) is the nature of an X?' In other words this definition of the essence of things is not the same as the definitions of terms found in scholarly papers today where the precise meanings of the terminology that a writer intends to use are explained. These definitions of the essence of things attempted to capture the eternal common nature, given once and for all, of all the substances belonging to a species, regardless of any capricious accidentals. It was obvious, therefore, that individuals could not themselves be defined.

The 'old' logic also contained elements of the theory of syllogisms and of topic and these will be dealt with thoroughly later in the book (see pp. 95 and 99).

The beginnings of judicial scholasticism

Logic is the science of valid forms of thought, directions on the use of mankind's acumen and wisdom. It lists a limited number of rules that can be tested in everyday conversation and exemplified in innumerable ways. Training in logic results in awareness of contradictions and obscurities in both speech and thought. Someone who has learnt the contents of *Perihermeneias* will be able to notice any errors in the arguments used by people who disagree with him. He will have a keener nose for possible disagreements in the different norms that restrict his actions. Such discoveries will lead to intellectual discontent and a strong desire to find out whether the contradictions are irreconcilable or whether they can be ironed out in some way or another.

One pressing task was to subject the judicial system to logical analysis. During the confused centuries immediately after the collapse of the Roman Empire small communities and families were forced to take the law into their hands and administer it as best they could. The most appealing and effective solution to legal wrangles was often to maintain one's right by force of arms. As life slowly became more civilized in the eleventh century, it turned out that it could be more profitable to explore the possibilities offered by laws and this in its turn encouraged the growth of a specialized group of lawyers. Laws, however, differed in different places. Sometimes they were based on ancient Roman practices, sometimes they reflected Germanic customary law. As it became more and more common for disputes to be settled by courts of law, the lawyers of the period often found themselves without the comforting authority of written laws.

In the eleventh century scholars, for the first time since the classical period, began to study the Roman legal sources in the form in which they had been codified by the Emperor Justinian in the sixth century. They approached these texts with the same reverence as that shown by the grammarians for Virgil. The classical texts radiated unrivalled clarity, the expression of the magnificent harmony and wisdom of a vanished age. Nevertheless, the laws, like poems, contained many obscure words and expressions, and they reflected a cultural environment that had long vanished. It was therefore necessary to explain and annotate the texts of the laws in the same way as for literary works: unusual words had to be explained with a synonym, obscure structures had to be rewritten and customs and habits that had long been forgotten had to be clarified with historical notes (glosses).

The glossators of Bologna

In exactly the same way as the systematic training of doctors had begun in Salerno, students of law began to travel from most of Europe to Bologna to study at the feet of the leading figure in the newly revived study of jurisprudence, Irnerius (who died in 1125). Their studies started with Justinian's collation of laws (*Institutiones*, *Codex*, *Digestum*, *Novellae*). *Digestum* was the subject of the regular lectures in Bologna and it is a text that is nothing more than a monumental collection of commentaries and interpretations by Roman jurists on philosophically important questions of legal principle and the casuistical application of these opinions in everyday affairs. In it the basic concepts are described: laws and rights, civil and common law, natural law, positive law and international law. The *Digestum* opens with the following distinctions:

Public law is the legislation which refers to the Roman state, *Private law* on the other hand is of value to the individual. Common law contains statutes about sacrifices, the priesthood and civil servants. Private law can be divided into three parts: it comprises regulations based on natural law and regulations governing the intercourse of nations and of individuals. *Natural law* is what is taught to all living creatures by nature itself, laws which apply not only to mankind but to every living creature on the earth, in the heavens or in the seas. It is this that sanctions the union of man and woman, which is called marriage, and likewise the bearing and upbringing of children: we can see that other living creatures also possess understanding of this law. *International law* is the [commonly recognized set of] laws applied by every nation of the world. As can be seen it differs from natural law in that the latter is the same for all living creatures whereas the former only concerns human intercourse. . . . *Civil law* does not deviate completely from natural law but neither is it subordinate to it. . . . It is either written or unwritten. . . . Its sources are laws, popular decisions, decisions of the senate, the decrees of princes and the opinions of jurists. . . . *Justice* is the earnest and steadfast desire to give every man the rights he is entitled to. The injunctions of the law are these: live honestly, do no man injury, give to every man what he is entitled to.

Institutiones
Codex
Digestum
Novellae

ius publicum
ius privatum

ius naturae

ius gentium

ius civile

'iustitia est constans et perpetua voluntas ius suum cuique tribuendi'

iuris prudentia	*Jusrisprudence* is knowledge of divine and human things, the study of right and wrong.[25]

Codex Iustinianus, the other textbook used for the regular lectures, is a collection of additions to Roman law and reflects markedly the social structure that prevailed after Christianity had been raised to the rank of official religion. Preeminent in this law is the Holy Trinity, followed by the Church, its property and its privileges, with the hierarchy of bishops, priests and deacons, the rules of ecclesiastical law, decrees about measures against heretics and pagans, and only after all this regulations about civil servants. The *Codex* finishes with a series of examples of how the laws were applied by the Roman emperors.

Digestum novum

The jurists at Bologna were then called on to study the second half of the *Digestum* (called the *Digestum novum* this is another example of how the accidents of fate affected medieval scholarship: the point separating the old from the new in the *Digestum* is in the middle of a paragraph, probably because the second half was part of a manuscript that was not available when the plan for the lectures on legal studies was established) as well as a number of shorter Roman and Lombard texts.

Corpus iuris civilis

This complete *Corpus iuris civilis* was to influence the thinking of both secular and ecclesiastical lawyers with its large number of definitions and universal rules of law expressed in the form of maxims such as 'Ignorance of the facts is an excuse, ignorance of the law is no excuse', 'No one may be sued twice for the same offence'. The studies were not restricted only to a careful examination of the texts, mock trials were also arranged and in them every possible application of the regulations of Roman law were tried out and rules for interpreting them in doubtful cases established.

Invariably a character called Titius figured in these fictitious trials always opposed by his adversary Seius, and sometimes also the unfortunate woman Seia. One of Irnerius' pupils, Bulgarus, wooed his listeners with thumbnail sketches of their daily life:

Seia, Titius' wife, lived in fear of the strokes and blows he dealt her

68

so generously (possibly because she spoke so often to strange men).[26]

On another occasion Titius and Seius were at odds because they interpreted an agreement in different ways:

Titius gave all his possessions to Seius on condition that the latter provided him with food. In doing so he did not think about the offspring that were later to arrive. Seized with misgivings, he asked for the possessions that he had once given away on certain conditions (the provision of food) to be returned to him, believing that he had the right to change his mind. The recipient challenged this, saying that Titius had no right to alter things, especially as both parties were bound by an agreement and that he had met all its stipulations fully.[27]

According to Bulgarus' statement on this case, the gift could not be retrieved, but if the size of the transfer had not been specified, Titius could, when he became a father, have claimed in the children's name, but not in his own, one quarter of their inheritance.

Irnerius and his successors, the glossators, used the 'old' logic in ways which excelled the standard found in the schools within the subject *dialectica*, one of the seven liberal arts. Here Boethius' legacy was put to good service. Repeated use is made of definitions like those described in earlier chapters: first the genus in which the object under examination is a species is established and then its distinctive characteristics are given. At the beginning of his commentary on Justinianus' *Institutiones* Irnerius defines 'justice' as a species in the genus 'virtue' and says that the genus contains three other species, namely 'prudence', 'fortitude' and 'temperance' (in other words the four cardinal virtues).

The glossator Placentinus goes at one point into a discussion of whether a definition in a legal text is adequate:

Prosecution is nothing else than the pleading in a court of law for the right that someone is entitled to. The definiens can be replaced by the definiendum. In fact every prosecution is the pleading in a court of law of the right that someone is entitled to, and vice versa.[28]

The glossators' more stringent demand for formal definitions is sometimes expressed in irritated comments about the traditional ways of expressing things:

'The beach is as long as the highest wave can reach.' This is not a definition of 'beach' but an explanation of how wide a beach is. A definition must state what the essence (*quid sit*) of the definiendum is, and this is not found here.[29]

The glossators also made use of the theory of categories and illustrated it with different fictitious cases but the effect was forced, systematization for its own sake: the examples are far too dissimilar to be illuminating and they do not provide any major help in surveying the problems of law. What was more useful was the theory of syllogisms (see p. 99) which in a limited form was part of the area covered by the 'old' logic. A gloss on a paragraph about the right to water consists of a syllogism of the first figure, although the order has been rearranged somewhat:

Things which can be described as 'common' are those awarded to the first possessor (major premise)
River water must be regarded as 'common' (conclusion)
As it is awarded to the first possessor (minor premise)[30]

The theory of topic, a collection of universal axioms formulated by Aristotle and Boethius (see p. 95), was a branch of study almost formulated for use in a court of law. The glossator Jacobus writes:

He who makes a law can also interpret law. *A minore.*[31]

locus a minore

These last words show the type of argument that can be applied here is 'from the lesser, the greater can be deduced', *locus a minore*. The axiom quoted is an application of the basic axiom: 'If something that one has only weak reasons to expect is true, stronger reasons will make it all the more likely to be the case': if a judge, who is himself governed by law, has the right to interpret the law, this right must be even more strongly ascribed to the originator of laws (the Emperor) who is above the law. Similarly the glossators use

70

example of *locus a definitione* ('what belongs to the definiens locus a definitione belongs also to the definiendum'), *locus a causa* ('when the locus a causa cause ceases, so does the effect'), and *locus a simili* (deduction locus a simili by analogy: 'the same judgements are valid for similar things').

The work of the glossators paved the way for systematic study of jurisprudence again for the first time since the classical period. The first attempts to organize the great mass of legal texts into manageable units can, on more than one occasion, appear to be naive demonstrations of scholarship which were probably of little practical help when they were needed. They do display the influence of logic on ways of thought, however, and its growing importance in education. One thing is obvious and that is that increasingly subtle analyses of legal concepts and the premises on which they were based contributed indirectly to realizing the aim of every good legislator – the exclusion of arbitrary and capricious judgements as far as possible from the application of laws.

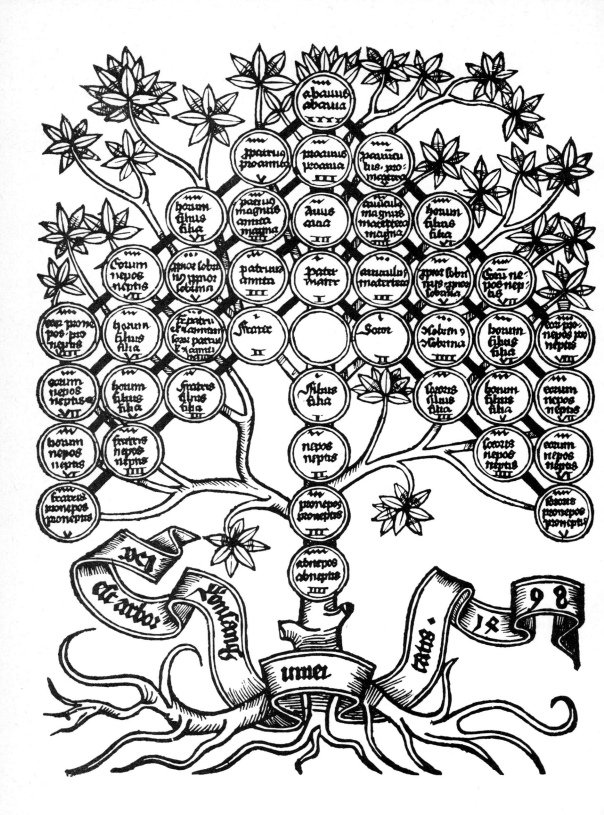

Canon law and the beginnings of historical criticism

The laws passed in different societies in different periods may appear to vary as capriciously as the demands of etiquette in different cultures. In Bologna the jurists contrasted the impressive cogency and lucidity of their classical sources with the confusing and contradictory regulations of later periods. Roman law impressed them greatly with its general common sense, and even if the rationality of some paragraphs was not immediately obvious deference was paid to their venerable antiquity. However, when it came to canon law the relationship was somewhat more complicated. *ius canonicum* For one thing this code was an 'animate law', continuously being built up as new decisions were made and, in addition, its validity was based on supranatural authority in the Bible, Church Councils and pronouncements of the Fathers and of the Popes. Often these could not be justified by rational argument but neither could they be questioned on the same grounds. Common sense could not, however, stand idly by

Fig. 12. A 'tree of kinship', *arbor consanguineitatis*. The tree shows the different designations of the kin of a certain person for the four generations directly above him and the four generations directly below him, as well as all his collateral relationships up to the descendants of the same great-great-grandfather. This table is more than a linguistic exercise. It was regularly included in editions of the canon law to illustrate the impediments to marriage based on kinship. Ecclesiastical law forbade marriage between blood relations up to and including the sixth degree. The fourth Lateran Council relaxed these regulations so that they applied up to and including the fourth degree. In other words this table covers all the relationships that preclude marriage. In addition marriage between a person and his godparents was prohibited as godparents and godchildren were considered to be spiritually kin to each other. *Arbor consanguineitatis*, printed by Jacob Thanner in Leipzig in 1498.

when these sources of the Church's teaching and canon law, which were both regarded as being expressions of the same (divine) authority, contradicted themselves in some way. It went against the grain to accept irreconcilable opposition in accepted ecclesiastical ordinances.

This was by no means a new dilemma. From earliest times Christians had had to commit themselves to one position when different parts of the Bible seemed to contradict each other. Augustine had laid down rules for the systematic exegesis of the Bible. What was new was that at some time around the year 1100 methodical systems were worked out for reconciling these inconsistencies using the 'old' logic as their basis.

The pioneer in this field was Bernold of Constance (who died in 1100). His starting point was the question of the validity of the sacraments performed by people who had been excommunicated from the Church and who were therefore no longer part of its communion. The relevant texts seemed to be in direct opposition to each other and when Bernold had described what his sources said he continued:

We can easily show that these different opinions are in harmony with each other. . . . Even when regulations point in different directions we should attempt to establish the validity of their implications so that we do not casually write off their dissimilarities as irreconcilably inconsistent. We do know that they have been promulgated and confirmed by apostolic authority. It is therefore our constant duty to attempt to discover an import in these regulations that will prevent them from ever conflicting with each other.

Bernold established the following rules for interpretation:

Take the total context into account.
Compare different decisions with each other. One is often explained by another.
Take account of the period and the environment, the people the regulations refer to and the reasons for making it.
Make a clear distinction between discretionary directions which apply until further notice and universal and eternal regulations.

Examine the authenticity of a text carefully and whether it has
   perhaps been falsely ascribed to an author or has been inserted
   spuriously in a genuine text.[32]

Here he has formulated concise rules for what was to be
known much later as the critical analysis of sources or
historical criticism. This regard for the reputation of the
authorities gave rise to the first impulses towards a critical
and scholarly methodology.

The Decree of Gratian

In the cities of northern Italy rudiments of the secular educational system seem to have survived the Dark Ages. The law school at Bologna was a lay institution. It was established to prepare lawyers for a career in the civil administration.

At some time in the 1140s however, it began to lose its predominantly secular emphasis. This happened when canon law developed into a subject of scholarly study in its own right . The clerical counterpart of Irnerius was a monk named Gratian (who died around 1160). He compiled a textbook which became so successful that all the texts that had hitherto been used in teaching canon law quickly fell into obscurity: 'The reconciliation of contradictory canon laws' or, to use the name more often used, the *Decree*. Apart from the Bible itself, the sources he used were decisions of the Church Councils, liturgical books, Roman, Visigothic, Franconian and Germanic legal codes and various pronouncements made by earlier canonists. Gratian put into practice the method formulated by Bernold and which was later to be introduced into theology by Abélard; his aims were to collect all the legal sources in one volume and to compare them with each other. At the same time he accounts continuously for the principles of interpretation used, defines the difficulties that arise (in the form of questions) and presents solutions. The first section of the *Decree* (the first 'distinction') deals with the fundamental question of the nature of justice:

Concordantia discordantium canonum Decretum

(*Gratian*): Two things govern the human race, natural law and custom. Natural law consists of those precepts in the law and in the Gospel which enjoin every man to treat others as he himself would be treated. For this reason Christ says in the Gospel: 'Whatever ye would that men should do unto you, do ye also unto them. For this is the law and the prophets.' It is for this reason that Isidore says in the fifth book of Etymologies:

All laws are either of human or of divine right. The law of God is manifest in nature, human laws are displayed in customs. The latter vary as different peoples follow different customs. The law of God is called *fas* (divine order), human law is called *ius*. The right to cross another man's fields is granted by *fas* and not by *ius*. fas – ius

(*Gratian*): This authoritative statement (*auctoritas*) demonstrates the difference between divine and human justice. auctoritas

All that is fitting or appropriate (*fas*) is called divine or natural law, but by human law is meant written or oral customary law. 'Justice' is a genus that includes many species. Therefore in the same book Isidore says that 'Justice' is a genus and that 'law' is a species within justice.[33]

Gratian's *Decree* deals not only with legal questions but also with matters of ethics and dogma. At this time theology had not been divided into separate disciplines, but one of the consequences of Gratian's book was that canon law became a separate subject pursued by specialists (known as decretists). Its relationship with the monasteries was broken and its scholars did not necessarily see it as part of a larger context. It became an independent intellectual pursuit.

The *Decree* was augmented as time went by with new papal decisions (decretals) on different concrete legal cases. These new legal sources – *Liber extra, Liber sextus, Clementinae* and *Extravagantes* – were grouped together as *Corpus iuris canonici*. Civil law had acquired an ecclesiastical counterpart.

decretales
Liber extra
Liber sextus
Clementinae
Extravagantes
Corpus iuris
canonici

The logic of revelation

The study of logic highlighted the question of the relationship of authority to rationality. 'Revelation' is by definition the disclosure of something that reason cannot on its own deduce, for otherwise revelation would not be necessary. But if the revelation contained the truth and if logic was the instrument for distinguishing true from false, a Christian philosopher could not make the assumption that theology and reason were two incompatible entities.

The abbot of the monastery of Bec in Normandy, Lanfranc, who was Archbishop of Canterbury when he died in 1089, in his commentary on the epistles of Paul, wanted to show that in dealing with the central feature of the Christian faith the apostle uses the same methods of argument as those recommended by Aristotle and Boethius. In the fifteenth chapter of the first Epistle to the Corinthians Lanfranc has indicated the organization of the presentation of the argument with terms taken from the study of topics (see p. 95):

Now if Christ be preached that he rose from the dead, how say some of you that there is no resurrection (*a genere*) of the dead? . . . (Answer): But if there be no resurrection of the dead, then is Christ not risen . . . Then (*a simili*) they also which are fallen asleep in Christ are perished. (Minor premise): But now is Christ risen from the dead, and become the first fruits of them that slept . . . If, after the manner of men, I have fought with beast at Ephesus, what advantageth it me, if the dead rise not? (Irony): 'Let us eat and drink, for tomorrow we die!'[34]

locus a genere

The type of argument called *locus a genere* involves the application of the axiom 'if a genus is excluded so also are its species', which is to say that if in this case general resurrection from the dead (genus) is denied, this implicitly denies the resurrection of Christ (species) and one's own resurrection (another species).

Lanfranc's successor as Archbishop of Canterbury had also earlier been a monk at Bec. Anselm of Canterbury (who died in 1109) was both an eminent logician and a speculative theologian. He was convinced that logic both could and should be applied to the knowledge of God. He took as his starting point a verse from the Book of the Prophet Isaiah which in the old translations read: 'If you have no faith you will not be able to understand'. Boethius had said something similar: 'As far as possible combine belief and reason.' Anselm saw it as a Christian duty to try to survey matters of belief rationally and by doing so to seek answers to intellectual objections to faith (the key word was 'faith which seeks to understand'). In order to demonstrate the rationality of faith he attempted, without using references to the authorities or to the Bible, to prove that there is irrefutable evidence for the existence of God:

fides quaerens intellectum

Some of my brethren have repeatedly implored me to speak in everyday language of the nature of God and His contemplation. . . . They have desired me to refrain from proving my argument with the help of quotations from the Bible and to present the results of each enquiry in straightforward language, ordinary arguments, and simple evidence, to formulate indisputable conclusions concisely and produce obvious proof of the revealed truth. They also desire me not to avoid facing naive or even unintelligent objections. . . . I do not see that anything I have said would clash with the writings of the Holy Fathers, or with Augustine's in particular. . . . If one regards the nature of things, it is soon apparent, whether we want to see it or not, that they do not all occupy the same rank in a scale of values: some take precedence over others by having a higher value. What man would deny that a horse is by its very nature higher than a piece of wood, or that a human being is higher than a horse? As one cannot therefore deny that the nature of some things is better than others, reason requires that there should be a supreme nature which has nothing above it. For if this scale was endless so that there was no highest value which has nothing above it, reason would be compelled to admit that there was an infinite multiplicity of natures. Everyone who is not himself insane will perceive the insanity of such a thought. There must, therefore, necessarily be a nature which is higher than any other or others and which is not itself below any other. . . . From this follows that there is a nature which is the highest of all those that exist. This could not exist if it were not what it is by virtue of its own power. . . . There is therefore a nature (or a substance or an essence) which by virtue of its own power is good and great and by virtue of whose power everything that is good and great, or indeed

79

anything at all, is what it is, a nature which is the highest good, the greatest and self-sufficient Being.[35]

As there must exist something that could occupy the highest position in the hierarchy of values, Anselm assumed that this being, which was the greatest conceivable, must also exist in reality, that the greatest conceivable is God.

This later became known as Anselm's ontological argument for the existence of God, and its validity was to be disputed both by Thomas Aquinas and Immanuel Kant. But the 'proof' aroused opposition from Anselm's contemporaries: a brother monk, Gaunilo, elected himself mouthpiece for the 'insane' and pointed out that the Islands of Bliss can easily be conceived without necessarily existing physically.

Abélard: reason takes precedence over faith

If faith for Anselm was the cognitive basis necessary if reality was to be understood, the approach adopted by Abélard was the direct opposite: for him reason was supreme. Only after critical and rational evaluation can one place confidence in an authority. Otherwise it would be pointless to try to convince a pagan or a heretic that he was wrong, he merely had to point out that faith was above all reason. Abélard supplies palpable evidence for the need for critical evaluation (the 'methodic doubt' that Aristotle recommends at the beginning of the Categories) in his essay *Sic et Non*. In it he enumerates 158 Sic et Non questions concerning the Christian faith and ethics on which the authorities, the Bible, the Councils of the Church, the Holy Fathers and other Christian writers seem to have contradictory opinions. Abélard supplies no answers to these knotty questions but leaves the solving of them to the reader's own perspicacity. To aid him in his task, however, he lays down some rules which appear to have been inspired by Bernold of Constance (see p. 74). Abélard extends the scope of critical analysis of sources to cover not only canon law but also Christian doctrine. The technique is refined further and the reader is told to find out whether the propositions contained in a text might be a survey of the opinions of other writers, hypotheses formulated for the sake of argument or are definite statements of opinion. Different writers use language differently and a given word cannot always be interpreted in the same way in different contexts. Textual criticism is also necessary and if a passage is difficult to understand it must be established whether this difficulty is the result of a mistake in copying the text, a translation mistake or caused by the reader's lack of sufficient knowledge. If at the end of this the authorities still disavow each other, they have to be balanced against each other. Only the Bible is above discussion, and second to its authority are the Holy Fathers insofar as the Church has adopted their pronouncements as its own. There must be complete freedom to interpret everything else:

I present here a collection of statements of the Holy Fathers in the order in which I have remembered them. The discrepancies which these texts seem to contain raise certain questions which should present a challenge to my young readers to summon up all their zeal to establish the truth and in doing so to gain increased perspicacity. For the prime source of wisdom has been defined as continuous and penetrating enquiry. The most brilliant of all philosophers, Aristotle, encouraged his students to undertake this task with every ounce of their curiosity. In the section on the category of relation he says: 'It is foolish to make confident statements about these matters if one does not devote a lot of time to them. It is useful practice to question every detail.' By raising questions we begin to enquire, and by enquiring we attain the truth, and, as the Truth has in fact said: 'Seek, and ye shall find; knock, and it shall be opened unto you.' He demonstrated this to us by His own moral example when He was found at the age of twelve 'sitting in the midst of the doctors both hearing them and asking them questions'. He who is the Light itself, the full and perfect wisdom of God, desired by His questioning to give his disciples an example before He became a model for teachers in His preaching. When, therefore, I adduce passages from the scriptures it should spur and incite my readers to enquire into the truth, and the greater the authority of these passages, the more earnest this enquiry should be.[36]

'dubitare de singulis non erit inutile'

Bernard of Clairvaux the antidialectician

All attempts like these to anatomize the revealed truth so that it could, as it were, be passed or failed aroused violent antagonism in a man like Bernard of Clairvaux. Abélard's ideas were not in themselves sensational or even particularly new. Augustine had expressed similar thoughts and Anselm of Canterbury could have been expected to have some sympathy for Abélard's critical (i.e. reflective, evaluative and balanced) programme in its desire to make the assent to articles of faith something more than the blind acceptance of authority. What shook Bernard to the core, however, was the new and non-traditional method of presenting arguments, which had aroused such violent interest in the schools:

Virtues and vices are discussed with no trace of moral feelings, the sacraments of the Church with no evidence of faith, the mystery of the Holy Trinity with no spirit of humility or sobriety: all is presented in a distorted form, introduced in a way different from the one we learned and are used to.[37]

The difference between Abélard and Bernard is the difference between two contradictory mentalities. Where Bernard was ecstatic in the face of ineffable mystery, Abélard saw an intellectual riddle which should be explained rationally as quickly as possible. In Abélard one can see quite clearly for the first time the seeds of a form of academic 'objectivity' in which problems are approached without the interpreter having first decided his personal relationship to the source that is to be interpreted. This dispassionate distance was new and ran counter to the centuries of monastic tradition that revered and loved the authorities as divinely inspired witnesses to the truth and in this new approach Bernard saw a dangerous threat to faith itself:

The faith of simple people is ridiculed, divine mysteries simplified, and the deepest matters become the subject of undignified wrangling. Human acumen presumes to everything and leaves nothing for faith. All that cannot be illuminated with the help of reason is regarded as trivial, something which it is beneath one's dignity to believe in.[38]

Bernard was not only an ardent mystic immured in a monastery, but also happened to be the most influential man of his day, a ruthless politician who could not tolerate any of his own unyielding convictions being gainsaid. He began a violent campaign against Abélard and did not rest until he had secured his conviction as a heretic before one of the provincial councils by quoting a number of dubious statements in his theological publications. But this was really a duel of personalities, a clash of temperaments. Abélard's methods had come to stay and they were adopted almost immediately by theologians of every school.

The form of the lecture is established

All teaching aimed to establish a relationship to the written traditions. In the twelfth century a form of teaching was worked out and standardized which was to be used in every area of study. The starting point was the text (*littera*) of the work studied, be it the Bible, laws, history, poetry or a medical treatise. The introductory session followed a fixed system of questions. Conrad of Hirsau, the headmaster whose dialogue between teacher and pupil has already been quoted earlier, presents the matter like this:

Teacher: You should know that when the ancients were about to expound a text they asked seven questions: author, the title of the work, its nature, the purpose of the author, the number and sequence of the books and then the interpretation of the text itself. Nowadays we are satisfied if four things are established about a work: its subject matter, its aim, its underlying purpose and what branch of philosophy it belongs to.
Pupil: Tell me what matter, aim and underlying purpose are.
Teacher: Matter is the substance something consists of. The word means roughly 'the mother of things' (*mater rei*). Matter is used in two contexts: one refers for example to the wood and stone which a house is built of, the other refers to genus and species and other elements of language used in the work the writer has undertaken. Aim (*intentio*) is the author's intention, the nature of the subject, its length and object. The underlying purpose (*causa finalis*) refers to its usefulness for the reader.[39]

The text shows traces both of Isidore's fanciful etymologies and the beginnings of Aristotelianism which was concerned to focus on and objectify the subject to be studied with the conceptual system of the new scholarship. During the following century hardly any text could be introduced without its four causes – material, formal, efficient and final (see p. 118) – having been established. The text was divided into different sections on the basis of logic and ascribed to a genus (practical philosophy for instance) and a species (ethics) with the characteristics that distinguished it from the other species (economics and politics) within the same

littera

intentio
causa finalis

genus. Only then did the interpreter begin to gloss the individual words and expressions in the text, a task that had become very necessary as most of the texts used in teaching were translations that followed the original languages very literally.

lectio
lectura

The whole of this method was called *lectio* ('reading' from which 'lesson' is derived) or *lectura*. In it the teacher was active and the pupils listened attentively and tried to remember as much as possible. To begin with they were not allowed to make notes and what they had learnt had to be recited from memory every day. However, as conceptual systems became more elaborate and the number of sections and subsections increased, it became necessary to note down the presentations. In the thirteenth century lecture notes gave rise to a new literary genre, which was known as

reportatio

reportatio ('carrying home'). The lectures of the most prominent teachers were circulated in the form of notes (at times these had been corrected and approved by the lecturer himself).

Delight in this new educational technique could in places give rise to excess. It could undoubtedly be used to provide effective help for the memory, but it could also turn into an end in itself which obscured the difference between the trivial and the important and destroyed any feeling for knowledge in its entirety:

In grammar they talk about the construction of syllogisms, in logic the declensions of cases. And, which is even more ridiculous, when commenting on the title of a work they go right through its contents. The first word has hardly been dealt with after three lectures. This is not teaching, it is a demonstration of ostentatious learning. Notice the fallacy in this approach: the greater the number of irrelevant details that are introduced, the less it is possible to discern what is important and remember it.[40]

Lombard – 'the master of the sentence'

The great systematizer in theology was Peter Lombard, the Bishop of Paris (who died in 1164). As the consummation of his work as a teacher he compiled a textbook in theology with the title *Sententiae* ('Sentences') which was in principle a more ambitious version of a florilegium in which the material had been arranged according to different themes, and there was a certain amount of commentary, presentation of problems and suggestions for solutions. The extracts were taken from the Bible, the Holy Fathers, the decisions of Church Councils, the works of Abélard and Gratian's *Decree*. It has been said of Lombard that he was an Abélard who was lucky and became a bishop. The *Sentences* were not the first summary of intellectual aspects of the doctrines of faith but they were the best, and, together with the Bible, they were to be one of the basic texts in theology until the sixteenth century. In Lombard's work ('the master of Sentences') Abélard's critical methods became part of the workday world of the classroom. *Sententiae*

magister Sententiarum

In the *Sentences* Peter Lombard describes an immense circle: from God, who is self-sufficient, proceeds all creation and it strives to return to its origin. The first book deals with God and the nature of God, the second with the creation and the fall of man, the third with the incarnation of Christ and the redemption, the fourth with the sacraments and the final things. To all of these he applies Augustine's teachings about reality (*res*) and sign (*signum*). There are two forms of reality, one is eternal reality, God, the goal we shall possess (*frui*), the other is the temporary, provisional reality that surrounds us, in other words created things, which we should utilize (*uti*) only as means to this goal. Both realities are signified by the sacraments which in and through material created things (water, bread, wine and oil) reflect and effect God's existence in man. *res, signum*

frui

uti

The relationship between faith and knowledge is dealt with by Lombard in a way that presages the thoroughgoing scholastic teaching method of analysing every problem that arises by formulating it as a question (*questio*), or more *quaestio*

87

precisely an indirect disjunctive question in which the second alternative is omitted: 'Whether X is Y (or not).' Put like this the question can give rise to paradox as a long list of

reasons can be produced which make it appear (*videtur*) that the only possible answer contradicts recognized, spon-

Fig. 13. The Creation. At the top is God the Father and from His mouth flows the Holy Spirit and the Word, which is to say Christ, who 'was in the beginning with God' and by whom all things were made (the Gospel according to St John 1:1–3, cf. Psalm 33, v 6). In this picture God, through Christ, creates Eve from the rib of Adam, who is asleep. In medieval Bible interpretation this was a 'prototype' for the creation of the Church, baptism and the Eucharist from the side that was pierced at the Crucifixion (John 19:34). The Bible in German, printed by Heinrich Quentell in Cologne around 1479.

taneous assumptions which are moreover supported by the authorities.

The solution to this lies in *distinctio* (distinction) of the different possible meanings of the concept X: It should be known (*sciendum*) that the word X is used in several different meanings. . . .' distinctio

sciendum

Lombard's writing shows obvious influences from his own teaching. The question presented here seems to have been used regularly for practice in the schools in Paris in his day:

Here the question is often raised: that as faith concerns invisible and unseen things (Hebrews 11:1) does it exclusively concern unknown things? If this is the case it would *appear* that the objects of faith can only be the unknown.

However, it should be known that there is external sight and inner sight. Faith does not concern what can be seen with external sight, its objects are what can be perceived in some way by inner sight. Certain things, can be the objects of faith while they can at the same time be obvious to natural reason, others will be believed even though they cannot be understood. Augustine clarifies the words of the prophet: 'If you do not believe, you will not understand' by saying: 'We believe some things even if we do not understand them, others cannot be understood if we do not believe them.' However, nobody can believe in God, if he has understood nothing as 'faith comes from hearing' preaching.

In his book On the Trinity, the same writer says: 'Firm faith is the beginning, however imperfect, of certainty, but complete certainty is not attained until after this life.' Ambrose said as well: 'Certainty does not enter immediately where there is faith, but where certainty exists there has also been faith.'

From this it should be apparent that there are certain things that cannot be understood or perceived unless first believed, whereas other things can be understood even before one believes them. But one does not understand them now in the way that one will understand them in the future, even so one can understand them better with the help of faith to purify the heart. For if one does not love God in faith, the heart cannot attain that purity which is necessary if one is to know anything about Him.[41]

Lombard's compendium lacks real originality and speculative depth. The author was himself aware of his limitations. In the preface he compares himself to the poor

Fig. 14. The theologians of scholasticism used the terminology of philosophy consistently to formulate the belief that Jesus was really present in the sacrament of Holy Communion, that the very substance of the bread and wine was transformed (transubstantiated) into the body and blood of Christ even though the accidental and fortuitous circumstances remained the same. The early scholastics were not, however, completely unanimous on the question of what degree of objectivity this transformation had. If, for example, a mouse were to consume the consecrated host, what is it in fact eating? Peter Lombard put the problem like this in his *Sentences* (book 4, distinction 13), 'It appears that what can be said is that dumb animals cannot receive the body of Christ, even if they appear to do so. What then does it receive, what is the mouse eating? God knows.' As this question was included in the *Sentences*, every teacher of theology had to take a definite stand on it. Unlike many of the problems in scholasticism this one could be expressed in simple and popular terms. Later generations have therefore been given the impression that the problem of the mouse's communion (or how many angels could be contained on a pinhead) were the main spiritual problems of the Middle Ages. This picture is taken from a handbook containing regulations to prevent irreverence for the consecrated elements (*Negligentie et defectus in missa contigentes*), printed by Heidericus and Marx Ayer in the 1490s. While the priest is devoutly concerned with his missal, a mouse snatches a piece of the host and at the same time a fly falls into the chalice.

widow in the parable who adds her mite to the Temple's treasury. However, just as the summaries compiled by Irnerius and Gratian on secular and ecclesiastical law gave rise to legal scholarship, Lombard's was to be the foundation of the study of theology in the schools and universities in the scholastic period. No less a figure than Dante acknowledges his position in allowing him to appear in Paradise together with Gratian and Thomas Aquinas. The latter was in fact to begin his brilliant career at the university in Paris in the 1250s as a commentator on the *Sentences*:

Next flames the light of Gratian's smile, who taught
  In either form, and in both gives pleasure
  To Paradise, by the good work he wrought.

That Peter next adorns our door, in measure
  Generous as she whose widowed means were small
  On Holy Church bestowing all his treasure.[42]

The 'new' logic

Abélard, Gratian and Lombard mark the threshold of a new era, the era of scholasticism. No mention has yet been made, however, of what provided both the real inspiration and basis necessary for this development: the new translations that led to the discovery of Aristotle's work in its entirety and to the growth of the universities.

logica nova

Abélard himself had had some knowledge about the sections of Aristotle's logic that were soon to be called the 'new' logic (*logica nova*). A contemporary chronicler tells us that the clerk James of Venice had in 1128 translated directly from Greek those parts of Aristotle that had not previously been translated into Latin. This translation was, however, regarded as being so obscure that the teachers in the schools in Paris did not dare to lecture on it despite the fact (or perhaps for precisely that reason) that it followed the original faithfully word for word. If one bears in mind that the texts of Aristotle's works seem themselves to have been notes for lectures written in an extremely laconic style in which many things are only implied, it is easy to understand that the translated texts often seemed to be complete gibberish. In his approach to the Greek originals, James made use of a technique that had been recommended by Boethius, which was to 'plank' the original text as far as possible, to give every Greek expression a fixed equivalent in Latin. The result was, not unexpectedly, extraordinary and without any literary value, especially as the original had been written in an extremely succinct and sometimes exasperating style. This literal translation did, however, have one immediate advantage in that its slavish copying conveyed to the reader who had become accustomed to its peculiar abruptness exactly what the author had intended as clearly as possible.

The learned humanist John of Salisbury wrote, around the year 1159, about the translations of *Analytica Posteriora* (see p. 103) in use at the time in a way that makes it clear that among his colleagues the conditions did not yet exist that would make the 'complete' Aristotle an indisputable frame of reference:

The second Analytics contains perspicacious scholarship and only a few people understand it. There are evidently several reasons for this as it deals with the science of argumentation which is the most difficult kind of exposition. It has fallen into almost total obscurity because so few scholars have concerned themselves with it. . . . It is without comparison the most impenetrable [of Aristotle's books] as a result of its extraordinary use of terminology and letters of the alphabet to stand for ideas, and the remarkable examples taken from different disciplines. Finally, and for this the author cannot be blamed, it has been so distorted by errors in copying that every new paragraph gives rise to additional obscurity, sometimes the number of obscurities simply exceeds the number of paragraphs. Most people ascribe the difficulty to the translator and maintain that the translation that is available now is inadequate.[43]

In Spain the situation was different. There a long tradition of Arabic scholarship had flourished and this also included Greek philosophy and the natural sciences. This contact with Arabic had been established through Syrian and in these conditions it is not remarkable that Aristotle's original ideas, to take one example, had been altered in many places both because of inherent inconsistencies in the translations and an accumulation of traditions of interpretation during the centuries. The flood of new impulses and new knowledge that swept in over Europe in the decades around the beginning of the thirteenth century from the translators in Toledo presented interpretations, sometimes re-interpretations and not infrequently mis-interpretations, of Aristotle. Not only his own works (which had been through a full cycle from Greek to Syrian to Arabic to Latin) now became available, but also a large number of Greek, Arabic and Jewish commentaries. Neoplatonism and Arabic accretions form part of the amalgam that is known as *Aristotelianism*. It was not only a new philosophical method. It was a coherent and extremely attractive outlook on life which in a period of general intellectual awakening ('the twelfth-century renaissance') filled many of the gaps left empty by Christian philosophy. Young teachers and students swallowed this Aristotle with the rapture such dazzling revelation deserved. No wonder that such intense illumination was also followed by a tidal wave that destroyed a

number of hitherto undisputed foundations and opened
yawning chasms in many young minds between the faith of
their fathers and the new gospel of scholarship.

But one thing at a time.

'Dialectical' scholarship: the art of convincing

After Aristotle's death (in 322 BC) his 'posthumous writings' on logic were collected together under the title of *Organon* (Tool). The contents of the *Categories* and *Perihermeneias* have already been described. The structure above them in the system thus erected was provided by the *Topics* and its appendix *Sophistici Elenchi* ('Sophistic argument').

    The *Topics* contains the theory of 'places' and is a handbook on different types of argument and the art of choosing suitable arguments for the thesis one has decided to defend in a debate. The method advocated is 'dialectic', which means that the starting point is not, as it was in the *Analytics*, true and self-evident axioms but merely plausible and generally accepted assumptions. The skill involved in dialectical argument is to persuade one's opponent to admit certain propositions and then to argue from them so that he has to yield. Concepts such as thesis ('a proposition to be proved'), problem (a question of the type 'is X Y or not?'), induction (which is to 'lead on' from the specific to the general, to move from species to genus in other words) are introduced in the work on topics and were eventually to become international words in the everyday language of educated people. The most important concept is, however, that of definition and Aristotle's teaching that definition is an indication of the closest genus and the specific characteristics had been made part of the textual basis of the 'old' logic by Boethius (see p. 64). Another aspect of topic that had been introduced in the same way was what was known as *loci* (places) – a number of types of argument in the form of generalized propositions. The ideal to be attained was probably to produce a comprehensive survey in this form of all possible types of argument and other rules for effective argumentation:

Everything contained in a species is contained in its genus. Several things can be the opposite of one and the same thing. That which gives rise to good is itself good. The end itself should be preferred

Organon

Topica
Sophistici Elenchi
loci

thesis
problema
inductio

definitio

95

to means of achieving this end. Part of something can never be predicated of the whole thing. A definition should be based on something close at hand and familiar. Every good definition consists of genus and specific characteristics which are closer to hand than the species itself.

It is a mistake to use verbose proof when it can be expressed concisely.[44]

Boethius formalized these rules even more and established a list of what he called principal propositions (*maximae propositiones*, cf. 'maxim') such as the following:

<table>
<tr><td>maximae propositiones</td><td></td></tr>
<tr><td>locus a definitione</td><td>What is asserted about the definiens is also asserted about the definiendum.</td></tr>
<tr><td>locus a causa</td><td>What is caused by good is itself good.</td></tr>
<tr><td>locus a maiore</td><td>If something which one has good reasons for anticipating does not exist, neither does anything which one has less good reasons for anticipating.</td></tr>
<tr><td>locus a minore</td><td>If something which one does not have very good reasons for anticipating exists so do things which one has better reasons for anticipating.</td></tr>
<tr><td>locus ab auctoritate</td><td>Confidence should be placed in specialists within their own fields.[45]</td></tr>
</table>

As we have seen in the extract quoted from Lanfranc, it was not unusual for medieval writers to add force to their argument by expressly citing the *locus* on which it was based.

Another rule laid down by Aristotle in the *Topics* was important for the concept of distinction and this was that if a concept has a number of possible meanings this is shown by the fact that it has more than one opposite. The adjective 'sharp' has more than one meaning as there are at least two opposites ('flat' and 'dull'). 'Sharp' can therefore describe the specific characteristics of two co-ordinate genera within the category of quality.

Sophistry: the art of deceiving

The work by Aristotle that made the greatest impression on the logicians of the twelfth century was however *Elenchi*, sophistic arguments, or, in other words, the art of confusing one's antagonists with apparently correct statements that on reflection turn out to be absurd. It was not Aristotle's intention to demonstrate these tricks as a skill in their own right. His intention was of course to draw attention to the possibility of deceiving oneself or others either in perfectly good faith or deliberately. *Elenchi* is a systematic catalogue of pitfalls in language or ways of thinking. The discipline within philosophy devoted to this study in the Middle Ages was called *sophistica*, sophistry. *sophistica*

Aristotle divides these deceptions into two main groups, those resulting from the inexactitude of language and those caused by breaches of the rules for thinking. The first group contains ambiguity (*aequivocatio*, cf. 'equivocal'), which can *aequivocatio* be illustrated with this obvious but perhaps not very convincing syllogism: 'Life is a journey, a journey is a trip, a trip is an error, therefore. . . .' It can be shown rather easily by using the method of distinction described in the *Topics* that the term 'trip' is ambiguous. Another form of linguistic ambiguity is that at one moment a subject can refer to the same time as its predicate (*sensus compositus*), as in 'the *sensus compositus* invalid has a temperature', but another time refer to a different time from the predicate (*sensus divisus*), as in 'the *sensus divisus* invalid is healthy again'.

Real transgression of the rules of logic is, however, more dangerous and often more difficult to discover. Among the fallacies listed by Aristotle are:

What applies under certain circumstances is taken to apply generally.
An adversary is dismissed by an attack on a caricature of his opinions.
'He who proves too much, proves nothing' – if a conclusion drawn from what one intends to prove also contains an error the whole argument is worthless.
Circular argument (*circulus vitiosus*) and begging the question *circulus vitiosus*

petitio principii	(*petitio principii*) – the proposition to be proved is contained in the premises.
	Transition to another genus – for instance that what can be conceived of must also exist in the material world (cf. Anselm's ontological argument for the existence of God).
post hoc, ergo propter hoc	'After and therefore because' – if B comes after A, A must be the cause of B.
fallacia consequentis	*Fallacia consequentis* was the name given to the false deduction that led to one possible reason being taken for the only possible reason – 'if you are drunk you drive badly, he drives badly therefore he must be drunk'.[46]

The beginnings of the academic approach
I: syllogisms (*Analytica Priora*)

Without wanting to detract from the value of these acute observations, it should be pointed out that they obtain in an area in which one can go far relying on intuition and common sense. Their main importance was in drawing attention to the imperfections of language.

In turning to Aristotle's first and second *Analytics*, however, we leave debating skills behind us and are confronted with the razor-edged exactitude of scientific thought. In syllogisms we are no longer dealing with plausible propositions which can be used in convincing our antagonists. We are solely concerned with incontrovertible premises from which binding conclusions can be drawn. The *Analytics* contained the science of argumentation. *Analytica Priora et Posteriora*

Aristotle defined the syllogism, the medieval schoolman's most cherished tool, as 'an assertion in which certain things are postulated which necessarily give rise to other things than those postulated'. By this he means that a syllogism always consists of at least three statements, and the last of these, the conclusion (*conclusio*), follows inevitably from the *conclusio* preceding statements (*praemissae*, the premises). The prem- *praemissae* ise that contains the conclusion's predicate is called the major (*maior*) premise; the one that includes the conclusion's *maior* subject is the minor (*minor*) premise. If both premises are *minor* true, the conclusion must therefore be true. Occasionally, however, false premises can by accident (*per accidens*) lead to true conclusions; for instance 'all chickens have wings' is formally the correct conclusion from the premises 'all animals have wings' and 'all chickens are animals', even though one of them is false.

The basic type of syllogistic argument is categorical argument, in which all the propositions confirm or deny something about something. A proposition that confirms something is described as affirmative; one that denies something is called negative (see p. 62). The propositions can be either universal in scope ('all' or 'no') or particular ('some' or 'some . . . not'). Medieval textbooks used letters of the

99

alphabet to designate the different combinations of propositions:

A = universal affirmative ('all X are Y')
E = universal negative ('no X is Y')
 I = particular affirmative ('some X is Y')
O = particular negative ('some X is not Y')

In a categorical syllogism each of the (usually) three statements belongs to one of these four groups. However the

major and minor premises and the conclusion must be arranged in one of nineteen possible arrangements if the argument is to be correct. A simple example of how this works can be taken from what was called the first figure (in which the major premise is always universal, i.e. A or E, and the minor premise always affirmative, i.e. A or I). In this case four combinations (*modi*) are possible and they are AAA, EAE, AII and EIO:

A   *All* people are mortal.
A   *All* Frenchmen are people.
A   Therefore *all* Frenchmen are mortal.

Fig. 15.   Logic depicted as a hunter. 'Logic is the study that hunts down truth and falsehood', is the description given in Pseudo-Boethius' *De disciplina scholarium*. From the hunter's horn emerges *sonus-vox*, the sounds of language. The sounds that carry meaning are the primary object of logic. Two *praemissae* emerge from the mouth of the horn in the guise of roses. In his right hand the hunter is carrying the *quaestio* method as a longbow, from his belt hangs the sword of syllogisms and the theory of *locus* forms a quiver containing the different types of argument as arrows. His breastplate is composed of *conclusio*, conclusions. His right boot is the categories, and his left the predicables, the main forms of the universals. The clog on the right foot is knowledge of fallacies not based on the inexactitude of language, the left clog is knowledge of the pitfalls of language. *Veritas* and *falsitas* are the two hounds that hunt *problema* in the form of a rabbit, the point at issue that cannot be decided with certainty. The hunter is still safely established on the rock of Aristotelian logic, behind him he has Parmenides, the pre-Socratic philosopher who according to legend invented logic while sitting on a rock in the Caucasian mountains. In front of him lie the Middle Ages' own discoveries in logic, *parva logicalia*, the shorter logical essays, the second half of Petrus Hispanus' *Tractatus*. In the middle distance can be seen *insolubilia*, paradoxes such as 'Everything I say is false.' In the background is *silva opinionum*, the wood of theory with the trees representing Albertists, Scotists, Occamists and Thomists, the followers of Albertus Magnus, Duns Scotus, William of Occam and Thomas Aquinas respectively. Gregorius Reisch, *Margarita philosophica*, printed by Johannes Schott in Basle in 1508.

E   *No* human being is perfect.
A   *All* politicians are human beings.
E   Therefore *no* politician is perfect.

A   *All* mammals are vertebrate animals.
I   *Some* household pets are mammals.
I   Therefore *some* household pets are vertebrate animals.

E   *No* bishops are atheists.
I   Some bishops are golfers.
O   Therefore some golfers are *not* atheists.

Aristotle described three figures (in the second of them one of the premises is negative and the major premise universal; in the third the minor premise is affirmative and the conclusion particular). A fourth was added in the thirteenth century by the Jewish logician Albalagus. So that these four figures could be kept in the memory a mnemonic verse was devised which was included in Petrus Hispanus' compendium on logic *Tractatus*. This became so well known that it was still being used in the teaching of logic in schools in the twentieth century:

Barbara Celarent

(1) Barbara Celarent Darii Ferio (4) Baralipton
Celantes Dabitis Fapesmo Frisesomorum
(2) Cesare Camestres Festino Baroco (3) Darapti
Felapton Disamis Datisi Bocardo Ferison

In this rhyme the vowels of course indicate the types of proposition and in addition the initial letters BCDF show how the syllogism in figures 2–4 can be reduced to the simpler forms in the first figure. The other consonants also indicate different logical characteristics. S and P show that the proposition indicated by the vowel preceding them can be converted, and M that the major premise can be turned into the minor premise and vice versa. Finally C indicates that the preceding proposition can be replaced by the contradictory opposite of the conclusion.

The beginnings of the academic approach II: the universal proposition (*Analytica Posteriora*)

For Aristotle exact knowledge (*scientia*) was always the result of syllogistic reasoning which took as its starting point principal premises whose truth could not be disputed (for instance 'the whole is always larger than any of its parts') and which could not be divided into smaller units, premises that were, in other words, axioms. The scholar uses these premises to prove through deductions (*deductio*) in syllogisms, preferably of the first figure, the reasons why something must be exactly as it is and why it cannot possibly be in any other way. The result would therefore be certain universal statements that would apply with no exceptions: Y must necessarily be ascribed to all X precisely because of their characteristics as X.' One example of this kind of scientific statement is the theorem from geometry that states that 'the sum of the angles in a triangle is the same as the sum of two right angles'. This is true of every triangle without exception and furthermore is true of triangles because of their qualities as triangles and not their qualities as 'geometrical shapes' or 'right-angled triangles'. In this second case the theorem is also true, but the reason for this is the triangularity of the right-angled triangle and not its right angle. In other words the class X must be the largest possible class for which Y is true.

A scientist or scholar also used definition, which in this context means that a term has an established meaning and that this meaning will be assumed in the reasoning, and hypothesis, which means the acceptance of a counterpart in reality to the term used. Geometry, Aristotle points out, must accept that dots and lines have certain qualities (definition) and that they really exist (hypothesis).

It would be easy to believe that this deductive procedure (inferring or deducing knowledge from truths which are already evident) would lead to disregard for the material world and the five senses. This is completely untrue of Aristotle, who, in fact, devoted a great deal of effort to the

scientia

deductio

definitio
hypothesis

observation of natural phenomena. He stresses the fact that deduction presupposes induction (in other words the universal propositions are based on a number of observations of individual cases) and that this is the only path to knowledge of the universe. For we are not born with any 'innate' conceptions or ideas but the impressions of our senses and the world as it is is the foundation of all our knowledge.

On the other hand Aristotelian scholarship was not interested in what was individual or *contingent* (not necessary, in other words what can take different forms or quite simply need not exist at all). As Aristotelianism became more and more dominant the methodology of different disciplines became increasingly stringent. At the same time interest in what could not be predicted waned and subjects such as history and literature ceased to be of interest for the scholastic philosophers.

contingens

It should also be pointed out that scholarship of this kind had set itself goals which are different from those of modern scientific research. There was no question of exploring new areas by adding information previously unknown to the existing store of knowledge. The aim was to find the eternal cause, the reason why everything was as it was and must necessarily remain so. The contents and methods of mathematics provide the model for this conception of scholarship.

At the beginning of the section in which he deals with *scientia* (in the second *Analytics*) Aristotle says that all teaching and all learning must begin with knowledge that already exists. The subject of study in the different disciplines varies admittedly, but they all share a number of axioms in common. There is a hierarchy of disciplines. Specialist fields of study are based on the more general ones. Although optics is based on the same basic propositions as geometry it does not try to prove these propositions but leaves that task to geometry. Optics takes geometry for granted. Seen like this geometry is a 'higher' science than optics, as it is more basic and less 'applied'. At the apex of the pyramid of sciences is metaphysics, which enquires into the basis of all knowledge of any kind.

Fig. 16. Geometry, one of the subjects in the *quadrivium*.
Theoretical geometry described 'unchanging quantities and
shapes'. In practice this knowledge was used, as this picture
shows, in building, surveying and in astronomy. Gregorius
Reisch, *Margarita philosophica*, Basle 1583.

The new professionalism

The 'new' logic upset the balance of subjects in the old educational syllabus. At the end of the twelfth century, at least in Paris, the city that had now become the leading centre of education for good, the seven liberal arts had become an idea rather than a reality. John of Salisbury describes how logical dexterity had become an increasingly absorbing interest and had outgrown its proper role, which was to serve as a tool for the more important branches of knowledge. Enmeshed in logic, scholars stop developing and fail to acquire the perfect, fully rounded learning which, in John's humanistic belief, was the object of the development of character:

I do not assert this in order to attack logic (it is after all an appealing and fruitful branch of study) but to show that they who devote themselves entirely to it, not for ten or twenty years but for a whole lifetime, have failed in fact to aquire its principles. When old age approaches, the body becomes weak, reason loses its edge and earlier enjoyments pale, logic is still the only thing they talk about and occupy themselves with. It distracts attention from all other interests. Even as old men scholars like this are absorbed with youthful follies, they scrutinize every syllable they read or hear, even every letter. They turn everything into a problem, they never stop asking questions. Nevertheless they never achieve clarity, in the end they only talk without saying anything, 'understanding neither what they say, nor whereof they confirm'. They discover new errors and remain completely ignorant of the ancient writers as they feel it would be beneath them to study their opinions. They compile every opinion, they quote and refer to the words and works of even the most trivial people because they have no opinions of their own. They cite everything as they cannot produce anything better themselves. The accumulations of opinions and contradictions are so large that not even their authors can keep track of them. The usefulness of logic is related to one's understanding in other areas. Nothing is easier for the specialist then talking about his own special field. It is more difficult to show the uses of one's knowledge. Show me a doctor who does not talk extensively about the elements, the bodily humours and temperament, of sickness and other aspects of medical knowledge. But anyone who is cured by all this might just as well remain ill. Any student of ethics can produce an abundance of moral rules as long as they are expressed in words. It is more difficult to demonstrate them through actions. In the same way it is exceedingly easy to talk about definitions, arguments and genera with one's colleagues. It is more difficult to show their usefulness in other fields of study.[47]

In logic inbreeding led to sterility. All-round education threatened to disappear and narrow-minded specialists interested in nothing but their own field began to appear. Professionalism was to triumph in the nascent universities.

The new physics (*Physica*)

Physica

Aristotle's *Physics* was translated in the second half of the twelfth century both from Arabic and from the Greek original. The word 'physics' is somewhat misleading for a modern reader. The Greek noun *phýsis* means 'nature' and the texts about nature (the books called *Physica*) also contained what we would call dynamics, chemistry and biology, as well as a number of metaphysical principles (see p. 117). Aristotle's physics is a science of the kind defined in the *Analytics*, as it is based on inevitable conclusions drawn from certain and obvious premises. It established the links in chains of cause and effect and accounts for the different ways in which knowledge can be acquired. It is a theoretical science and like mathematics and metaphysics it is concerned with finding out the nature and essence of things and not with how they can be exploited usefully.

motio

In *Physics* Aristotle studies what he called 'motion' and by this he meant any change from one state to another in the categories of quality (an apple changes from green to red as it ripens), quantity (growth or decline) and place (movement in space). Physics observes the 'nature' of things, the innate tendency to undergo such changes in the course of a process and the consequent realization of the innate possibilities in one of these areas. There is a transition from potentiality (*potentia*) to actuality (*actus*), from possibility to reality (cf. 'potential–actual')' When bricks and planks of wood are combined to form a building it is the same potential in them that is realized ('actualized') and that makes it possible for us to describe them as building materials. Processes such as learning, moving a stone, creating and destroying, maturing and aging, are, seen from this point of view, nothing but the progress of this innate motion towards its goal, either directly or by stages (through different degrees of potentiality).

potentia
actus

loco-moto
motio naturalis

In its basic meaning, motion is motion in space (*locomotio*, cf. 'locomotion'). All such movement is either 'natural' or 'compelled'. A stone moves 'naturally' downwards. If we see a stone rising in the air, we can deduce that its

motion is 'compelled', and, according to Aristotle, this is motio violenta
caused by a moving force in immediate contact with the
stone (in this case air). On the other hand the natural
movement of fire is upwards.

There is a similar relationship involved in motion in the
category of quality. A source of heat is in immediate contact
with what is heated. In the category of quantity whatever
causes growth or decline is in immediate contact with
whatever grows or declines. This 'motion' has always existed
in the universe and there has never been a time before which
everything was still. Nor will 'motion' ever cease. Time itself
is defined as a measure of motion.

All motion must be caused by something other than that
which is in motion, something which in its turn is moved by
something else, and so on. This sequence of cause and effect
cannot continue to infinity (*in infinitum*) however, but must   in infinitum
have its origin in a mover that is not itself moved by anything
else (the 'unmoved mover' or 'the prime mover', *primus*   primus motor
motor). Motion has always existed in some form, it is eternal,
and the prime mover must therefore also be eternal.

Aristotle foresaw and met an obvious objection to his
assertion that an object in motion is always in direct contact
with the immediate cause of motion. How is it possible, for
example, for a stone that cannot move itself to continue to
move even after it has left the hand which threw it? Aristotle
is forced, he says, to make an assumption that the hand
transfers the motive force to the *medium* (the air) in which the   medium
stone moves and this motion is propagated, in the same way
that sound is, until it exhausts itself. At that moment the
stone will stop moving.

The Aristotelian picture of the world

Aristotle described the universe as a system of spheres that were embedded within each other like the rings in an onion. At the very centre is the globe, immoveable, composed of equal proportions of four elements, earth, air, fire and water. This 'sublunary' world, in other words those things that were to be found beneath the moon (*sub luna*) were influenced by the sphere of the moon which was 'moved', in the Aristotelian meaning of the word, by the moon. This in its turn was 'moved' by a large number of spheres and among them were those of the sun and the other planets. Encompassing the planetary spheres were the spheres of the fixed stars and finally, itself unmoving, came the sphere which directly or indirectly kept the whole system in motion, the prime mover. (Medieval astronomers simplified Aristotle's model, which contained no less than fifty-five spheres, to produce a more manageable system of between eight to fourteen spheres.) The parts of the universe that lay outside the sublunary world were not composed of the four earthly elements but of a fifth element, ether, and the only movement to be found outside the sublunary world was movement in space.

In the sublunary world all 'motion', in other words all alteration within the categories of quality, quantity, and place, was caused originally by the prime mover and transmitted by the heavenly bodies. As a rationalist, Aristotle had no time for astrological speculation. His theory that the heavens were subject to an eternal and unchanging divine order did not however expressly contradict the different beliefs in fate that were to arise later and which saw the lives of men ordained by an implacable celestial mechanism.

Aristotle had also said that the prime mover moves everything else 'by being loved'. These words were to have an enormous influence on medieval theology. According to the apostle John, God is Love. It now appeared that Aristotle confirmed that this love was the energy that kept the whole of the universe in motion. ''Tis love that makes the world go round', or the final lines of Dante's *Divine Comedy*: 'l'Amor che move il sole e l'altre stelle.'

sub luna

quinta essentia

110

Fig. 17. A theologian and an astronomer debating the number of heavenly spheres. According to Albertus Magnus there were eight of them (the seven planets, the Moon, Mercury, Venus, the Sun, Mars, Jupiter and Saturn and the sphere of the fixed stars). During the late Middle Ages astronomers used to assume that there were nine spheres and called the sphere outside the sphere of Saturn 'the first moveable' (*primum mobile*), meaning that it was the one most directly affected by the influence of the prime mover (*primus motor*). The maximum number of spheres used by astronomers was fourteen: next to the globe were placed the 'sublunary' spheres of the four elements (earth, water, air and fire) and between Saturn and the *primum mobile* lay the 'firmament', the stanchion of the heavens which according to the Book of Genesis 1:6 'divides the waters from the waters' together with the *caelum crystallinum*, the crystal heaven with the 'waters above the firmament'. Outside everything was the *empyraeum*, the abode of God and the saints. Lecture notes made at the University of Uppsala in Sweden in the 1480s show that Aristotle and Albertus Magnus allowed for eight spheres, astronomers for nine, theologians for ten, and the author of *Computus chirometralis*, John of Erfurt took all fourteen into account. 'The natural philosopher does not need to postulate more spheres than he can deduce from the evidence of his senses and, as only eight can be observed, philosophers postulate eight spheres. But astronomers postulate nine because they have observed the contrary movement of the firmament . . . and they too are correct. But theologians postulate ten as they have placed outside the ninth an immoveable sphere which is called the abode of the saints. They too are correct. The author of *Computus chirometralis* also assumes that there are ten spheres but in addition to these he distinguishes the four spheres of the elements.' These last were characterized by the fact that they could both influence and be influenced; unlike the heavenly spheres they were subject to continuous generation and corruption. Petrus de Alliaco, *Concordancia astronomie cum theologia*, printed by Erhard Ratdolt in Augsburg in 1490.

Aristotelian psychology (*De anima*)

For Aristotle, the soul (a term that now fills Europeans with unease) was everything that distinguished a corpse from a living body and to it he ascribed the following functions, listed here in reverse order of importance:

(potentia)		
vegetativa	1	nutrition and reproduction
sensitiva	2	sensation
desiderativa	3	desire
secundum-locummotiva	4	locomotion
imaginativa	5	imagination
intellectiva	6	reason

Among the living organisms plants possess only the first of these functions and it is only human beings that possess the last, whereas animals were endowed with the five preceding functions in varying degrees. In a summary of its functions the 'soul' was described as 'the first actuality in a body that has potential life'. This reflects the same way of seeing things as that found in the *Physics*, in which the whole of material existence is in constant 'motion' from one state to its opposite, from potentiality to actuality, from possibility to its realization. In this description the soul is the fundamental realization of the potential life of the body. Its relationship to the body can be compared to the relationship of applied (actuality) to merely acquired (potentiality) knowledge, or of sight (actuality) to the eye (potentiality).

Body and soul are one, like the imprint of a seal and the wax that bears it. In other words, Aristotle did not see the soul as an appendix independent of the body, as Plato did, and even less did he regard the body as the prison of the soul. Aristotle could not accept the idea of immortality for the functions of the soul. He does, however, make one important exception and accepts that the soul's highest function, the function that human beings alone possess, *active* intellect, is 'immortal and eternal'. Unlike the other functions, intellect cannot be localized to any specific part of the body and is therefore independent of the body and can as a result be described as immortal.

What Aristotle meant by active and receptive intellect is by no means clear, however. He describes as receptive intellect the receptive faculties admitting the impressions provided by the senses. Active intelligence, on the other hand, is the constructive power of conceptualization which makes sense of these impressions. The relationship of these two faces of intellect can be compared to that of colours and light. Colours do have an objective existence even in a dark room but light is needed before they can be distinguished. Active intellect is what transforms the potentially understandable into what is actually understood. It is this active aspect of intellect that is the only immortal part of human beings. This is not to be understood to mean that there is individual immortality but rather that while alive a human being shares in some kind of supra-individual constructive intelligence. *intellectus agens* *intellectus possibilis*

Hardly any other section of the philosophy of antiquity has, understandably enough, given rise to so many or so varying analyses as this one has.

The impressions of the senses are, Aristotle maintains, infallible in themselves. Our mistakes are made in interpreting them. In addition to the five senses there is also a general sense (*sensus communis*), which co-ordinates the functions of the other senses and combines their information to create an overall impression of, for instance, movement, size, shape or number. *sensus communis*

The senses, drives and urges, mobility and power of conceptualization are closely interrelated. Only those creatures that can experience pain and pleasure (in other words animals and man) can have a concept or memory of what is pleasant and unpleasant and they are driven ('moved') by such concepts to seek out what is pleasant and to shun the unpleasant. Human beings are preeminent among animals because their concepts can, in addition, be shaped by reason. Animals are guided entirely by the memories they have acquired while human beings can also be steered by reason, so long as this has not been obscured by emotions, sickness or sleep.

When we are born we have no innate concepts or ideas. The receptive intellect can be compared to a clean table of

Fig. 18. These are a student's notes from a lecture on Aristotle's *On the Soul* given at the University of Uppsala in November or December 1482. The widely spaced lines of thicker script are the text of the book itself (*littera*), in this case the beginning of the second book. The lecturer's 'glosses' (*glossae*) on individual words and phrases have been added above the lines in finer script (the student turned the quill pen over and used the back of the quill). The substance of the lecture (*commentum*) has been closely written in the margin adjacent to the relevant parts of the text. In the top left-hand corner the three words *Sube at maxie* (which stand for *Substantie autem maxime*) show that the commentary that follows refers to the section in the seventh line of the text that begins with these words. In the same way the three words *Quare omne corpus* in the margin just below the middle of the page refer to the same words in the tenth line of the text. To keep up with the presentation of a lecturer students were forced to use a form of semi-shorthand, which soon became standard in university studies. Apart from the abbreviations that were used by all late medieval writers, a large number of abbreviations were introduced for specific terms in the study of philosophy and law. The first line of the text reads as follows (the glosses have been given in parentheses): *Que quidem (recte) a prioribus (id est, antiquis) tradita (tractata), dicta sunt (solum in capitulo de erroribus) de anima (id est, de cognicione anime). Iterum autem* . . . As can be seen this technique also saved paper. Uppsala University Library, MS o 600. fol. 105^v.

tabula rasa

anima est
quodammodo
omnia

wax (*tabula rasa*) capable of receiving any shapes at all. The human soul is, however, able to absorb an immaterial copy of the material universe and therefore it can be described as 'in some ways everything'. The human soul has the power to understand and master its environment. It is like the human hand and just as the hand can produce clothes, tools and weapons that can compensate for the natural endowment of animals, so can human being *become* everything by perceiving and understanding everything that is potentially conceivable and comprehensible.

Aristotelian metaphysics (*Metaphysica*)

The works of Aristotle compiled under the title *Metaphysics* (the word merely means in fact 'the works that come after the Physics') were collected after his death and reflect several different phases in the development of his thought. Frequently one section contradicts another. The thinking contained in the *Metaphysics* gave rise in the Middle Ages to a separate discipline in philosophy (metaphysics), which was described as the supreme study, the crowning consummation of all others. Interpretations of Aristotle's own opinions in this, the most abstract section of his philosophy, have aroused controversy over more than one point. The natural starting point for surveying them is not 'the historical Aristotle' but the versions of his ideas that were dominant within Aristotelianism.

The subject of metaphysics is 'being in its very quality of being'. Aristotle asserted that the verb 'to be' is ambiguous and is used in as many meanings as there are categories (see p. 61). For the smallest common denominator of all these meanings, what we can say in some way *is*, he uses the term *the being* (*ens*). This being (and the participle is to be understood as a noun, which includes both what does exist and what *can* exist) is therefore a collective term that covers anything at all that can be conceived by thought. It is the fundamental object of the intellect and has at one and the same time the greatest extent imaginable, because it can be said about everything, and the smallest imaginable content, because it is the most indefinite predicate. *[margin: ens qua ens]* *[margin: ens]*

About every individual being, that is to say about everything that is not nothing, three things can be said. It is *one*, indivisible in itself and distinct from everything else (it can however be composite, but if one part is removed the being in question ceases or changes into some other form of being). It is *true*, which means that it can be perceived by thought to be a being to the same extent that it is so. It is *good*, that is to say desirable and corresponds to a need (an innate tendency) in some other being. These characteristics were later to be *[margin: unum]* *[margin: verum]* *[margin: bonum]*

117

transcendentia
(transcendentalia)

'ens et unum
(verum, bonum)
convertuntur'
pulchrum

called by the schoolmen the transcendental attributes, and like being itself they 'extend over' the boundaries between the categories. They are mutually convertible. What is one is also true and good, what is true is one and good and so on. The Franciscan philosophers in particular usually added as well that being is *beautiful*, it is greeted by the senses as being pleasantly natural and simple.

This being in its basic meaning is the being which is a substance, which supports the other categories (the accidentals). A substance can be analysed and is held in tension

potentia – actus

between two poles, potentiality and actuality. In the change from potentiality to actuality the substance remains unchanged while the accidentals alter. This is Aristotle's answer to the philosophical paradox about how something can be altered and yet always remain the same. A being identical to itself (a substance like, for instance, a person) changes from potentiality (infancy) to actuality (maturity) without its identity being lost or changed. All the time it is the same person but the accidentals (such as the categories, quantity, quality, time, place, relationships for instance) change continually.

The first and most fundamental of all principles, the basis for all thought and discussion of opinion, is as follows: 'It is impossible for something to be at the same time and in the same meaning A and not-A.' This principle was called the

principium
contradictionis

law of contradiction (*principium contradictionis*).

After this, metaphysics devoted itself to four principles which have been give the somewhat misleading name 'the

quattuor causae:
materialis
formalis
efficiens
finalis

four causes' (*quattuor causae*). These are the material cause (*causa materialis*), the formal cause (*causa formalis*), the efficient cause (*causa efficiens*) and the final cause (*causa finalis*). Instead of the term 'cause' it would be better to describe them as 'fundamental principles' in two respects.

Everything that *exists* was thought of by Aristotle as being

materia – forma

a combination of matter and form, as consisting of shapeless matter that had been given a form in the same way that molten wax is impressed by a seal. Everything that is *altered*, alters because of an efficient (active) principle (or cause in its real meaning) and for the purpose of attaining some end, a goal, the desired. This purposefulness (finality) exists both

118

in nature ('in nature nothing occurs in vain') and in the deliberate actions of human beings. 'natura nihil facit frustra'

'All men naturally desire knowledge' is the often quoted beginning of the *Metaphysics*. One proof of this is the high value we give to our senses not only because of their usefulness but also for their own sake. The power we have to retain the impressions of our sense in our memory creates in us what is called experience, and experience is the basis of knowledge. One sign of knowledge is the ability to teach others. The highest form of knowledge is that which aims to understand the 'causes' or principles described here. Aristotle calls this knowledge wisdom (*sapientia*). The wise man, the philosopher, is driven by his awe to investigate these ultimate causes far beyond the teeming confusion of minute details. He disregards practical applications to penetrate the supreme relationships and seeks knowledge for its own sake. Speculation of this kind grants to its practitioner the purest, most unadulterated satisfaction that can be envisaged. It is the highest form of human existence. sapientia

Metaphysics was to provide scholastic philosophy with an inexhaustible source of speculation about the relationship of form and matter in the composition of existence, how it had been created by the Prime Cause and sought to return to its Goal, the absolute Being, pure Actuality, now identified as the God of the Christian revelation.

Fig. 19. Astronomy teaching her arts to Ptolemy, the Greek astronomer, here wrongly identified with his namesake the King of Egypt. Ptolemy's book *Almagest* was the most important classical work on astronomy. As its name suggests it had been transmitted through Arabic traditions and it was the basis of John of Holywood's *Sphaera*. Gregorius Reisch, *Margarita philosophica*, printed in Basle in 1583.

Arabic philosophy: Aristotle meets Allah

Parts of this enormous mass of literature with its new ideas and new ways of thinking had reached Europe in the form of translations from Arabic. This was the case with the *Analytica Posteriora* and its theory of knowledge, with the *Physics* and the *Metaphysics*. It confronted European scholarship and the Christian faith with a well-thought-out and previously unknown philosophy that was bound to collide with accepted systems of thought over some points and on others to appear to contradict the dogmas of the Church. The Aristotelian view of nature postulated an impersonal Prime Mover. It argued against the idea that the world had come into existence at a fixed moment in time, created from nothing. It denied personal immortality. It had no supernatural perspective but described the supreme form of human existence as the speculation of human intellect on the ultimate axioms and causes and effects.

These aspects of the system had already disturbed Arab philosophers who confessed the Muslim faith. The Koran describes a personal creator and the eternal accountability of the individual, whose final reckoning will result in reward or punishment in the hereafter. If one wanted to remain a faithful Muslim and an Aristotelian it was necessary to reconcile these discordant ideas in some way.

Al-Fārābī, a philosopher who died in Bagdad in about 950, identified the active intellect described in *De anima* as the prophetic power that spoke with Mohammed's voice in the Koran. The Prime Mover was the same as Allah, or the One of neo-platonist thought, from whom everything created emanates in a chain of 'intellects' and heavenly spheres. The lowest of these intellects was active intellect, a link between God and human reason. Immortality was attained, according to Al-Fārābī, only by those who had acquired philosophical insight through the enlightenment of the active intellect.

Ibn-Sīnā (a Persian who was known in western Europe as Avicenna and who died in 1037) continued working on a theological superstructure for the Aristotelian world-view.

intelligentiae

121

God, the unmoved Mover, is the only being that exists of necessity, whereas everything else, in other words everything that has been created, is contingent (not necessary).

essentia – esse

Avicenna introduced into metaphysics the distinction between essence and existence. Essence (which is the answer to the question: 'What is the nature of an X?') does not necessarily presuppose existence. We can talk about dragons, monsters or Utopia and define the essence of such phenomena exactly, even though they do not really exist. Their essence does not therefore include their existence because they are contingent. The only being whose essence does include its existence is God. He, unlike everything else, exists of necessity. God is also the absolute Good. A number of autonomous intellects originate from God and the tenth of these is active intellect. This is the power that gives matter its form, which, in other words, determines the potentiality in matter as actuality.

Avicenna also attempts to provide a theodicy, in other words, he also tries to show how faith in an all-powerful God of love is compatible with the existence of evil. According to Avicenna, evil is the price we pay for the existence of free will. Responsibility is what raises human beings above the rest of creation. Evil in particular can lead to something good in the long run. Individual guilt and the tragedy of life serve the final atonement. Despite everything, the universe is in fact an ordered totality and is reflected in the soul of man. These ideas were to meet with response in Thomas Aquinas.

The most influential Arab thinker was Ibn-Ruschd (known as Averroes in Latin, he spent his career in Spain and Morocco and died in 1198). He produced commentaries on more or less the whole of Aristotle's work, and just as Aristotle is often called the Philosopher, Averroes is referred

Philosophus
Commentator

to quite simply as the Commentator. It was Averroes who laid the basis of the veritable cult of Aristotle in later days and who saw in him the Genius of geniuses, a reflection of divine reason. As an interpreter Averroes' only ambition was to be the prophet of the one Philosopher and to prepare the way for exact understanding of the true doctrine. In theology Averroes gave rise to the attitude which in its pure form requires 'the double truth', the belief that what is philosophically impossible can very well be religious truth. Admittedly Averroes professed the Islamic faith and accepted that God created and sustains the universe, but for him the creation had no beginning in time. The world is eternal. Active intellect is a power distinct from individual human beings and even the receptive intellect is one in all men. Therefore personal immortality is a philosophical impossibility but, nevertheless, reference to eternal reward and punishment can have a healthy and sobering effect on simpler minds.

Averroes' massive commentary became available in Paris in its entirety at some time round 1230. He was soon to have faithful disciples among the admirers of Aristotle in the arts faculties.

Armandus

De declaratiõe difficiliũ termino:
ru; tam Theologicalium ꝗ; Phi:
losophie ac Logice.

The University: Form and Contents

The origin of the University of Paris – a social invention

Abélard's life had been filled with intrigue. For a short period he had been able to teach at the cathedral school in Paris but he was forced to leave it because of personal enmity with its scholasticus, William of Champeaux. He was fortunate enough to be able to start his own series of lectures in the shadow of the church of St Geneviève on the left bank

Fig. 20. Scholastic philosophy exploited the resources of Latin to the limit and in doing so created a specialized language of unique clarity and flexibility. The impetus for this creativity was to be found in the enormous translations that were produced. Both Greek and Arabic provided greater possibilities than Latin for expressing nuances of thinking but this lead was soon narrowed, above all by John Duns Scotus and his followers. The inventiveness of the schoolmen when it came to making up new words and expressions still affects modern languages and is seen most clearly in the number of English adjectives ending in *-al* and *-ive*, nouns ending in *-ity* and *-ist* and verbs ending in *-ize*. The two last-mentioned were originally Greek but the schoolmen had no scruples about adding them to Latin stems and the new hybrid forms that resulted proved to be so useful that they became part of modern European languages after they had been banned from Latin during the Renaissance as typical products of 'gothic' barbarity. This illustration is the title page of Armandus de Bellovisus' *Explanation of difficult terms in theology, philosophy and logic* (*De declaratione difficilium terminorum tam theologicalium quam philosophie ac logice*), printed in the printing house 'behind the Franciscans' (*Retro minores*) in Cologne at the end of the fifteenth century.

125

of the Seine. The church was in the charge of a college of priests who were not under the jurisdiction of the cathedral and therefore outside William's control. For several decades he worked there, devoting himself to his beloved logic and developing his theological methodology. His personal magnetism attracted students from all over Europe. It has been said that twenty of his pupils later on in life became cardinals and that fifteen became bishops. Abélard's teaching methods were soon generally imitated—one example can be seen in Lombard's *Sentences*. They were in fact to be institutionalized but not in Abélard's own school. This, in fact, scarcely survived its founder. The personal magnetism of one individual is not an adequate basis on which to build a new institution. Economic resources and a stable system of organization are also needed.

The university was a social invention. Like other social inventions – the guild system, trade unions and the ombudsman – the university developed to protect the collective interest of one group of people against other forces in society. The new institution did not spring fully armed from the earth, with an established organization, troops of functionaries, acknowledged status and accepted terminology; decades were spent preparing the ground. Institutionalization took place gradually and the reality existed before the name did. The outlines of the new university emerged gradually from a background of strife between different bodies. It is impossible to give a precise date for the birth of the new institution.

The University of Paris was the product of a synthesis between charisma (Abélard) and institutionalization (William of Champeaux). During their lifetimes they were irreconcilable adversaries. But heresy in one generation can often be orthodoxy in the next.

In the period following the death of Abélard, the second half of the twelfth century, Paris became a city of teachers. The process that took place between this state of affairs and the existence both in name and form of a university (or, as the schoolmen would have described it, the university's transition from potentiality to actuality) cannot be described in detail. The evidence is too scanty. It can be described as a development of the teachers' feeling of belonging to a guild, from the adoption of guild statutes to the recognition of its existence by the society they lived in.

It has been pointed out earlier that when a large body of students is gathered together in one place it is very likely that some of them will consider taking up the lucrative teaching career themselves. When after many years of endeavour a student had managed to obtain his first degree (had become *baccalaureus* in the terms used) and then after more years of study had procured permission to teach (*licentia docendi*) from the scholasticus, it is more than likely that he would feel some sort of solidarity with those of his fellows who had managed the same feat, with all those who had by their own efforts attained official recognition that they had reached a certain intellectual level. The actual admission to the circle of teachers was marked by a series of special initiation rites. After a candidate had been awarded his licence (and therefore become a licentiate) he was, after consultation with the teachers' corporation, installed in his teaching post in accordance with the practices of Roman law. This ceremony had two elements. He was invested with the insignia that denoted his new dignity: a square cap (biretta), a gold ring and an open book which were given to him by the appropriate teachers on behalf of the complete corporation of teachers. Afterwards he received the blessing and the kiss of peace and was attended to the cathedral. The new master then availed himself for the first time of his newly acquired right to teach by giving a lecture (*inceptio*, 'commencement'). This ceremony had been inspired by the consecration ritual of bishops. The new member of the teaching body had from this moment the right to entitle himself and act as a *magister*, a title that later in certain contexts was replaced by *doctor* (teacher). It was also customary for the newly installed *magister* to entertain his colleagues to a good dinner (it could not be too lavish, however, as there were statutes in some places that regulated the permitted extent of this generosity).

The human instincts that require that everybody who is to become part of a group that has a higher status than those around it should have to pay for this dignity in some way also

baccalaureus

licentia docendi

inceptio

magister
doctor

inspired the efforts of the teaching guild to safeguard their mutual interests and make sure that the existence, autonomy and privileges of their corporation were recognized by lay and ecclesiastical authorities.

It has been estimated that around the year 1200 Paris had a population of between 25,000 and 50,000 and that not less than ten per cent were students. So important a group was at the same time a cause of social antagonisms and an economic force to be reckoned with. The earliest legal documents that refer to the students of Paris as a separate group also imply that the relationship between citizens and scholars was not always without friction. In 1194 Pope Celestinus III laid down *privilegium fori* for the 'clerks who reside in Paris', which meant that, with the exception of criminal suits, legal cases in which students were involved would be tried by ecclesiastical courts. In order to take advantage of this privilege, however, a student had to prove that he was officially registered in a *matricula* (a register). At the turn of the century, the year 1200 was a historic year in the development of the emerging university. The event that gave occasion for the first direct and written privileges for a corporation was a series of student riots. A German student who belonged to an aristocratic family and who had been elected Bishop of Liège had an attendant who had been attacked and beaten in an inn in Paris. The bishop-elect was no coward and with the help of some of his compatriots he took revenge on the innkeeper who, like the traveller from Jerusalem to Jericho in the gospels, was left 'half-dead'. Violence as we know gives rise to more violence. It was not long before an armed band of citizens attacked the hastily assembled German students and several of them, including the bishop-to-be, were killed.

King Philippe II Augustus was obviously afraid that after this brawl the masters and students would leave Paris for more peaceful surroundings (a possibility that might, on the other hand, have appealed to the citizens). He therefore issued letters patent that stated with marked emphasis that all crimes committed by students from this time on were to be tried by an ecclesiastical court and that this right should be confirmed on oath by the population of the city of Paris.

privilegium fori

matricula

128

Freedom within limits

At some time around the year 1210 the corporation of teachers and students (regularly referred to from this date as *universitas magistrorum et studentium*, cf. p. 139) was granted legal recognition with the right to be represented by a spokesman. The outlines of the new university became even clearer as the result of a long controversy between the teachers and the chancellor of Notre-Dame. It has earlier been pointed out that the office of scholasticus, often held by the chancellor of a cathedral, was of vital importance as it was this individual who had the power to grant the right to to teach. The chancellor of Notre-Dame also claimed the sole right to judge in cases in which students were involved. The fact that one person could possess such power without himself being a teacher not unexpectedly gave rise to dissension. For their part the masters could oppose the chancellor's 'personell management' by refusing objectionable licentiates the right to be installed as master. During the first decades of the thirteenth century this led on several occasions to open conflict. It finally went so far that the chancellor used his ultimate and most effective weapon: he quite simply excluded the whole of the mutinous University of Paris from the fellowship of the Holy Church by excommunication. His reason? The corporation of masters had, without consulting the bishop, the chancellor or the cathedral chapter, adopted its own statutes.

    The result was stalemate. There were no precedents and it was obvious that the whole issue could be settled only by some higher outside authority, the Holy See in Rome. Its occupant, the mighty Innocent III, who represents the heyday of papal reputation and influence on matters temporal for all time, had himself been a student in Paris. He was eager to carry out an active policy for the universities and to safeguard the University of Paris as a stronghold of Christian learning with an autonomous relationship to the local ecclesiastical and secular authorities. In 1215 he gave the teachers and students further evidence of their status as a

universitas magistorum et studentium

free corporation in the right to adopt their own statutes and to elect their own officials.

In August of the same year Robert Courçon, the papal legate, confirmed the agreement that had been reached between the university and the chancellor and in the same document laid down the main points in a syllabus that was later to set the pattern for university teaching in the arts faculties (what today would often be called philosophical faculties) for the rest of the Middle Ages.

artes

Lectures may be given on Aristotle's works on logic, both the old logic and the new, not cursorily but as regular lectures. Likewise the two books of Priscian, or at least the second book, shall be

treated in the same way. On holy days no lectures will be given apart from those on philosophy, and rhetoric, on the quadrivium, Barbarismus, Ethics (faculatative) and the fourth book of Topics. No lectures may be given on Aristotle's Metaphysics or natural philosophy, not even in summary form, and neither on the teachings presented by the master David of Dinant, Amalric the heretic, or the Spaniard Mauricius.[48]

Some of the details in this syllabus are interesting. It is obvious that of the seven liberal arts little more remains than the word *artes*. The major emphasis is on *grammatica* and *dialectica*. Priscian was a Roman grammarian and his book is more advanced than his colleague Donat's. His 'two books',

Fig. 21.   A hunter cooking his soup, an alchemist at his retorts, a tilt hammer and a suspicious housewife in the marketplace. Alchemy nursed the hope of being able to produce silver and gold artificially. A common theory about the nature of metals was that all metals were a mixture of quicksilver (*argentum vivum*) and sulphur in different proportions. The same theory said that quicksilver was composed of water and air, which explained its clarity. Its mobility was caused by its moistness and its weight. The more quicksilver a metal contained, the lower its melting point. If nature was allowed to run its course with quicksilver and sulphur these minerals would stabilize as silver and gold. Alchemists wanted to help nature on its way. They called quicksilver *mercurium* as it could form compounds with all other metals, just as the planet Mercurius could, according to astrology, combine its influence (*influentia*) with all the other planets. In his 'Pearl of philosophy', however, Gregorius Reisch warns against alchemists, especially those who joined the retinues of princes and noblemen, 'because if they really knew this secret of scholarship, they would of course conceal themselves, give thanks to God for such a treasure, give charity to the poor, but hardly live on the wealth of others. . . . As this practice causes society great harm the authorities and others who attend to the interests of society should intervene against their fatuous impudence. For they appear to belong to that group of people of whom Paul the Apostle says, "They are continually learning but can never attain knowledge of the truth."' Bartholomaeus Anglicus, *De proprietatibus rerum*, printed in Westminster by Wynkyn de Worde in 1495.

which were called *maior* and *minor* dealt in great detail with the morphology and syntax of Latin respectively. The teaching in rhetoric provided was not intended to impart any eloquence to the students but was restricted to presenting patterns for correct and elegant letters and legal documents (*ars dictaminis*). *Barbarismus* is the third section of Donat's 'Great art' (*ars maior*), which cautions against language errors and goes through figures of style. 'Ethics' meant the 'old' ethics and, as was the case with logic, Aristotle's *Ethics* was first known in a limited form. The manuscripts available covered only the second and third books which contain philosophically neutral passages on virtue as the middle way between extremities and a catalogue of vices (see p. 179). The fourth book of the *Topics* deals with definition.

The second half of Courçon's syllabus contains more controversial items. Aristotelian metaphysics and natural philosophy were quite simply not allowed, not even in 'summary form'. This last term probably refers to compendia (*summae*), derived from Arabic sources, with disturbing tendencies. They paid too little reverence to the revealed truth and may even have presented ideas about the eternal nature of the world and the mortality of the individual as irrefutable philosophical dogma.

Priscianus maior et minor

ars dictaminis
Barbarismus
Ars maior Donati

summae

Resistance and submission

The rediscovery of Aristotle as a complete philosophy rather than a system of logic confronted Paris with an awe-inspiring and coherent synthesis that had been created without any influence from Christian beliefs. It is not in the least surprising that the encounter between the two turned into a collision. We know that in 1210 a local synod of bishops, to add emphasis to its decisions, commanded that all notes from lectures given by the master David of Dinant should be burnt. Amalric of Bène was hounded ruthlessly. He was by this time already dead but it was decreed that his body should be exhumed and reburied in unconsecrated ground. At the same time both public and private study of any of Aristotle's works on natural philosophy was completely forbidden. Robert Courçon's letters patent of 1215 can therefore be seen as merely confirming these measures.

This intemperate antagonism may seem remarkable if one remembers that because of the work of Thomas Aquinas, Aristotle was later to become a model of philosophy for the Church in many important matters. For centuries to come theological disagreement was to be considered, formulated and expressed according to the standards he had laid down. But other sources than those so painstakingly destroyed by the synod of bishops confirm that David of Dinant and Amalric of Bène went further in their disregard of Christian beliefs than orthodox Aristotelianism did. Their teachings contained elements of pantheism and materialism. If God really existed, He was to be found throughout creation but only there: If, as the Apostle says, God 'worketh in all' (1 Corinthinians 12:6), then He is also to be found in what is evil. Moreover, the world could not possibly have been created from nothing. The art of interpreting dreams made it possible to see into the future.

This goes a long way further than Aristotle and was enough to disturb any bishop or believing Christian. Not unnaturally, all these new false doctrines were ascribed to the great Stagirite and the prohibition against expounding his metaphysics and physics probably originated in the theological faculty, in which Robert Courçon was himself a master. The prohibition was reiterated, though rather more circumspectly ('until the works on natural philosophy have been examined and found free of any suspicion of error') by the Pope himself in 1231 and in 1263. This prohibition applied only in Paris and not, for instance, in Toulouse or Oxford, which, at this period, had begun to compete with Paris as the home of philosophical learning.

Prohibitions of this kind have, however, an inherent tendency to be ineffective, or at least to have results different from those intended by their originators. Aristotle had no peer. His system was unopposed. A large number of theses which, rightly or wrongly, had been ascribed to Aristotle were explicitly condemned by Estienne Tempier, the Bishop of Paris, in 1277. These will be dealt with later (p. 230). Actions of this kind, however, rather stimulated interest in the forbidden and a completely orthodox argument began to make itself heard in this context which was that in order to oppose error it was necessary to have studied it thoroughly. Finally in 1366 a Papal document made lectures on the works that had hitherto been forbidden (on paper at least) obligatory for the degree of master of philosophy. Aristotle had conquered western Europe and had been given the highest endorsement he could require.

Privileges, the organization of faculties and the office of rector

In a circular dated 1299 the masters of Toulouse point out with pride that anybody who 'wanted to enquire into the innermost mysteries of nature' had always been able to find what they wanted at Toulouse. The foundation of this university was connected with the series of ideological and social disputes that had taken place in Paris between 1228 and 1231. The letter was in fact nothing more than a 'special opening offer', greater academic and intellectual freedom than could be offered in Paris, which was dominated by theologians. The disputes in Paris had been ended by a Papal Bull *Parens scientiarum* ('The mother of sciences') of 1231, which has been described as the *magna carta* of the University of Paris. Among the privileges it confirmed were these:

The right to establish its own statutes
The right to punish transgression of these statutes itself
The right to have criminal cases tried by ecclesiastical courts
The right to suspend teaching until recompense had been made
  for the ill-treatment or imprisonment of students by authorities
  not empowered to deal with them.

From this moment on it is possible to talk about the university as an institution distinguished by characteristics which in many cases it was to retain until well into this century. Among these are fixed syllabuses, academic degrees, its own system of jurisdiction, the power to decide on the form and content of the teaching independent of any outside influence, and the right to strike as an effective means of upholding its privileges. The name *universitas* was not, however, to be used as a generally understood term until the fifteenth century. Up to that time the only official name for a university was *studium generale*. When a seat of learning had been recognized as a *studium generale*, the degree it issued were also recognized officially by all equivalent universities. This state of affairs helped to create an international intelligentsia and its members could, at least in

universitas

studium generale

theory, act as teachers within their own faculty at any other *studium generale* merely after having presented their master's degree. This licence to teach anywhere (*ius ubique docendi*) was issued by the university as a result of special permission from the Pope. It was one of the measures taken by the Holy See in its endeavour to make the universities a unifying

ius ubique docendi

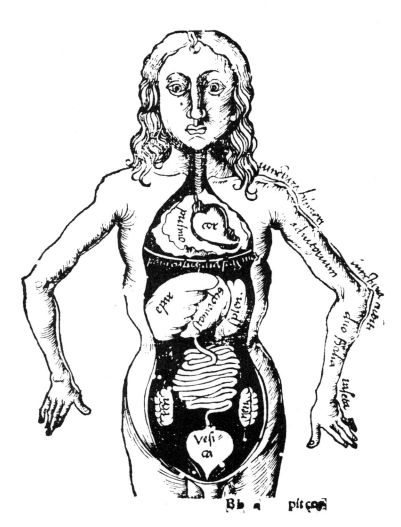

Fig. 22. An anatomical plate. Gregorius Reisch, *Margarita philosophica* (first printed in 1469), printed in Basle in 1583 by Sebastian Henricpetri.

136

factor in Europe, but its effect was often undermined by different forms of local patriotism.

Even in Abélard's time a careful distinction had been made in Paris between theology and philosophy (*artes*). Not long after the death of Irnerius, the lawyer of Bologna, civil law began to form part of the university syllabus, but it soon had to give way to the study of canon law, which was already well established in Paris in the 1170s. Medicine was also being studied there on a rather modest scale by the end of the twelfth century. The four 'faculties' (*facultates*), a term that in this context means 'branches of learning', had begun to take real shape by the year 1200 even if the legal and terminological distinctions had not yet been given unambiguous clarity. An agreement from 1213 between the university and the chancellor recognizes the right of each faculty to approve candidates for the relevant degree of master, and in practice this right also gave them control over the organization of the teaching. Not until 1252, however, did one of the 'higher' faculties (so termed because they required completed studies in the 'lower' preparatory philosophical faculty), in this case theology, establish its own statutes for admission to the degree of master.

The office of principal (*rector*) did not evolve until the end of the thirteenth century. Originally the impartial chairman at meetings between all the faculties, in the fourteenth century he became the university's chief spokesman and governor and his consent was needed before the university's decisions could take legal effect. The details about the different stages in this development are, however, not very clear.

facultates

rector

Bologna – student democracy and the nations

Up to now most of our attention has been devoted to Paris. The reasons are fairly obvious. It was not only prototypes for the philosophical and theological faculties that developed there. Paris also became the model for what were later called masters' universities, universities where a convocation of masters had the power to make decisions about the running of the university.

There was also a more democratic type of university. In Bologna it was the students themselves who had the power to make or break professors or the rector. It may be remembered that the law school there had originally been a secular university founded to provide teaching in Roman civil law which would be of direct usefulness to students in their future careers. Because of the growth of importance of canon law in Gratian's time, Bologna also came an important centre of learning for the Church.

The early history of the University of Bologna is not unlike what was later to happen in Paris. Bologna became institutionalized more quickly, however, and this was in some part thanks to the active interest of the Imperial court. It was particularly proud of the letters patent it had received from Emperor Frederick Barbarossa in 1158, *Habita*, which it regarded as its charter of foundation and which were later incorporated in Justinian's *Codex*. In recognition of the glory reflected on the city by the law students they were granted legal immunity by the emperor himself:

Inasmuch as all who do good deserve Our praise and Our protection. We feel that it is with particular love that We should shield from injury all those through whose knowledge the world is enlightened and Our subjects nurtured in obedience to God and to Us, His servant. Who feels no sympathy with those who out of love for knowledge have submitted voluntarily to exile? They who were rich have become poor and have humbled themselves, they expose themselves to perils of every kind and sometimes endure physical mistreatment from the vilest of men.[49]

The emperor's compassionate letter confirmed the students' right to be judged either by their teachers or by the bishop of the city. If their adversaries attempted to bring the case before any other judge it lapsed automatically.

The driving force in Bologna was the students, or rather the students' union. The feelings of alienation that Emperor Frederick hints at, made the students pouring into the city combine in organizations similar to trade unions which were called *universitates* (corporations) followed by the name of their place of origin. This was the prototype of the organizations that were later to be called generally *nationes* (nations). The term *universitas scholarium*, meaning the 'student body in its entirety', can be traced back to the year 1193.

universitates

nationes

universitas scholarium

As the teachers lacked a corresponding 'trade' organization, these corporations had for many years extensive powers to influence the selection of teachers and the conditions under which they worked. This student-power, which on several occasions became pure dictatorship, gave rise to considerable tension and finally had to be restrained by some form of agreement. In the 1250s both the city of Bologna and the Holy See acknowledged the distinct nature and the statutes of the student university, but at the same time awarded teachers the fundamental authority of invigilating examinations and issuing licences to teach. The students continued, however, to have more or less complete control over the university's relationships with the outside world. As one can imagine, the relationship between teachers and students remained tense. How students could retain control of such power is perhaps easier to understand if it is remembered that they were on the whole men with a certain amount of maturity and not teenagers as the majority of the arts students in Paris were. In many cases they had already completed their studies of philosophy. The background becomes even clearer when it is realized that the students in Bologna were drawn mainly from the most influential classes in their respective countries. Their social position was sound and they were men who were used to making decisions for other people.

In Bologna lecturers were kept on a tight rein with the help of an extensive system of checking and fines. A lecturer was fined if he began or ended a lecture after the time announced; he had to have reached an agreement with his students about the syllabus for the year; he had to keep within the limits of each section dealt with and there were set fines for different breaches of these rules. The same rules applied if he attempted to talk his way out of difficult questions or try to gloss over obscure passages. For safety's sake, teachers deposited a sum of money from which these fines could be taken when occasion arose. Special informers were used to denounce particularly bad lecturers. Complaints from no more than two students meant that the rector (who, naturally, had been appointed by the students) was obliged by the statutes to intervene 'so that the doctors' disobedience might be punished'.

That this unbending system of control could be exercised for so long – although the statutes almost certainly give a rigid picture of what really happened – was also due to the fact that the students had an economic grip on the teachers. Salaried teaching posts were not established before the end of the thirteenth century and before that teachers had to send round a collection plate. By the middle of the fourteenth century, the city of Bologna had completely taken over the responsibility of paying the teachers. The result was inevitably that the unlimited power that the students and the rector had enjoyed was curtailed. The apparatus of root and branch student democracy moved too slowly. The more flexible system of government that had by now been established in Paris was, in the long run, better suited for the encouragement of collective responsibilities.

The nations of students were, however, an invention that came from Bologna. The simplest division of students who came from elsewhere was between those who had come from places 'beyond' or 'this side of' the Alps (*ultramontani* and *citramontani*). In the fifteenth century the former group was divided among seventeen nations, the latter among sixteen. New administrative ideas and principles cannot possibly, however, have come from the mass meetings of these unwieldy nations. In the nations there were officials who were called advisers (*consiliarii*) and with the rector they prepared matters that were to be discussed.

ultramontani
citramontani

140

The rector's position gave him amazingly high status. He was in fact placed higher than even a cardinal. When he was installed in office this was done at a resplendent ceremony in the cathedral and he was then escorted in triumph by all the

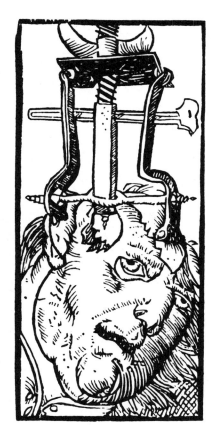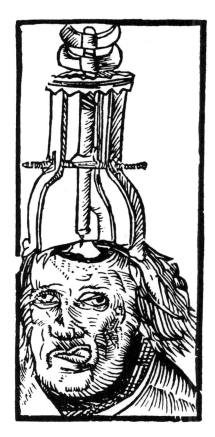

Fig. 23. An instrument for trepanning. The school of medicine in Salerno had worked out instructions for the treatment of limb and skull fractures, on how to carry out an amputation, stitch wounds together, stop bleeding, perform bloodletting and so on. In monasteries in Scandinavia the following types of surgical instruments have been found: cups for bloodletting, bloodletting lancets, examination needles, catheters made of lead, different surgical knives, tweezers, scrapers of iron and bronze, probes of lead and bronze, needles for stiching wounds and clips for holding the edges of a wound together. Hieronymus Braunschweig, *Handywarke of surgeri*, printed by Peter Treveris in 1525.

students in the city. It goes without saying that this kind of ceremony involved very heavy expenses for the holder of the office and special regulations were made about how much the festivities were allowed to cost. One bizarre and particularly expensive custom was to rip the clothes from the newly installed rector's back and then compel him to buy the rags back for fantastic sums of money. This helps to explain why more than one potential candidate fought tooth and nail to avoid being elected rector. The result was that a new stipulation was made forbidding anyone elected to refuse the post.

Lectures and degrees

A doctorate in law awarded by the University of Bologna was the equivalent of a master of arts degree from the University of Paris. They were both official recognition of the right to teach, which at that time was regarded as being both a 'degree' and a title. The number of active teachers at Bologna was fairly small and the work was lucrative.

At Bologna there developed the custom of dividing the lectures into ordinary lectures and extra-ordinary ones. The ordinary lectures were given on the books that were regarded as being the most important of the legal texts. In civil law these were *Digestum vetus* ('the old classification') and *Codex* ('the Book', cf. p. 67ff.).

The first requirement of a student, imperative if he wished to be able to claim legal immunity, was enrolment in a register. The student's day was taken up with an ordinary lecture in the morning and two shorter extra-ordinary lectures later in the day. To begin with these were given in private houses; later on school buildings in the city were rented and for especially popular lecturers one of the city's public rooms or a marketplace could be used.

According to the statutes, after every section of the text the doctors were supposed to read the glosses (see p. 69). The extra-ordinary lectures were, as a rule, given by students who had been studying for a sufficiently long time. At Bologna as in Paris these students were called *baccalaurei*, but at Bologna this was more a descriptive term than a formal academic degree. What was demanded for the title of baccalaureate was five or six years of active study and permission from the rector to lecture on a chapter (a *titulus*) or a book in civil or canon law. These lectures were regarded very much as training in the art of academic presentation rather than real teaching. It was known for students to bribe their fellows to make up an audience for these delicate occasions. The degree proper, the doctorate, was conferred in the same way as the dignity of master was in Paris and the candidate was given a book to betoken his authority to expound the law. At Bologna, where all power was vested in

iuris doctor

magister artium

lectiones ordinariae et extra-ordinariae

Digestum vetus Codex

baccalaurei

143

the students, this ceremony was one of the few privileges that the teachers had. To create a parallel to the system that prevailed north of the Alps, Pope Honorius III intervened and declared that in future no doctor's degree was to be awarded without the permission of the archdeacon of the cathedral, an office he had once held himself. This official therefore became chancellor of the university. In Paris there had been constant warfare between the chancellor of the cathedral and the university for most of the thirteenth century, but the relationship between the University of Bologna and the archdeacon was nearly always amicable. The wealth of the average student meant that the office of chancellor was an unfailing and abundant source of income.

Theology challenged by Aristotle

During the eleventh century as we have seen Aristotelianism slowly but surely found its way into every branch of learning. The combination of its methods of thinking with theology was to be a particularly fertile union. Terms like principal propositions and axioms could easily be reinterpreted so that they fitted the supreme articles of the Christian faith embodied in the creeds. How far this procedure meant that theology could be described as a science (which used syllogisms to deduce irrefutable conclusions from certain premises) was something that the scholastic theologians were to decide differently according to their varying temperaments. In contrast to the natural (in other words, tangible for human intelligence *ratio*), sciences, articles of   ratio
faith such as the Holy Trinity or the incarnation were not susceptible to verification and had to be believed because they had been revealed by a higher power (because of the *auctoritas* of the source, which in this case was ultimately the   auctoritas
Holy Spirit). Boethius' teaching on *locus* was, however, well known to everybody and one of its assertions was that an argument that finds its support in authority and not on rational insight was the weakest kind of argument (*locus ab auctoritate est infirmissimus*). How was it then possible to say that theology was the supreme science? What, if anything, was the basis for believing in it?

The Bible gives no explicit answers to questions like these. Scholars had reached the stage when they were well aware that the Bible, like all other authorities, was something that had to be interpreted, and that the principles on which this interpretation was based had to be accounted for candidly. The confrontation of the new philosophy with faith primarily gave rise to a number of questions and we shall see later that the *quaestio*-form was the most typical and fruitful genre produced by scholasticism.

However, this new way of thinking and the increasingly subtle language that arose as a result of studies of philosophy also provided theologians with the possibility of expressing the dictates of faith in more exact and less elusive words. One

Fig. 24. A lesson in anatomy. Three scenes showing an autopsy, a lecture and a decorative landscape have not here been combined to give a realistic picture of the teaching of medicine. The text reads, 'Here is shown the correct position for a body for an autopsy and where and how the first incision should be made. It refers to the adjacent chapter in which everything is described.' A sixteenth-century edition of Mondino dei Luzzi's anatomy (*Anatomia Mundini*).

example will illustrate this. It had always been believed that Christ Himself was really present in the Sacrament of the Altar in the species of bread and wine. Although they were ordinary created things, in the course of the Mass they were changed or transformed in some way into the body and blood of Christ. Aristotle's theories about categories proved to be serviceable when it came to attempting to define more exactly how this alteration could take place.

It was obvious that what faith knew was the true body and blood of Christ retained all the attributes that the senses experienced as bread and wine. In Aristotelian terms the accidentals remained the same; quantity, quality, disposition in time and space did not change in any way as the priest pronounced the words of consecration. The human senses are, moreover, infallible and there was no reason for believing that our senses were deceiving us in this case. But when He who is Himself the Truth asserted: 'This *is* my body', Christian faith had to accept that the category which in the highest degree *is*, namely substance, undergoes a transformation into the body of Christ. This is the miracle of the Mass: the substance of the bread, the carrier of the accidentals of bread, departs but the accidentals remain in some miraculous way through the direct intervention of God. The miracle had been given a rational explanation:

If one wonders in what substance the accidentals have their basis (form, taste and weight), I would answer that it appears as if we have to acknowledge that they exist without any basis rather than rest on some basis because there is present no other substance than the body of Our Lord and His blood, which are not affected by these accidentals. For the body of Christ does not take such a form but appears as it will when He will one day return to judgement. These accidentals are therefore their own basis.[50]

This alteration of essence with no change in the accidentals was called by the theologians transubstantiation (change transsubstantiatio from one substance to another). This explanation was given supreme endorsement when in 1215 the fourth Lateran Council declared it to be a dogma, an article of faith enjoined on every Christian.

Lectio and disputation

The most striking characteristic of the atmosphere of the universities was that everything was continually questioned. There was discussion not only of debatable points but even of matters that were already accepted with full conviction. People wanted to know why what was obvious was so obvious. This habit of asking questions, inspired by the methods presented in Abélard's *Sic et Non* and the mock trials that had become part of the teaching methods of the University of Bologna, gave rise to a form of teaching called *disputatio*, which in importance took second place only to the lectures. Lectures were confined to explanation of the texts but the disputations suffered from no such constraints and in them students were given the chance of marshalling all their perspicuity and dexterity with syllogisms. With the help of ever more finely drawn distinctions, they had to show the number of different meanings contained in almost every expression. To make sure that they did not finally become bogged down in desperate hair-splitting, these disputations were terminated by one of the masters, who summarized the arguments that had been presented and provided his solution to the problem (*determinatio*). In some cases the master's summary was written down and circulated, possibly after corrections and other editorial improvements had been made, and this genre of literature (if one can use this term to describe writing of such a 'technical' nature) was called *quaestio disputata*.

An even freer form of disputation was what was known as *disputatio de quolibet*, disputations about 'anything at all'. The name was well deserved as the subjects of disputations of this sort could range from the supreme Being and its nature to ridiculous trivialities suggested by someone in the audience and prompted by inquisitiveness, malice or puerile cleverness. The aim was to nonplus the respondent and leave him at a loss for words. This form of disputation, which occasionally gave rise to anthologies of *quodlibeta* (the determinations provided by some eminent master), were, understandably enough, something of a popular amusement

(margin notes: disputatio; determinatio; quaestio disputata; disputatio de quolibet; quodlibeta)

and could draw their audience from outside university circles. They could at times include the city's authorities and other notables, and on such occasions the questions raised could have close connections with contemporary political concerns or current plots and machinations.

Medical theory . . .

With the few exceptions already described (see p. 44) there was little to medicine except the intuitions and illusions behind popular remedies until some time in the middle of the twelfth century when it was elevated to the rank of an academic discipline able to hold its own as one of the four faculties in the university system. The major reason for this was the capacity for translation shown at the school of Toledo. In medicine as well as in philosophy the advanced Arab civilization was to be the factor that released the enormous amount of latent energy dormant in Europe as it awakened. The sudden rise and rapid institutionalization of the universities can hardly be explained without any reference to the Arab world. Higher education in the Muslim world was based on small fraternities of pupils assembled by the personal magnetism of the master they followed. It can hardly have been an accident that in its earliest stage the university in Europe consisted of similar groups of wandering students centred round a few renowned teachers who were, to begin with, without any local ties in the shape of buildings or the like. In Arab civilization can also be found models for – or at least parallels to – the *lectio* and *disputatio* of scholasticism.

The academic study of medicine, like all the other subjects, consisted principally of the study of authoritative texts. There was a definite body of knowledge to be acquired, a suitable subject for detailed conceptual analysis and profound argument and controversy. The official texts for study contained works of Greek origin and the impressive and scholarly synthesis of classical medicine and Arabic Aristotelianism which was Avicenna's mammoth *Canon*. In printed form the million words that this work contains cover over a thousand folio pages. As are all of his works, it is irradiated by Avicenna's lucidity and his ability to digest learning. In the preface he describes the basis of medical science in a way that would have satisfied Aristotle's most stringent requirements. Medical insight is the habit acquired by practice of recognizing the causes of illness and

Canon

150

health. Its material causes are the separate parts of the body, the bodily fluids (blood, phlegm, choler and melancholy) humores and, in a larger perspective, the elements themselves. The formal causes are the different combinations of the elements and the fluids, their *complexio (temperamentum)*, which complexio, governs a human being's character, temperament temperamentum ('humour') and state of health. The effective causes are changes in the weather, food, drink, good and bad habits and the final cause is the functioning of the organs.

The *Canon* covers the complete field of medicine: anatomy, physiology, surgery, the pathology of the organs, histology and it also contains general rules for doctors.

At the school in Salerno physiology and pathology were based on the theory of temperament. Sickness was a sign that one or several of the bodily fluids had begun to dominate the body and disturb the finely balanced equilibrium. Diagnosis was made after observing pain, the temperature, the pulse rate and urine samples. Galen's works on anatomy were studied and the fact that students were asked to dissect the bodies of animals probably helped to make the subject clearer and more interesting.

A syllabus for the four-year course in medicine at the University of Bologna has been preserved. Four lectures were given each day, two in the morning on theory and two in the afternoon with practical applications of the theory. The whole of the first year was devoted to the introduction to Avicenna's *Canon*. The first lecture each morning dealt with subjects such as the inevitability of death, sickness in general, children's diseases, dietary regulations and medical instructions *(regimen sanitatis)*. The second lecture dealt regimen sanitatis with the fevers, and in the afternoons students practised foretelling the kind of crisis different symptoms would lead to. During the second year Galen, Hippocrates and new sections of Avicenna were covered and the afternoons were given over to revision. In the third year the students started to read Hippocrates' *Aphorisms*, some new works by Galen and a book by Averroes, which had a Latin title, *Colliget*, which is a distortion of the Arabic original. The fourth year was devoted to continuous revision. Medical authors never tired of repeating things, feeling that it was impossible to

151

teach other people things that they had not ploughed through themselves: *sapius repetita placebunt* ('repetition makes the contents more digestible').

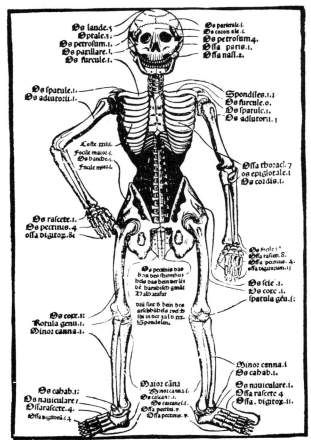

Fig. 25. 'The South-German late-Gothic skeleton.' The charts used in teaching anatomy were inspired by religious art. In the original of this illustration the names of the different bones were inscribed on small 'pennants' around the skeleton. In this picture the terms have simply been printed and lines drawn to the appropriate parts of the body, later these lines were to be ruled lines. However, the heading over this beautiful skeleton still bears witness to the unclear division that existed between religious knowledge and other forms of knowledge. It uses a quotation from the book of Job to remind medical students of the transience of life and the gravity of eternity: 'Man that is born of a woman is of few days, and full of trouble.' *Anatomia*, printed by J. Grüninger in Strasbourg in 1497.

. . . and practice

From Salerno the impulses from Arab scholarship spread to the newly established medical faculties at Bologna and Montpellier. The first case of an autopsy on a human being is recorded from Bologna some time around the beginning of the fourteenth century. It was not carried out because of medical curiosity but for legal and forensic reasons to establish whether a death was the result of natural causes or whether some individual had assisted nature in some way. From here it was but a short step to the inclusion of anatomy as an obligatory subject in the medical faculties. In 1396 King Charles VI of France awarded the University of Montpellier an annual grant of the body of one criminal executed either by hanging or drowning, 'in consideration that the said study of anatomy must take place, that it is of necessity for the welfare of the human race and in order to advance appropriate experiment in the said science of medicine'.

In Montpellier the lectures of William of Congenis followed faithfully a textbook written by a master from Salerno. Students were also obliged to go to the hospital of the Holy Spirit in the city to observe and practise the extreme responsibilities of the surgeon. Seeing with one's own eyes 'encourages boldness, as an important part of the surgeon's skill is daring'. They had to watch while the master himself operated on the bowels or on the internal organs. 'On one occasion while the master was trepanning an injured man one of the students fainted when he saw how the brain throbbed. My advice is, therefore, that nobody should perform an operation before he has watched it being done by someone else.'

One can wonder whether these operations were successful. They do represent considerable progress from the days of 'pre-scientific' medicine as the Syrian surgeon Thabit records. During one of the crusades he was attending a Frankish knight who had an abscess in one of his legs. Thabit had applied a poultice and observed that the abscess had burst and seemed to be healing when a Frankish doctor burst

Fig. 26. The oldest series of anatomical illustrations in print, Johannes Peyligk's *Philosophiae naturalis*, printed by Melchior Lotter in Leipzig in 1499. Top left is an explanatory illustration showing how the human being divides into three sections. Counting from the top down, these are firstly the animal limbs or, in other words, the inner senses (conceptualization, imagination, thought, memory and *sensus communis*) and the five senses, and then in the central section the 'spiritual organs', the lungs and the heart. The lowest part consists of the 'natural' organs, the digestive system and its component parts.

At the top right is a picture of the stomach (*stomachus*), the spleen (*splen*) and the liver (*hepar*). The feeling of hunger (*appetitus*) is explained in this way. When any part of the body is empty it attracts blood from the stomach through the liver and arteries. This causes the stomach to crumple up and a feeling of sorrow ensues. The spleen is a storage vessel for black bile (called here *melancholia*) and excess of this substance gives rise to melancholy and deep depression ('spleen'). The three other bodily fluids are produced in the liver and they are blood (*sanguis*), bile (*chole*) and phlegm (*phlegma*). Excesses of these fluids give rise to lasciviousness, bad temper or sloth respectively.

The illustrations in the centre of the page are of the kidneys and the heart. The function of the kidneys is to separate excess water from the blood, and the function of the heart is to heat the body with the vital spirit which it receives from the lungs. The heart is the warmest part of the body and the basis of life.

The five illustrations at the bottom of the page are, from left to right, a lung, the cranium, the ventricles of the brain, the empty space (*lacuna*) at the centre of the heart, and an eye. The sounds of the voice are created in the lungs. The larger the lungs, the more breath they can transmit to the heart and the warmer a person will be. For this reason women are not so warm as men and have weaker voices. The cranium is formed of several bones joined together and excess brain fluid can escape between the joins. Below the cranium there two membranes, the hard mother and the soft mother (*dura mater* and *pia mater*), which shield the brain from contact with the bones of the cranium. Arteries are embedded in these membranes to provide the brain with nourishment. The brain is a white, bloodless organ that contains a great deal of marrow and breath. Every nerve in the body originates in the brain. In it there are three chambers (*ventriculi*): the front, the back and the central one. These 'cells' contain the inner senses. In the front chamber are *sensus communis* and imagination, in the central chamber conceptualization and thought, and the memory

154

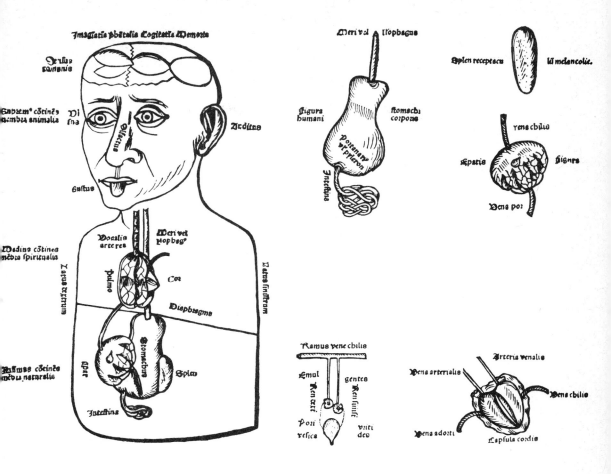

is at the rear. The brain is the coldest organ in the body and its coldness is balanced against the warmth of the heart to maintain the temperature of the body. Excess phlegm collects in the hollows in the brain and drips down into the nose. The eye, finally, consists of three fluids and seven membranes.

in and brusquely asked the patient whether he preferred to live with one leg or die with two. The choice was not a difficult one to make and to his amazement Thabit found himself watching with revulsion as the Frankish field-surgeon sent for a sturdy soldier with a sharp axe. The amputation was finally a success but 'the poor patient died instantly'.

Like the teachers in the other faculties, the teachers of medicine guaranteed collectively that candidates for the degree of baccalaureate met certain minimum standards. Part of the instruction in the faculty consisted of repeated disputations on selected sections of the texts studied. After four years of study a candidate for the baccalaureate was required to defend a theoretical thesis in public. If he acquired this first degree, he could then, under the direction of his own teachers, give basic lectures so that after an oral examination in the presence of masters from all the faculties he could become a licentiate, a degree that naturally led up to a doctorate.

theorica
practica

physicus
medicus

The Arabs had been careful to distinguish between the *theorica* of medicine and its *practica*. In the late Middle Ages a clear differentiation was maintained between those who pursued these two branches of medicine: the theoreticians were called *physicus* and practitioners *medicus*. The general contempt of the academics in other faculties for the practitioners, who were looked on as the tradesmen of the medical guilds, led, especially in Italy, to greater emphasis being placed on the speculative side of medicine as a branch of scholarship in which sure and certain knowledge was deduced from eternally valid universal axioms. In the fourteenth century Gentilis de Fulgineo, a commentator on Avicenna, composed elaborate *quaestiones* that applied the metaphysical system to medicinal herbs and similar physical realities. One of his questions concerns how the plants that are potential medicines are 'actualized' in the body:

The question is this: to what extent are the herbs which are called potential medicine given their efficacy by the influence of the warmth of the body and if so, how. The cause of this perplexity is that we clearly experience the heating effect of pepper and the

156

Fig. 27. The first urine test? Then, just like today, urine analysis was one of the obligatory routines before a diagnosis was made. Medical science laid down elaborate rules for how the sample should be dealt with. It had to be taken when the patient made water for the first time in the morning, and was not to be allowed to stand for any length of time. The patient should not have been involved in any physical exertion and the sample had to be kept in a clean and transparent vessel of glass or crystal. It had to be examined with light shining through it but could not be exposed to direct sunlight. Urine samples were thought to yield information primarily about the condition of the liver, arteries and the bladder. According to Avicenna urine should be analysed in accordance with the Aristotelian categories: substance (degree of purity, admixture of foreign substance), quantity (a great deal, very little or normal), quality (colour, smell), the relationship of different stratifications in the liquid, the place of precipitation (upwards, downwards or in the centre) and the time for sedimentation. A miniature from *Ms Harley 1585*, British Museum (*c.* 1170–1200).

157

cooling effects of poppy but if we touch them they both appear to possess the same quality to begin with. This gives rise to conjecture which would be without motivation in the case of glowing iron or ice or something similar, for instance. It was this that started Galen's speculation and led him to conclude that these medicines, pepper and poppy, are medicines *in potentia*.[51]

Such a question can arouse a certain amount of interest but it can hardly have given rise to any major advances in basic medical research, especially as this research was in no way based on empirical experiment. The practice of medicine did, however, have tangible effects on public health. In the wake of the study of medicine came a growing interest in public hygiene and this can explain in part the decline in the prevalence of leprosy in Europe in the fifteenth century.

Scholasticism: the Masters and their Schools

The questions that Aristotle posed accepted patterns of thought were to remain dominant from the thirteenth century, the period that was the golden age of scholasticism. Before the ideas of its leading exponents are presented, however, a word of warning is necessary. The certainty with which the early schoolmen make pronouncements about 'the thing in itself' may be surprising. Their optimistic approach to the theory of knowledge was based on Aristotelian metaphysics and on Paul's belief that even the invisible nature of God can be perceived and understood in the physical creation (Romans 1:20). The innermost realities are therefore accessible to the senses, thought and language. It is possible to conceive of every being (see p. 117) as it really is, and everything in the universe is in itself good and beautiful and ordered in all-embracing system of mutual interdependence. This is also true, albeit merely by analogy, of the supreme Being, in other words God, the absolute, necessary existence, unalloyed and independent Truth and Goodness. All other forms of existence, truth, beauty or any other value is what it is by virtue of its participation in the supreme Being. This optimism was to endure until confronted by William of Occam.

The mendicant orders reach Paris

When the Cathars and other extremist lay movements that threatened the unity of Christendom arose at the beginning of the thirteenth century two 'begging' mendicant orders were founded. The Dominicans or the order of preachers was founded by the Spaniard Dominic, and the Franciscan order

Fig. 28. Fantastic drawings intended to be used to help to remember things. *Ars memorandi nova secretissima*, printed by M. Greyff, Reutlingen, the end of the fifteenth century.

(the little brothers) by Francis in Italy. These movements in the Church were based on the New Testament ideals of poverty, property in common and obedience and were intended to win back lost ground with the very weapons the heretics had used.

From the very beginning the Dominican order was an order of priests and it was only natural that its members should devote themselves to advanced studies, especially as they were supposed to convince those who were in error by argument and reason. The founder of the Franciscan order, however, had intended its members to follow literally in the footsteps of Christ and his apostles. The order soon experienced a metamorphosis and adopted a style very similar to the Dominicans; they purchased buildings in the cities, laid down courses of study and began to acquire libraries. The mendicant orders established themselves with amazing speed in Paris; the Dominicans in 1217 and the Franciscans in 1219, in the first case one year, and in the second nine years after the orders had been granted approval in Rome. Unlike the monastic orders, which followed rules like that of Benedict, the mendicant friars were not confined to a specific monastery isolated in the countryside but were in fact enjoined to be on the move and to be active at the very heart of communications and trade, in the market squares. They travelled from place to place in pairs. They formed an international movement in a Church that was still organized statically on the basis of geographical divisions protected by the local bishop, an organization that had not changed in principle since antiquity. The mendicant orders were in the service of the universal Church, bearing with them the new learning and spreading ideas and impulses across the length and breadth of Europe. They were compatible with the universities (both organizations had indeed been created in response to new social conditions).

In Paris the mendicant orders were, on the whole, given a friendly welcome and in 1221 the master Jean de Barastre assigned a building on Mont-Sainte-Geneviève to the Dominican order. From this time on it was they who were to set the tone.

During the riots between 1228 and 1231 the mendicant

orders remained in Paris and started their own teaching. This was the first step towards total domination of the theological faculty. In 1254 only three of the fifteen teaching posts in theology were held by teachers who were not attached to either the Dominicans or the Franciscans. Infiltration on this scale did not take place without a certain amount of complaint from university teachers who were not themselves members of the orders.

The seraphic doctor: knowledge and wisdom

Giovanni Fidanza, better known as Bonaventura or 'the seraphic doctor', was the most imposing of St Francis's doctor seraphicus spiritual heirs. In 1250 he was responsible for the Franciscans' courses in theology in Paris. He was first and foremost a theologian and he made a clear distinction between theology and philosophy. Philosophy is concerned only with those aspects of reality that are accessible to the enquiry of reason. This field covers only a small part of the potential of human beings and in it are to be found no adequate answers to the question of how they are to reach their true destiny. Additional knowledge is needed to supplement philosophy and this is granted only through revelation, theology, which for Bonaventura was the same as the Scriptures. Theology begins where philosophy ends.

To what extent, however, is biblical theology a science? Admittedly it contains truth revealed by God, but this is presented in a way which makes absolutely no systematic use of rigorous distinctions, definitions and syllogistic deduction. Can it then be described as a strict science (*scientia*) in the Aristotelian meaning, which starts from certain premises and by means of syllogistic reasoning derives incontrovertible deductions about its subject (God, the creation, redemption, the sacraments, etc.)? Moreover the Bible deals with individual events, it is a story that describes events which could have turned out differently from the way they did.

Bonaventura was aware of these difficulties but maintained nevertheless that theology is a science. He did not accept the restriction of the concept of science to the purely 'theoretical'. Science also involves practical guidance. One branch of science, ethics, provides norms for behaviour and its aim is, according to Aristotle, 'to make good people out of us'. Theology has a similar function and its aim is to prepare us to achieve salvation on the supranatural or transcendental plane. Every science must be organized in the way most suited to its aims. Theology therefore appeals to more than reason, and its methods are different from those of other

163

sciences. It does not use abstract definitions of concepts but employs different types of narrative and in this way it speaks to as many different forms of personality as possible.

How can a method like this lay any claim to certainty? Bonaventura distinguished between two kinds of certainty. One is acquired step by step as a result of logical deduction and the other is based on unquestionable sources in which one can place complete confidence. In point of fact, however, God alone possesses the capacity of being able neither to deceive nor be deceived. For this reason He has so arranged it that all the information that human beings need apart from the data provided by the senses and reason is imparted infallibly and not through the results of human research and enquiry, which can err, but in the form of divine revelation. This involves the 'disclosure' of certain relationships that human reason would never be able to deduce despite all the evidence available in the universe (such as the Holy Trinity,

revelatio →

Fig. 29. The medieval conception of the world (cf. Fig. 17). At the centre is the globe with the spheres of earth, water, air and fire. Next comes the Moon, Mercury, Venus, the Sun, Mars, Jupiter, Saturn, the firmament, the crystal heaven and the sphere of prime movement. Empyreum, the realm of God, his angels and the saints, surrounds everything. In the sphere of the firmament the twelve signs of the Zodiac have been depicted. In the realm of the saints Christ is enthroned as ruler of the World, and His feet rest on the spheres. He is surrounded by saints and the nine different classes of angels arranged in three hierarchies. In a sermon which was obligatory reading for all priests and monks on the Feast of St Michael (29 September) every year, Pope Gregory the Great (who died in 604) had described the classification of the heavenly host: 'The testimony of the Holy Scriptures tells us that there are nine classes of angel – angels, archangels, principalities, powers, mights, dominions, thrones, cherubim and seraphim. Cherubim and seraphim are described in the Old Testament. Paul the Apostle lists four classes in the Epistle to the Ephesians: "far above all principality, and power, and might, and dominion". In the Epistle to the Colossians he wrote: "whether they be thrones

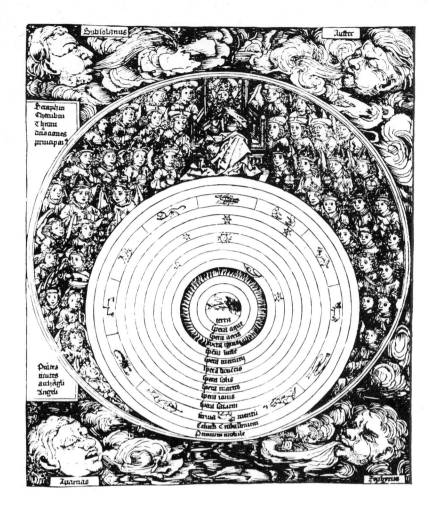

or dominions or principalities or powers". If thrones are added to the four classes named in the Epistle to the Ephesians, there are, therefore, five classes. Added to the angels, archangels, cherubim and seraphim this adds up to a total of nine classes in all.' These creatures of spirit were described in the language of philosophy as independent intelligences by whose agency God governed the universe. This concept combines aspects of Arabic Aristotelianism with the neo-platonic interpretations of the Bible found in the pseudo-Dionysius the Areopagite. The four winds – counting clockwise from the top left-hand corner they are the easterly, southerly, westerly and northerly winds (*subsolanus*, *auster*, *zephyrus* and *aparctias*) – have been added here purely as ornamentation. Schedel, *Liber chronicarum*, printed by Anton Koberger in Nuremberg in 1493.

165

the Incarnation). The patterning of the Scriptures to meet every human need demands that theologians must spare no pains to recover every layer of meaning from the holy text. Bonaventura described the multifarious nuances of meaning in the words of the Bible in the tradition that has been described earlier (see p. 28).

Philosophy deals with things such as they appear in nature or in the soul within the realms of inborn or acquired natural knowledge. But theology, the science based on faith and the revelation of the Holy Spirit deals with matters of grace, glory and the eternal Wisdom. For that reason she places herself above the methods of philosophy and takes from [the contemplation of] the nature of things as much as is needed to be able to hold up a mirror in which the divine can be reflected. . . . The structure of the world is beautiful, but even more beautiful is the Church, adorned with gifts of divine grace, and the greatest beauty of all is to be found in the heavenly Jerusalem. Beauty above all beauties exists in the highest and most blessed Trinity. For this reason Holy Scripture does not only contain the most sublime content imaginable but also grants joy to human reason and raises it to the heavens; it is itself incomparably beautiful and delights our understanding in a miraculous way. By ever accustoming ourselves to this delight we enable it to elevate our reason so that it can lead us upwards to contemplation of the divine mysteries.[52]

Bonaventura could never have accepted Aristotle's belief that intellectual speculation and the satisfaction that it can bring with it is the highest form of human activity. Knowledge must lead upwards to experience. This had been Augustine's concept of the role of theology and Bernard of Clairvaux had praised experience of God as the greatest thing to be desired. Bonaventura also transcended the intellectual categories. Man's aim is wisdom (*sapientia*), and wisdom is to achieve mystical union with God and 'taste of His delights'. In saying that creation is a reflection of the ideas of God, Bonaventura was using ideas based on Augustine. This attitude (exemplarism) comes ultimately from the teachings of Plato. These divine ideas are seeds which in the act of creation spring into an infinite variety of natures:

sapientia

166

In the eternal Wisdom there is a procreative force which conceives, nourishes and brings forth all substance. For every
archetypal seed is begotten by eternity in the bosom and womb of
eternal Wisdom.

It is hardly possible to travel further from Aristotle's
intellectualism and his rejection of the ideas of Plato about
pre-existing ideas in the divine mind.

Research with awe

Bonaventura was also critical of Plato, however. He had denied that it was possible to acquire knowledge through our senses and claimed rather that the material world was a deceptive mirage that decoyed people away from genuine reality, which was the world of ideas. In Bonaventura's opinion this attitude must lead inevitably to inescapable philosophical scepticism. Human reason can undeniably achieve philosophical knowledge but the more it tries to grasp truths which transcend the material world the more it will feel its own impotence. It is for this very reason that theology is needed. The fact is that it is impossible for us to win through to the eternal, universal and unchanging truths merely through the contemplation of created things. These things change continually. Nor can we find the necessary point of stability in our own intellects as our inner life alters constantly. If, however, we can achieve absolutely positive insights, and this we can do, we must conclude that God Himself, the ultimate cause, the eternal and unchangeable illuminatio truth, assists with enlightenment and edification (*illuminatio*) in the act of knowing. Seen like this theology becomes the supreme study to which all others must be subordinated:

If, therefore, in order to acquire full insight we resort to the absolute unchanging and immoveable Truth and the absolutely infallible light, it is also necessary to resort to the highest study (*ars superna*) as it embodies this light and this truth. The light accords unerring truth to our knowledge, and the truth endows what is known with unchanging constancy.[53]

Bonaventura was therefore an eclectic. He borrows and uses general terms from Aristotle such as the contrast between form and matter, potentiality and actuality, substance and accidentals, and so on, and he shares Aristotle's view that the senses are the necessary channels of information about reality. But it is from Augustine that he has taken the theory of illumination that explains how, despite everything, we can acquire absolutely certain knowledge about

168

reality. The Christian revelation also colours the whole of his philosophical approach. Men should regard the universe as a stairway to God. There is nothing in creation that is not a trace, a small image of the Creator, and from this point of view the senses too function as paths to God.

It is difficult to understand how a Franciscan like Bonaventura could reconcile the ideals of his order with his career as an academic teacher. Francis himself had mocked the rich and wise of this world. Could it not be said that this preoccupation with philosophy was unnecessary and dangerous for true Christians who had immediate access to the highest truths? Bonaventura, was aware of the contradiction but finally came to the conclusion that scholarship was a religious task that must be taken seriously by the new mendicant orders. The difference between the Dominicans and the Franciscans in this respect was, in his opinion, that the Dominicans started by contemplating the supreme truths (*speculatio*) so that afterwards with the help of the unction (*unctio*) of the Holy Spirit these could be preached in praise of God, whereas the Franciscans' approach was the direct opposite and they first preached the revealed truth and then devoted themselves to contemplation of the perfection with which it was composed. Both of these approaches were necessary if the mendicant orders were to fulfil their task of giving bread and not stones to people, and all forms of human appetite must be satisfied:

The reader must not be lulled into believing that it is enough to study without the blessing of the Holy Ghost, to speculate without piety, to enquire without awe, to survey without exultation, to labour without reverence, to know without loving, to possess intelligence without humility, to learn without God's grace, to explain the world without the divinely endowed wisdom of God.[54]

Oxford – experiment and experience

Not very much is known about the early history of the University of Oxford. In 1167 King Henry II prohibited his subjects from travelling to Paris in order to study. This prohibition had political motives but its effects were to be felt in the sleepy country town of Oxford where the schools that already existed underwent something of a boom. Oxford was never to measure up to Paris as a centre of theological studies but in philosophy it was to choose its own paths and was to exercise a major influence on the history of ideas. More emphasis was placed on practical and empirical studies in Oxford than in Paris.

Fig. 30.   A lesson in astronomy at the University of Oxford. At the desk a master is giving a lecture and the two students at his feet are making notes. The five figures at the bottom of the page almost certainly represent *baccalaurei* in a practice disputation and they are showing passages in their textbooks to each other. To the left in the picture is a clock driven by weights and a sphere, to the right is an hour-glass, a candle marked with hours and an astrolabe. These three ways of measuring the time (clocks, hour-glasses and specially marked candles) all began to be used in the fourteenth century. By the end of the century mechanical clocks were being constructed which not only told what time of day or night it was, but also the position of the sun in its passage through the zodiac, the times at which the sun, moon and planets would rise, what point had been reached in the ecclesiastical year and the saints' days. It is obvious that constructing these devices required a high degree of mathematical and astronomical knowledge. The sphere is described in Fig. 40. The astrolabe was invented in the second century BC by a Greek astronomer. At the beginning of the eleventh century it had reached France by way of the Arabs. With its help it was possible to fix the height of the stars, the time of day, the time of sunrise and sunset and the length of dusk and dawn. The standard textbook in astronomy was *De sphaera (materiali)* by the English mathematician and astronomer John of Holywood (Johannes de Sacrobosco), which was written at some time around 1240 and was used up to the final breakthrough of the Copernican system. *Compotus manualis ad usum Oxoniensium*, printed by Charles Kyrfoth in 1519.

171

The first individual to emerge in the history of Oxford is a truly imposing figure. Robert Grosseteste (Great head) became chancellor of the university around 1215, bishop of Lincoln in 1235, and died in 1253. He wrote commentaries on Aristotle's works on science in the second *Analytics* and the *Physics* and he knew enough Greek to be able to translate, with some assistance, the *Nichomachean Ethics* (see p. 179) into Latin. His greatest contributions were however in the field of natural philosophy, and a succession of pamphlets flowed from his quill on different branches of this study. He also believed that form and matter were indivisible elemental constituents in every substance. Grosseteste was extremely interested in the study of optics and this was naturally accompanied by metaphysical speculation about the nature of light. He saw light as a substance half way between spirit and matter, the active force and prototype of all substances. He carried out experiments on the refraction of light and described the evaporation of water and applied his observations as mathematical formulae.

doctor mirabilis

A more interesting personality, although a less important one, was Grosseteste's pupil Roger Bacon, 'the wondrous doctor' (*doctor mirabilis*). After he finished his studies at Oxford he travelled to Paris where he did everything he could to show his contempt for the general ignorance there of Greek and Hebrew, not to mention the natural sciences. He never tired of lavishing his sarcastic comments on the narrow-mindedness and lack of respect for empirical studies that he found. This did not mean, however, that Bacon was a sceptic and he had complete and confident belief that God had revealed the mysteries of nature to the Jews and to Aristotle and that they could be penetrated provided that one had sufficient intelligence and lived an irreproachable life. He was passionately interested in astrology and alchemy. On the other hand he regarded blind respect for authority as the most dangerous of all poisons, the downfall of the masses, such as those who had called 'Crucify him!'. True insight was reserved for a select few who would always be in contradiction to the great masses.

The aims of philosophy for Bacon was not truth for its own sake but the improvement of the world. Theories are necessary but experience is even more necessary: 'anyone who desires to rejoice at the truth of something without evidence must also learn to survive without experience'. Everything must be tested experimentally.

Albertus Magnus the Encyclopaedist

doctor universalis

One of the people whose reputation in Paris had been a mystery to Roger Bacon was 'the great Albert', Albertus Magnus, who was honoured by posterity with the title *doctor universalis*. The reason for this title was that Albert had aimed to make all the knowledge of antiquity accessible to his contemporaries. Albert was a Dominican from Germany and he became a master of theology in the 1240s. He intended to summarize all the new learning in an enormous encyclopaedia and assess it critically to see how it might be used fruitfully within the confines of orthodox Christian beliefs. He regarded this as a suitable and pressing task for himself and for his order. He pleaded therefore for the study of all branches of knowledge in the Dominicans' own schools but this was not accomplished without a certain amount of complaint. 'There are some people who know nothing but who fight tooth and nail against philosophy, especially among the Dominicans, where they meet no resistance. They are like wild animals and what they do not understand they tear to pieces.'

Fig. 31. Albertus Magnus, later Bishop of Regensburg, surrounded by his students. One of them is crowned with a halo and in all probability is intended to represent Thomas Aquinas. The picture illustrates an idea rather than a genuine teaching situation. Then, just like today, it would have aroused a great deal of amazement if a university teacher had appeared to teach dressed in a mitre. Thomas was canonized in 1323, while Albertus had to wait until 1931. In this picture from 1491 he is depicted with radiance around his head. In the 1450s among the Dominicans in Cologne an Albertist school developed which rejected some aspects of Thomist philosophy. This led to the kind of dispute that was later used to make fun of scholasticism such as the question of whether logic was a practical science, as the Thomists maintained, or whether it was speculative, which is what the Albertists believed. *Aristotelis De anima cum commentario secundum doctrinam venerabilis domini Alberti Magni*, printed by J. Koelhoff in Cologne in 1491.

In order to make every item of knowledge, whether it had been revealed to the Greeks, the Muslims or the Jews, open and accessible to those who could read Latin, he wrote innumerable paraphrases and commentaries. (A critical edition of his works is about to be published and when complete it will consist of forty folio volumes.) He went extensively through physics, mathematics, metaphysics and ethics and collected as many writers and opinions as possible,

irrespective of where they were to be found. He displays historical interests which were unusual for the period and attempts to follow an opinion as far back in time as possible in order to work out its exact meaning when it was first used. He is closer to Aristotle than anyone else, he cites his own experiences, demands empirical evidence and carried out experiments to establish the anatomy and behaviour of animals and never merely accepts uncritically the assertions of authorities:

I have examined the anatomy of different species of bees. In the rear part, i.e. behind the waist, I discovered a transparent, shining bladder. If you test this with your tongue, you find that it has a slight taste of honey. In the body there is only an insignificant spiral-shaped intestine and nerve fibres which are connected with the sting. All this is surrounded with a sticky fluid.[55]

Albertus is a precursor of more modern thinking when he tries to make a clearer distinction between theology and philosophy. He gives an affirmative answer to the question of whether one can describe theology as a branch of scholarship which is different from other disciplines. One reason is that its subject is 'that which is to be enjoyed' or in other words God according to Augustine's teachings (see p. 87) and not as in the other branches of scholarship that which is to be made use of in order to achieve this goal. In addition the supreme principles from which everything else is derived are revealed articles of faith and not axioms which are obvious to all and sundry.

In his philosophy Albertus follows no one thinker or school of antiquity uncritically. As a general rule he considers that a synthesis of the ideas of Plato and Aristotle is to be preferred (a union he himself was unable to produce as Plato was on the whole unknown at that period).

Albertus adopts the Aristotelian definition of the soul as 'the physical, organic and potentially alive body's primary actuality' (see p. 112) but gives this a Platonic reinterpretation. The soul is not merely the form for the matter or body but is in itself a substance which admittedly cannot subsist without the body but which is nevertheless not a part of it.

Its relationship to the body is that of a navigator to his ship. The navigator can be identified with his ship; he uses it as a tool to achieve his purpose and without the ship he is unable to carry out his task. Albertus has taken the simile from Avicenna. He took another illustration from politics when, in order to illustrate the unity of the soul despite its different functions, he compares it to the central power that governs the whole of society but does so through different subordinate authorities. Nevertheless it constitutes a united whole as it is directed towards one supreme function, that of the king.

Albertus' contribution was to make an overwhelming flood of ideas and interpretations available. He did not have the time to weld this colossal mass of information into a Christian synthesis. This task was taken on by a pupil who was to become greater than his master, Thomas Aquinas.

The complete Aristotle direct from the Greek

Ethica

Politica

Grosseteste's translation of the *Ethics* made the content of Aristotle's moral philosophy available. There was another major work by Aristotle that had been waiting for a translator and that was the *Politics*. A Dominican called William of Moerbeke who came from Flanders and was later to be the archbishop of Corinth in Greece was encouraged by his friend Thomas Aquinas to undertake a revision of the most important of Aristotle's texts using the Greek originals, which, as a result of the fourth crusade, had become accessible to western Europe. William was one of the few people in the centuries preceding the Renaissance who had more than second-hand knowledge of Greek. Since the days of Boethius hardly anyone had been able to draw his own conclusions about the original texts of the major works in philosophy or the New Testament. Of the important *Politics* only a translation of the first two books was available for Albertus Magnus. William of Moerbeke is probably the first person to have translated books III–VIII to Latin. Thomas Aquinas had therefore reasonably reliable texts of Aristotle's works to hand when he began to write his commentaries. Before looking at this work, however, it is necessary to survey the contents of the *Ethics* and the *Politics*.

Aristotle's *Ethics* (*Ethica*)

All human actions have some definite purpose. This purpose is either an end in itself or the means to another end. In other words there has to be an ultimate purpose for all human activity and behaviour and this aim is called the good. The good is what everybody is striving for but, however, there is no unanimity about what it consists of, whether it is pleasure, wealth, reputation or something similar. This good, which is the aim of all human actions, can be divided up into the *useful* (*bonum utile*) or the *delightful* (*bonum delectabile*). The useful is desired only as a means to an end and can never be an end in itself, on the other hand the delightful, because it appeals to our senses, can be an end in itself. There are also actions, however, which produce feelings of gratification which have nothing to do with sensual satisfaction and these are actions which are in harmony with the highest and best of human functions, the organizing intellect. Exercising this supreme form of goodness (*bonum honestum*) produces a state that Aristotle calls felicity or bliss (*felicitas*). Bliss for human beings is the active use of all the mental faculties in accordance with virtue. Virtue (*virtus*) takes two forms: intellectual virtue (for example wisdom or practical intelligence, 'that which enables us to do the right thing for the right purpose') and moral virtue (for example generosity or sobriety).

Intellectual virtue is acquired by education, moral virtue by usage, by the constant repetition of moral actions. Virtue is therefore an acquired habit (a *habitus*, something that one has). The same is true of its opposite, vice (*vitium*). Virtue and vice are both therefore species in the genus of 'habit' and the distinguishing characteristics (see p. 60) of moral virtue must therefore be defined more precisely. Moral virtue is the habit a person has of choosing the correct middle way between the two extremes of too much and too little, 'the golden mean'. Courage is the correct balance between fear and foolhardiness and a large number of other virtues are the correct balance between extremes. Evil, the extreme, is the easy choice but the correct middle way is difficult to follow.

bonum

bonum utile
bonum delectabile

felicitas

virtus:
intellectualis

moralis

habitus
vitium

All extremes are vices, but not all vices are extremes – delight in the misfortunes of others, adultery, theft and murder are evil thoughts or actions in themselves and not only failures or excesses in some respect.

All adult persons who have full use of their senses are ascribed responsibility. The extent of this responsibility is however related to degrees of freedom and actions can be more or less free. Actions that take place as the result of external obligation or ignorance are involuntary. Human beings alone are completely responsible for all their actions and cannot blame circumstances and excuse actions, for instance, by saying that they were compelled by lust or fear. Each human being is also responsible for his or her own moral character as this is the habit of being disposed to good or evil and it is acquired by practice. If nobody acts voluntarily when he acts badly, neither can anybody be said to do good from choice and if this were true, nobody would deserve either praise or blame, which would be absurd. Every voluntary action is the result of deliberation and one thing has been preferred to another.

iustitia:

Preeminent among the virtues is justice. This is the essence of all virtues which affect our relationships with other people. It can, in its turn, take two forms – distributive and commutative. Distributive justice involves seeing that every individual gets his due in matters like reputation, wealth and so on. Commutative justice governs barter and trade and enjoins fair compensation for goods, services and damage that may arise. Justice is the principle by which as a result of considered choice a man acts justly in sharing things among other people or with other people. What is just in society or in international relationships (*iustum politicum*) has two aspects. One is that of natural law, the rules and code enjoined by nature itself, and the other is positive law, the additional legislation that is required if all the particulars of society are to function without unbearable strife.

distributiva
commutativa

iustum politicum
ius naturae
ius postivum

There are five intellectual virtues and they function as a standard of what is true and false:

scientia

(1) Strict knowledge, *scientia*. Its subjects are what is essential, non-contingent and eternal. It is acquired through observation of individual facts (induction) which makes it

180

possible to establish the supreme principles. From these axioms indisputable syllogistic reasoning is used to deduce incontrovertible knowledge about cause and effect. Scholarship is therefore among other things a virtue that is acquired by repeatedly establishing proofs and the knowledge thus produced is not innate in any human being but has to be taught and learned. It leads finally to certainty.

(2) Art, *ars*. The acquired characteristic of being able to produce something with one's own hands in the most suitable way, to create something contingent. All artifacts and all works of art are contingent as they could differ in many ways from what they finally became. ars

(3) Prudence, *prudentia*. The acquired characteristic of choosing the correct course of action. Acting correctly is an end in itself (whereas art has as its object a product of action). prudentia

(4) Intellect, *intellectus*. The intuitive process that enables us after the observation of a number of individual facts (i.e. by induction) to deduce the universally valid truths. intellectus

(5) Wisdom, *sapientia*. A combination of scholarship and intelligence that results in lasting insights into the most important causal relationships. sapientia

The most noble activity of mankind, the absolute fulfilment of man's principal function, his reason, is the active application of the virtue of intellect. This sublime condition is intellectual *felicitas*, speculation about the truth for its own sake, the only aspect of man which is divine, indeed the only activity we can envisage of the gods (in the Arabic and Christian interpretations this was expressed as if it referred to the angels). It is not pleasure but intellectual speculation which is most in harmony with human nature, which is the unalloyed satisfaction and which more than anything else makes a human being human. felicitas
intellectualis

Mention should also be made here of the four 'cardinal virtues' which were to become a constant motif in the literature of the Middle Ages even without influence from Aristotle's *Ethics*. They were prudence (*prudentia*) justice (*iustitia*), fortitude (*fortitudo*) and temperance (*temperantia*). They originated in the works of Plato and were regarded as collective terms that covered every single aim or attitude which was correct in the life-long battle against the tyranny virtutes cardinales

prudentia
iustitia
fortitudo
temperantia of human urges and impulses. The 'virtuous' were those who had achieved such a state that they could with joy and tenacity do good in spite of internal or external opposition.

The most important influence of Aristotelian ethics almost certainly lay in its insistence that the human character was the result of systematic moral training. Personal misfortune and suffering were, in this light, not seen as catastrophes but quite simply as necessary requirements if a human being was to become truly human – persevering, unselfish, sympathetic, and humble – and as valuable opportunities to practise the habit of moral virtue.

Aristotle's *Politics* (*Politica*)

The state is a commonwealth that has been established to
attain the common good. Man is by nature a political, or in   bonum commune
other words social, being and therefore the establishment of   animal politicum
states is in accordance with natural law. Nature does nothing
in vain and the 'purpose' of the state is to remedy the obvious
fact that no individual human being can alone provide for all
his or her needs. Natural law also lays down a division
between those who rule and those who are ruled, between
master and slave, between man and woman as between body
and soul. The use of money arose as a more convenient
method than barter, which is a natural and honourable
occupation, but to earn money by the use of money
(loaning on interest) is contrary to nature.

In the *Politics* Aristotle examines a number of existing and
utopian constitutions. The communistic property-sharing
society proposed by Plato in *The Republic* (a work which
Averroes had written a commentary on as Aristotle's *Politics*
was not available) and which suggested that free men should
share everything, even their wives and children, was rejected
as such a system would make the practice of two of the
virtues – sexual temperance and personal generosity –
impossible. It is naive, according to Aristotle, to believe that
sharing all property would lead to universal friendship, it
would, on the contrary, lead to continual friction. The reason
why people squabble about possessions is not lack of
communism but common envy. The nature of the state is to
be a commonwealth of mutually disparate groups with their
own interests, tasks and responsibilities. No individual or
single group must be permitted to become too influential.
Citizenship should involve as a minimum participation in
the work of the law-courts and in a consultative assembly.
There are three forms of government which are natural:
monarchy, aristocracy (where those who best merit it
exercise power) and polity or constitutional rule (*politia*).   politia
There is a debased form of each of these – tyranny, oligarchy
(government by a few) and democracy in the meaning 'direct

government by the lower classes', The following words were in the late Middle Ages to be given great importance:

It can be shown satisfactorily that power should be held by many rather than by a few.

According to this, assemblies of people should be 'sovereign' in achieving the purpose of the state, the greatest common good, in other words a guaranteed minimum of the necessities of life for everyone.

Aristotle makes a distinction between a good human being and a good citizen and the two qualities are not necessarily found in one and the same person even if the aim of the ideal state is that this should be so. It is possible to fulfil one's obligations as a citizen without being impelled to do so by any moral convictions. The state, however, must have some moral aim as a guiding principle and turn its citizens into good people by encouraging certain actions and punishing others.

Material wealth should be discouraged as over-abundance is damaging for those who have it. Nobody, however, can become too rich spiritually. The best form of life is either active (social activity conforming with the virtues) or contemplative (philosophical speculation on the lines laid down in the *Ethics*), but speculation is the more praiseworthy occupation for those who can devote themselves to it. This demands, however, leisure and economic independence. Whatever the circumstances it should, however, be the goal of active work as well. We work to provide ourselves with leisure and so that we can enjoy the free time (*scholé* in Greek) which has, in fact, given its name to formal education, the school (*schola* in Latin).

[margin: vita activa]
[margin: vita contemplativa]
[margin: schola]

Thomas and the scholastic synthesis

Thomas Aquinas, *doctor communis* or *angelicus* was born in Roccasecca near Naples in 1224 or 1225 and studied *artes* at the University of Naples between 1239 and 1243. He became a member of the Dominican order in 1244 and was sent to Paris where he studied under Albertus Magnus. His first subject of study was biblical exegesis and the *Sentences* of Lombard. In 1257, the same year as Bonaventura, he was given a teaching post in theology and he began to write extensively. Commentaries on the *Sentences* were valued much more highly at this time than the exposition of texts as they gave the lecturer in theology full scope for the authoritative presentation of his entire conception of theology and of philosophy. Thomas also taught in Orvieto, Rome and at the Papal court at Viterbo. It was there and in Paris that he completed his two great Summae, *Summa contra gentiles* ('Summa against the heathens', in other words an authoritative guide for missionaries to Muslim areas) and *Summa theologica*, an enormous digest in the form of *quaestiones* of theology in its entirety. The organization of both works was similar to that of the *Sentences*, and the number of problems discussed allowed the author to give full rein to his enormous knowledge and his powers of speculation. He had not fully completed his life's work when he died in 1274, again the same year as Bonaventura, while travelling to the council of Lyons. By then he had, with the help of William of Moerbeke's translations and revisions, also written commentaries on all of Aristotle's major works.

Thomas followed in Albertus' footsteps in so far as he assimilated elements of Augustinian philosophy including the neo-Platonic mysticism represented by the Pseudo-Dionysius the Areopagite (see p. 26f.) as well as the most important innovations in Arabic and Jewish philosophy. It has been said of Thomas that he never forgot anything that he had read and, even if this is an exaggeration, one never fails to be amazed by his majestic awareness of all the texts of different kinds which are relevant to the problems he discusses.

doctor communis

Summa contra gentiles

Summa theologica

Thomas exploits the *quaestio*-genre to its full but does not allow it to lose its flexibility and become a sterile formula. 'In accepting or rejecting an opinion one must not be governed by love for or hatred of the person who defends it but only by the truth.' In a *quaestio* there is a recurrent cycle. The disjunctive question 'Whether . . .' (*Utrum . . .*), precedes reasons based on authority or common sense against (*videtur quod non*) and for (*sed contra*), the author or lecturer gives his own answer and the reasons he adduces in support of this answer, his *determinatio* (*Respondeo : dicendum quod . . .*) and finally corrects the counter-arguments introduced initially (*ad primum*, etc.). The *Summa theologica* contains 38 main sections (tractates) on 631 *quaestiones*, and these are divided up into 3,000 articles that discuss a total of roughly 10,000 opinions advanced.

Theology was the subject most based on authority as it dealt with things that could not be verified or falsified by empirical investigations. What was imposed by the articles of faith or had been defined by the councils of the Church was therefore, or so it would appear, above all discussion. What object could the methodical questioning of truth possibly have in a discipline like this?

One form of disputation is magisterial disputation, which is conducted in front of students not in order to dispel incorrect conceptions but in order to guide the listeners to realizing themselves the truth of the thesis proposed. In such cases one should use arguments which encourage the truth to grow, to show how what is being said is true. If the master is content merely to present the solution to the question in the form of bald statements from the authorities, the listener will admittedly learn what the truth is but his scholarship and his understanding will have gained nothing and he will leave the disputation empty.[56]

This method was questioned by many different groups. For Roger Bacon theology should principally consist of exposition of the sacred texts:

but for the last fifty years theologians have been concerned mainly with *quaestiones*. This is made obvious by all the tractates and *summae* by every possible author which are so big and so heavy that you have to have a horse to carry them.[57]

Theology – the study of the meaning of life

Some form of picture of the kind of academic world in which continual controversy of this kind is the most dynamic element can be gained from the beginning of Thomas's *Summa theologica*. The first *quaestio* is entitled 'On theology, its nature and the extent of its validity' and is divided up into ten articles: (1) Is theology necessary? (2) Is it a science? (3) Is it one science? (4) Is it speculative or practical? (5) Is it of more importance than other sciences? (6) Is it 'wisdom'? (7) What is its subject? (8) Does it use argumentation? (9) Should the Bible use metaphorical language? (10) Does the Bible have different levels of meaning?

Some of these questions seem justified while others are more far-fetched. They show that theology had been challenged by Aristotle. In fact it is he who formulated the questions when he established the criteria for science and the theologians now felt that it was up to them to justify the existence of their subject.

It is interesting to examine Thomas's answer to the second article (Whether theology is a science):

The second question is dealt with thus: Ad secundum sic
It would appear that theology is not a science,   proceditur: videtur
1) Every science starts with self-evident principles. But theology starts with the articles of faith, which are not self-evident. 'For all men have not faith', as it says in the third chapter of the second epistle to the Thessalonians. Theology is not therefore a science.
2) *Furthermore:* science does not deal with [contingent] details.   praeterea
Theology however does deal with details such as the behaviour of Abraham, Isaac and Jacob and the like. Therefore theology is not a science.
Against this however there are the words of Augustine (from book   Sed contra
XIV On the Trinity): 'Only those things are included in this science that inspire, nourish, safeguard and strengthen our faith'. This refers to no other science than theology. Therefore theology is a science.
I answer: one must admit that theology is a science. But *it should be*   Respondeo:
understood that there are two kinds of 'science'. One of them   dicendum
comprises sciences which start with basic propositions that are   (sciendum) est

obvious in the light of natural reason, for example arithmetic, geometry and so on. The other comprises those that are based on principles that are revealed by a higher science, as for instance optics is based on principles known from geometry and music on principles from arithmetic. In this second meaning theology is a science as it is based on principles revealed in the light of a higher knowledge, in other words the knowledge (*scientia*) possessed by God and the blessed. Theology therefore relies on the basic propositions (*principia*) which have been revealed by God just as the science of music relies on the basic propositions which have been taken from mathematics.

Ad primum *On the first point* it should be said: the basic propositions of every science are either self-evident or derived from the information yielded by some higher science. As has been shown, this latter is true for theology.

Ad secundum *On the second point :* details are used in theology not as chief objects but either as illustrative examples from real life (as also happens in ethics) or to endorse the authority of those who have helped to convey the divine revelation which is the basis of the Bible, and therefore of theology.[58]

As is often the case, the paradox is resolved by making a distinction (*sciendum*): the original formulation of the question can confuse anybody who does not remember that one term in the question (*scientia*) can stand for two distinct concepts, at least.

Thomas resolves other questions with the same deliberate patience. Theology is necessary in addition to philosophy because all human actions must be carried out with the intention of attaining some supreme final goal. Philosophy does not provide us with such a goal and revelation is therefore needed to give human existence its supreme purpose. As theology therefore shows us both the nature of God and how human actions should be arranged for us to attain our final goal as surely and as expediently as possible, it is at the same time both a theoretical and a practical science.

sapientia God is the supreme cause of everything and therefore theology is eminently 'wisdom' as it is described in the *Metaphysics*. God is also its fundamental subject because everything it deals with is examined only to the extent that it conforms with the final purpose, which is God.

188

The language of mystery

Scientific demands for stringency seem to conflict with the symbolic language of the Bible, and the more important a truth is, the clearer its wording ought to be. The confusion of symbols and similes seem merely to cause more confusion in an area in which only a little can be said unambiguously. Thomas rejected this view and pointed out that the highest and most important truths are spiritual ones but they cannot be communicated without the use of physical conceptions. The whole of our knowledge starts in the senses. This is one of the characteristics of human beings, therefore God had adapted His revelation to satisfy it, and moreover human beings find more pleasure in similes and parables than in bald statements of the truth. For the same reason the words of the Bible support several dimensions of meaning and are not merely the sterile and bare chronicle of historical events in some period in the past. Words are symbols of things (the literal meaning) and yet God uses allegorical, tropological and anagogic meanings (see p. 28) to extend these perspectives into uncountable new realms and in the same way the things which are referred to become signs for new things, ultimate reality. Only in this way can the truth in all its profundity be expressed in human terms.

The language of men is incapable of describing God and His characteristics adequately. The only truly meaningful statements about God are about what He is *not*. He is not subject to any limitations in time or in space, cannot increase and cannot perish or be influenced in any other way. This is called negative theology.

theologia negativa

In Thomas's eyes, however, it was not completely pointless to try to describe God in positive terms. The most apt name of all for God is 'He who is', which was revealed to Moses in the burning bush (Exodus 3:13–14). Admittedly God *is* in an incomparably greater way than anything else. He is the one, and the only one, whose essence is to exist (see p. 122). Human statements about God can contain truth by analogy.

'Qui est'

analogice

Some things can be said by analogy about God and the creation. The fact is that we cannot refer to God except with names taken from things which have been created. . . . Whatever is said about God and creation must accord with the order in which all things created are by degrees related to God, their origin and very cause.[59]

Analogy is the middle way between literalness and a confusion of possible meanings. Requirements must be made of the language used even in this field. Language is not

Fig. 32. A motif from 'the poor man's Bible', *biblia pauperum*. It was here that the outlook of the scholars and ordinary people was to meet on common ground. The poor man's Bible intended to illustrate how the New Testament was concealed in the Old Testament and how it could explain the Old Testament. The oldest manuscripts for this series of pictures date from the thirteenth century and the chief importance of the work was as a source of inspiration for church painters. It consists of scenes from the life of Christ, his death and his glorification. Each scene is always placed between two scenes from the Old Testament and quotations from the Prophets interpreted to refer to Christ. In the centre of the illustration here we see Christ ordaining the Eucharist surrounded by his disciples. On the left is Melchisedech, King of Salem, priest of the all-Highest, who on one occasion went out to meet the patriarch Abraham with bread and wine (Genesis 14:18–20). On the right the miracle of the manna during the wanderings of the children of Israel in the desert is depicted (Exodus 16). Both these events are seen as foreshadowing Christ's Eucharist. In the New Testament itself (Epistle to the Hebrews 7 and the Gospel according to St John 6) they were interpreted as 'types' of Christ's eternal High Priesthood and the eucharistic sacrifice. In the top left-hand corner is King Solomon who ascribed these words to Christ (Wisdom personified) 'Come, eat of my bread' (Proverbs 9:5). To the right is his father, King David who wrote in Psalm 77: 'Man did eat angels' food'' (v. 25). Bottom left is the prophet Isaiah saying: 'Hearken diligently unto me, and eat ye that which is good'' (Isaiah 55:2). Bottom right King Solomon is again depicted. Proverbially wise, he was the accepted author of the book of Wisdom (which in the Middle Ages was regarded as one of the canonical works of the Old Testament) and the pennant he holds bears the words 'You gave them bread from heaven' (Wisdom 16:20). Beneath the scenes from the Old Testament is the distich:

Sacra notant Christi quae Melchisedech dedit isti.
Se tenet in manibus, se cibat ipse cibus.

('What Melchisedech gave him foreshadowed Christ's holy bounties. In his hands he holds himself, of himself he gives to eat.') All of these biblical motifs were interwoven poetically and with great artistic effect by Thomas Aquinas in his Office for Corpus Christi. One stanza, *Panis angelicus*, was given a well-known musical setting by César Franck. *Biblia pauperum*, a block book edition, a copy in the Bibliothèque Nationale, Paris.

adequate but it is not completely useless either, otherwise
→agnosticism would be the only possible standpoint. Only
God *is* certainly to the highest and most complete degree,
but everything else *is* by virtue of its participation in the
existence of God. The existence of God and the existence of
creation are not therefore completely different things but
neither are they identical. They are analogous ('the analogy

analogia entis   of being', *analogia entis*).

Authority and common sense

The eighth question is dealt with like this:
It would appear that theology does not use argumentation.
1. For the fact is that Ambrose says in his first book *On the Catholic Faith*: 'If you are looking for faith, forget arguments'. Faith is, however, the primary object of the enquiries of theologians. For this reason the 20th chapter of St John's Gospel says: 'But these signs are written that ye might believe'. Therefore theology does not make use of argumentation.
2. If you use arguments, they are either based on faith (*fides*) or on reason (*ratio*). If theology uses arguments based on authority this would seem to conflict with its importance as the supreme science as, according to Boethius, arguments based on authority are the weakest of all. If theology, on the other hand, is grounded in reason this contradicts its aim. In one of his sermons Gregory says: 'The faith that is confirmed by human reason has no merit.' Therefore theology does not make use of argumentation.

fides – ratio

Against this however are the words used in the Epistle to Titus about the bishop: 'Holding fast to the faithful word as he has been taught, that he may be able by sound doctrine both to exhort and to convince the gainsayers.'
I answer: one must say that just as other sciences do not use arguments in support of their own basic propositions (*principia*) but use these [in this context unproven] propositions as a starting point to demonstrate other truths within the science, neither does theology use argumentation to prove its own basic principles, which is to say the articles of faith, but uses them as a starting point to prove something else. For instance in the First Epistle to the Corinthians the Apostle begins with the resurrection of Christ and goes on to prove general resurrection.
One must however consider (*considerandum est*) that within the disciplines of philosophy the lower sciences neither prove their own basic principles or counter arguments against them. This is left to the higher sciences. The highest of them all, metaphysics, will counter arguments against its principles for as long as the protagonist accepts any of its points. If, however, he will accept nothing at all, nobody can carry on a debate with him but can merely dismiss the objections that have been made. There is no higher authority than the Holy Scriptures and therefore we can argue with someone who disputes its supreme principles as long as our antagonist acknowledges something at least of the revelation

of God. In this way we can debate with heretics and use reasons taken from one of the articles of faith to counter the rejection of another. If our antagonist, however, does not believe in any aspect of the divine revelation, there is no way in which we can prove the articles of faith by using reason and all that is left to us is to demonstrate the falsity of the arguments that have been used against the faith. As our faith is founded on infallible truth it is impossible to use any truth to prove anything that contradicts our faith. For this reason 'evidence' adduced against the faith must be invalid evidence, arguments which can be dismissed.

On the first point it should be said that although arguments based on human reason cannot prove aspects of faith, theology nevertheless starts from the articles of faith to go on to prove other things, as has already been said.

On the second point it should be said that it is appropriate in theology that there should be arguments based on authority because the principles on which theology is based have been granted us through revelation. This in no way diminishes their importance. Even if arguments based on the authority of human reason are the weakest arguments, on the other hand arguments based on the authority of the divine revelation are the most effective.

Theology nevertheless makes use of human reason, not to prove faith for in doing so it would deprive faith of its value, but to prove gratia non tollit, other corollaries in the science. As grace does not take away nature sed perficit, but perfects it, natural reason should be placed at the service of naturam faith just as the natural desires of the will are used in the service of love. It is in this significance that in the Second Epistle to the Corinthians the Apostle says: 'And bringing into captivity every thought (*omnem intellectum*) to the obedience of Christ.' It is for this reason that theology makes use of the pronouncements auctoritates (*auctoritates*) of philosophers whenever philosophers have with the help of human reason achieved insight into the truth just as Paul quotes the words of Aratos: 'Just as some of your own poets have said: "We are also His offspring".'

Theology uses such pronouncements, however, because they are convincing arguments derived from extrinsic sources. Its authentic and compelling arguments come from the canonical Scriptures. Our faith rests on the revelation conveyed to us by the writers of the canon of the Scriptures, the apostles and the prophets, but not, on the other hand, on anything that may have been revealed to any other teacher. Thus Augustine in his letter to Jerome writes: 'I have learnt to revere only what are called the

194

canonical books in the Scripture so highly that I am completely convinced that not one of their authors erred in any way in producing them. I read everything else without believing that the contents must be true only because some writer or another so thought or described something, however saintly or learned he may appear to be.'[60]

Grace perfects nature

The article that has been quoted, which is the eighth in *quaestio 1* in the *Summa*, shows the steadfast confidence with which Thomas believed that he could combine the new philosophy with the true Christian faith and its traditional forms of expression. Faith is infallible, Aristotle is obviously true and reasonable and therefore the two must agree with each other. All of Thomas's works are devoted to demonstrating this miraculous agreement between *fides* and *ratio*, the way in which grace is the consummation of nature, and his serene, thorough and magisterial tone uses the style and forms of expression familar from the discussion of philosophy. *Semper formaliter loquitur* are the words used by his principal commentator, Cardinal Cajetan, 'he always speaks formally'. This was not because he had no other choice, or because of inability to use language. As a poet Thomas shows remarkable adroitness in his use of rhythm and assonance and alliteration, demonstrating there his mastery of language. In the lecture room, however, it would have been out of place to woo the listener's ear with eloquence. Science seeks to express itself precisely, even at the cost of repetitions and over-explicitness.

'nihil est in intellectu quin prius fuerit in sensu'

Like Aristotle, Thomas was convinced that knowledge starts with the senses and that there is nothing in the intellect that did not begin as a sense impression. No higher knowledge about non-material things can be achieved without laborious deliberation starting with data yielded by the senses. We experience reality in three stages. We first perceive the undivided unities in their essences (which can be expressed in the form of definitions). The next stage is to combine or separate these unities, for instance by using simple affirmative or negative statements (X is Y, X is not Y). The last stage is deliberation in the form of syllogisms.

As a philosopher, Thomas is primarily interested in understanding Aristotle and making him understandable. Where Bonaventura follows Augustine in saying that God illuminates human reason directly in the act of knowledge (see p. 168), Thomas prefers the Aristotelian idea of active reason (even if at times this is identified as a form of divine illumination). According to Thomas, we have been given the task of trying to understand, with the help of reason, everything in the realm of 'nature' (its opposite is the realm *natura – gratia* of 'grace', in which supernatural revelation must be granted us). In this the Aristotelian pattern is of great service to the student of philosophy and makes it possible to describe the structure of reality, its inner dynamism and its purpose in simple statements. The foremost task is to describe the structure of the world as an autonomous reality. Only then is it necessary to introduce the widest perspective and include the supernatural information about relationships not accessible for philosophical enquiry yielded by theology.

The disciplines within philosophy are divided up according to whether their subject is practical, the study of how human beings should arrange their active life (practical or moral philosophy with its three specialities, ethics, economics and politics), or theoretical contemplation of the nature of things in themselves without reference to practical application (theoretical philosophy and its three branches, physics, mathematics and metaphysics). All science deals with principles of eternal, unchanging and necessary validity and it demonstrates why something must be as it is, and cannot possibly be in any other way. The theoretical sciences are classified according to their level of abstraction and the more abstract they are, the higher they are. Physics deals with the 'motion' of bodies (see p. 108) purely from the point of view of 'mobility' and pays no reference to the concrete nature of different kinds of body. Physics is therefore more abstract than the study of matter. The next level is mathematics, which disregards everything but numbers, quantities, lines and so on. The third and final level is the science that in its real meaning can be called theoretical, metaphysics or 'the prime philosophy', which disregards everything except *philosophia prima* being as being and the causes in their causality (see p. 117). All of these sciences are based on logic, which in effect is merely the tool of all valid thought.

Dazzled by the obvious

The path to the highest and supreme philosophy leads from logic, which is merely the learning of a method, through mathematics, which even a child can learn, and then on to natural philosophy, which demands experience, and ethics, which presupposes maturity, until it reaches its final goal when the accomplished philosopher perceives the first causes. In actual fact these prime causes are the most obvious of all, but they have the same effect on our intellect as daylight has on a bat and we are blinded by their obviousness. The greatest bliss (Thomas adds an important proviso to Aristotle's assertion with the words 'in this life') is contemplation of the first causes.

causa materialis, formalis, efficiens, finalis

in potentia

in actu

materia prima

forma substantialis

All that does exist or can exist is determined by four 'causes' – matter, form, efficient cause and underlying purpose. What *can* exist is said to exist potentially, what does exist does so in *in actu*, as an actualized potentiality. Matter is in itself indeterminate (*materia prima*). The primordial form that turns something into a substance (the 'substantial form') gives the shapeless matter its first impression, endows what can exist potentially with existence and also imbues it with certain innate tendencies (its nature). For instance the prime matter can coalesce through the influence of a substantial form and become a human being. Other effects

forma accidentalis

will produce accidental (i.e. which does not belong to the nature of the substance) determination so that the same material will also become a fair-skinned, linguistically gifted . . . human being.

Matter which has been given some form in this way is continually subject to alteration (increase and abatement) in potentiality and actuality in different directions. These changes are brought about by the effects of two principals working externally – agent and purpose, in other words the efficient cause and the final cause. All 'natural' agents (all causes that have any influence except human beings with free will) are predetermined to act in order to achieve some natural goal. In other words nature is not blind but 'acts' with some definite purpose. The ultimate agent is the prime mover. Because of their free will, however, human beings are agents that can establish their own goals.

These are the broad outlines of the picture of reality that Thomas derived from Aristotle. It was not difficult for him to fill this framework with Christian contents. However, at times some slight alterations were necessary.

Aristotle rejected the idea of creation from nothing, and for him the supreme being was an impersonal prime mover. He had no conception of the idea of individual immortality and there are several other points where it would be difficult to reconcile thorough-going Aristotelianism with orthodox Christianity.

Thomas explains the concept of the creation within the Aristotelian system in the following way. Among everything that exists there is only one being which does not owe its existence to anything else: this being is God. His essence (*essentia*) is the only essence in which existence (*esse*) is a essentia
necessary component, to quote Avicenna. Everything else esse
apart from God can either exist or not exist, it possesses Deus:
existence because of God and everything else that it possesses is an imperfect participation in perfection, God. Everything has been generated according to a model in God's thinking. For this reason God is the prototype of everything, its exemplary cause. In addition as the creator causa exemplaris
He is the efficient cause of everything and also the final causa efficiens
purpose and aim of everything, its final cause. The fact is that causa finalis
everything has been created so that it can participate in His perfection. God has granted existence to everything that has been created and has afterwards become the maintenance of that existence. In this meaning as well He is the cause of everything.

This does not imply that God is to be regarded as the normal direct cause of everything that happens. He does not intervene directly in events which can just as well be caused by secondary causes. If He were to do so, the system of cause and effect in nature would be a fiction and there would be no point in things being endowed with their own nature. God functions as the cause of everything only insofar as He is the final goal of everything, the sustenance and force of everything. In all other respects, however, the normal laws of

199

causality function and the actions of human beings are not determined by influences from outside but are the result of deliberate free choice. Fundamentally everything is involved in the designs of divine providence and God foresees everything, even the slightest effect of any of the secondary causes. This is because He is not subject to time but is able to survey simultaneously the past and the future (seen from the finite perspective of creation). For God everything is eternally now. The fact that God foresees everything does not impose any outcome on a course of events any more than human knowledge of events in the past influences these events.

The universe is a whole, composed of beings and things and they have different degrees of perfection (see p. 26). If the universe is to be entire, it is also necessary that some events take place of necessity and others as the result of coincidence. The effect of coincidence is sometimes disorder and lack of goodness (in other words evil, cf. p. 27). As things are, everything is supported by the providence of God, which sees to it that in the end everything turns out for the best. The alternative to this contingency in the creation and the possibility it gives for the existence of evil would, however, be that everything happened because of absolute necessity. An arrangement like that would make the completeness of the universe an impossibility and preclude the governing of the world through the providence of God and the free will of human beings. Together these disadvantages would outweigh any evil present in the imperfection of the prevailing organization of creation.

It was pointed out earlier that according to Thomas everything created is non-necessary, contingent and dependent on something other than itself, namely God, the only necessary being. God has, from pure goodness, brought creation into existence in order to be able to share His goodness, not for any imperative reason but because that was His will. Everything created is a combination of potentiality and actuality, and the nearer it has come to its actuality, the more perfect it is, the greater is its participation in God, who *actus purus* is the 'pure act', the completely fulfilled being that has no potentiality left to be actualized.

The creation, the existence of God and the problem of evil

When it came to the sensitive question of whether the world was eternal, Thomas sought to provide as elastic an interpretation of Aristotle as possible. He claimed that the problem was philosophically neutral. It cannot be proved that the world is eternal, but neither can it be disproved.

The reasons that Aristotle cites are not proof in its general meaning but only in the limited context of his intention of refuting the arguments of earlier philosophers when they claimed that the world had begun to exist in some specific way which was in reality impossible. This becomes evident in three ways. To begin with, both in the eighth book of the Physics and in the first book of 'On Heaven' he cites opinions from Anaxagoras, Empedocles and Plato and then presents counter-arguments. Secondly, when dealing with this subject he always quotes the arguments of earlier philosophers, so that this is not the presentation of evidence but argument based on plausibility. Thirdly, in the first book of the Topics, he says explicitly that there are certain dialectical problems to which there are no incontrovertible solutions, such as, for example, 'Whether the world is eternal'.[61]

Thomas avoids direct confrontation with the philosopher by presenting his standpoint as nothing more than hypothesis. However he does not go as far as Albertus, who admitted that on this point Aristotle had given evidence of his own human imperfection.

Like Anselm, Thomas was interested in the possibility of producing evidence which, purely on the basis of rational argument and without any reference to the opinions of authorities, would prove the existence of God. He dismissed, however, Anselm's ontological proof of the existence of God as one form of illegitimate transition from one genus to another (see p. 79), from the world of conceptualization to the physical world. For Thomas it was impossible to make pronouncements on the existence of God purely on the basis of an analysis of the concept of God ('the highest conceivable: therefore the highest existing'). Human beings have not been endowed with direct intuitive insight in the supreme things. Instead they have to use more indirect reasoning on the basis of Aristotle's theories about causes. According to Thomas there are five methods (the 'five ways', *quinque viae*) of approaching the question of the existence of God, and they yield conclusions which can be taken as different degrees of evidence (compare the final phrase in each paragraph below):

quinque viae

1. Everything that is in motion which changes from potentiality to actuality must be set in motion by something else. This chain of causes cannot be extended infinitely. There must, therefore, be a first unmoved mover, 'which expression is understood by everyone to mean God'.
2. In the physical world everything takes place as a result of a series of effective causes. Nothing can be its own cause. This series cannot be extended infinitely. Therefore there must be a first effective cause, 'which everyone calls God'.
3. All things can either exist or not exist, they are produced and decay. They are, in other words, contingent and not necessary. Therefore everything that exists has at some time not existed, but has been given existence by something else at some moment in time. This process cannot continue to take place in a never-ending cycle. Therefore there must be something which is in itself necessary, the utmost cause of all necessary causes 'and everyone calls this God'.
4. In everything there are degrees of perfection, just as there are degrees of temperature. Therefore within every genus there is something which is perfect in the highest degree and the cause of everything else in that genus in the same way that fire is the warmest and the cause of everything warm. Therefore there is something which is the cause of everything's existence, perfection and so on in every genus, 'and we call this God'.
5. Nature and natural phenomena lack knowledge but always, or at least most often, they act purposefully and reach a definite goal not by chance but because of some intention, exactly in the same way as an arrow is directed by an archer. Therefore an intelligence exists which directs everything towards its goal, 'and we call this God'.[62]

In order to reject the existence of God, it can be pointed out that in the concept of God is assumed the idea of infinite goodness. Therefore no evil can exist if God exists. Therefore God cannot exist. Thomas's answer to this was:

In his Handbook Augustine says: 'As God is perfectly good He would not allow any evil among his creature but for the fact that He is so almighty and good that He even created good from evil.' This is therefore part of God's infinite goodness and He allows the existence of evil in order to win goodness from it.

It must be remembered that for the tradition that Thomas represented and whose sources were, in this respect, neo-Platonism as interpreted by Pseudo-Dionysius the Areopagite, evil was not something that possessed independent existence. Evil is not a being in itself, it is a lack, a deficiency of good which should exist (*malum est privatio boni debiti*). (Blindness is something evil, but only when there should be the faculty of sight: and the fact that a stone cannot see is not evil as the stone has no eyes and therefore there is no transgression of natural order.) Neither is moral evil anything in itself but consists of deviation from behaviour dictated by nature or by reason, just as sickness is deviation from the natural condition, which is health. Evil reveals itself as a deficiency when compared with good, or normal or what ought to exist just as the hole in a piece of cheese is nothing other than a deficiency of cheese. Evil is a non-being.

malum est privatio boni debiti

'malum est nonens'

The senses, instinct, imagination, thought and the memory

Thomas also saw himself as an interpreter of Aristotelian psychology but this too needed correction on one or two points if it was to be brought in line with the Christian faith. Thomas's view was that the rational element in the soul *anima intellectiva* (*anima intellectiva*), man's noblest and most eminent faculty, survives the death of the body and is immortal. He postulated, as Albertus Magnus did, that it has in one sense independent existence (that it subsists, is itself its own basis) as the *forma* of the body. Its imperishability is hinted at by its natural drive to continual existence, as no natural drive can be abortive this one must have a real goal such as all the others have:

> One sign that this is in fact the case [that the soul is immortal] is that everything longs for the form of existence that is natural for it. In beings that have the power of knowledge this longing is the result of knowledge. The senses cannot envisage their existence in *hinc et nunc* anything but the here and now, but the intellect, on the other hand, experiences its existence absolutely and independent of time. Everything that has been endowed with intellect by its very nature longs for eternal existence. Now there does exist a true goal for every natural drive. Therefore every intellectual substance is imperishable.[63]

A thesis that came originally from Averroes that the receptive intellect is one and the same in all men (see p. 123) was dismissed by Thomas as absurd. If this were the case, all human beings would only be able to conceive of things in the same way, and think in exactly the same patterns. It would be impossible to explain why there were different opinions about one and the same thing.

In its ideas about the senses, the sources of all knowledge, Thomas's psychology is a synthesis of Aristotle and Avicenna. The five external senses are defined as passive potential prepared to be changed by external sense impressions just as warmth is absorbed by the sense of touch and shape is experienced by the eye. Following Avicenna, Thomas postulates five inner senses that correspond to these external senses; with their help human beings and animals can retain sensual stimuli and if necessary activate them again: quinque sensus interiores

A living being needs not only to receive sense impressions through the senses at that moment when the stimulus exists but also needs to retain and preserve them. But receiving and retaining are two separate functions for bodies, as wet bodies have no difficulty in receiving things but cannot retain them easily while dry bodies function in the opposite way. As the sensitive capacity is the actualization of a bodily organ there must be one faculty which receives impressions and another which retains them. It must be borne in mind that if an animal were only influenced by pleasant or unpleasant sense impressions, it would be unnecessary to believe in the existence of any other feelings in animals than pleasure and fear. However, it is vital for their existence for animals to search for certain things and to avoid others, not only because they affect the senses pleasantly or unpleasantly, but also because they are of vital importance or are dangerous. The sheep flees from the wolf as soon as it sees it approach, not because the wolf has any terrifying colour or shape but because it is a natural enemy. In the same way small birds collect straw, not because it is pleasant to their senses but because straw is used to build nests with. In other words it is of vital necessity for animals to perceive essentials even if they escape the external senses. The faculty of perception of this kind must therefore be placed in something else, as perception of palpable features depends on sensual stimuli while this form of perception does not. . . . In order to retain and preserve, the powers of *fantasy* or *imagination* have been established as a form of storage vessel for the shapes which have been received through the senses. In order to perceive relationships which are not apparent to the senses *estimation* has been created. In order to retain all this there is the *memory* like a treasure chest for these notions. . . . Notice that concerning the forms which are experienced by the senses there is no difference between animals and human beings. . . . There is, on the other hand, where the essentials mentioned are concerned, as animals experience them because of natural instinct whereas human beings do so as a result of inner deliberation. What is called natural estimation in animals is therefore called cogitative power in human beings. . . . Students of medicine place this in a special organ in the middle of the head. It makes inferences of individual

actus organi corporalis

phantasia sive imaginatio

vis aestimativa
vis memorativa

naturalis instinctus

vis cogitativa

objects of thought whereas the intellective reason makes inferences of universal concepts.[64]

sensus communis

The collective sense, *sensus communis*, functions as a coordinating faculty. It relates the impressions of one sense to another to produce an impression of the whole. Movement can be perceived by sight, touch and hearing simultaneously.

Later on scholasticism was also able to determine exactly where the inner senses were placed. Thought and conceptualization were not situated where we would expect them to be because of the knowledge we have of modern medical research. Physicians and philosophers of that period did not consider that they were part of the substance of the brain but that they were placed in the ventricles of the brain, the hollow spaces that are filled with cerebro-spinal fluid.

tabula rasa

When we are born, our intellect is like a tablet of wax that has been cleaned and is free from impressions, a *tabula rasa*.

Fig. 33. A drawing by a student named Fabian Wachter from Külsheim which he drew while studying psychology at the University of Leipzig some time around 1488. Here there is absolute certainty about the position of the 'inner senses' and their relationship to each other. They are *sensus communis*, the coordinating sense that perceives the entirety of the other sense impressions: *imaginativa*, the imaginative faculty that can summon forth pictures of an object even when it is not present itself; fantasy, *fantasia*, which can arrange these pictures even in combinations which the senses have in reality never experienced; *estimativa*, judgement, the instinct of animals and the rational capacity of human beings which draws conclusions from the sense impressions that are not obvious (about danger, usefulness, etc.); and finally *memorativa*, the memory, which is where the final products of all these operations are stored. These senses are covered by a single mnemonic SIFEM. Each is situated in its own cell (*cellula*) in the brain. The figure of five arose because the front and rear ventricle of the brain are divided into two cells, while the central one was thought to consist of one cell. The five inner senses correspond to the five external senses, sight, hearing, touch, smell and taste. Norrköping Public Library, MS 426 fol.

It is a mere potentiality (a receptive intellect, which is susceptible to any external form at all). When the senses are affected by the reality that surrounds human beings, an immaterial copy, a 'perceptible form' of the object registered is transferred to the senses. Here active intelligence takes over and filters out all of the individual and coincidental circumstances in the picture the senses have formed of the object. What is left is a 'comprehensible form', the eternally valid

intellectus possibilis

species sensibilis
intellectus agens

species intelligibilis

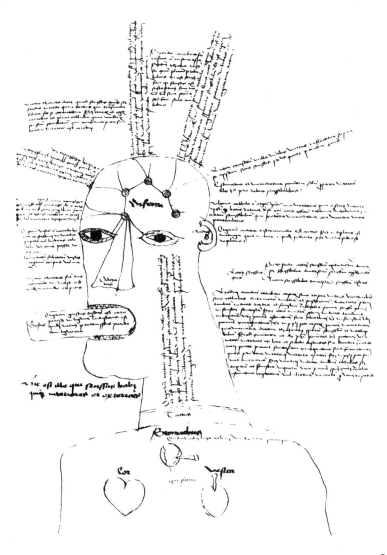

207

essence of the universal, the object in question seen as a substance stripped of its accidentals. The senses can in other words, only register details in the 'here and now'. It is the intellect that first can grasp the unchanging essence of things.

hinc et nunc

In this lies the ability that human beings have for self-realization, to conceive of everything that is conceivable. In one sense human beings *become* everything by registering and conceiving it and for that reason it is possible to say that man is in some ways everything (cf. p. 116).

homo est
quodammodo
omnia

Reason and nature as the highest norms

The *Nichomachean Ethics* was not written from a religious perspective in our sense of that concept. When Aristotle defined the utmost goal of man as happiness, the highest form of which was intellectual contemplation of the supreme principles, satisfaction as it were of the intellectual urges, this can hardly be accepted by a Christian philosopher like Thomas Aquinas as a complete description of human aims. Augustine had described mankind's ultimate purpose as 'the enjoyment of God', *frui Deo*. Thomas combines this idea with Aristotle's intellectual contemplation and describes the true and eternally valid 'happiness', bliss in the world to come, as the contemplation of God by the intellect face to face, directly, after having been obliged in this life to trust to the revealed articles of faith from which, with the help of reason, conclusions can be drawn about proper conduct.

The task for human beings is therefore to achieve this goal as expediently as possible by choosing courses of action. This involves observing the natural law which dictates the foremost norms concerning good and evil and this law is implanted in mankind as a natural inclination for the good and for actions that will lead to the good. Thomas pays reason more honour than the will. It is the intellect which guides the will and love.

The will governs all the function of our soul except the vegetative ones. The principle of free will is a necessary requirement for ethics, for without it it would be pointless to talk about good and evil. Because of reason and free will human beings are masters over their own actions and they 'hom est dominus differ in this respect from animals, which are constrained by suorum actuum' instinct. Ethics is not concerned with the unconscious actions of human beings (*actus hominis*), such as, for example, actus hominis moving one foot or scratching one's beard, while preoccupied with something else, but only with the human actions which are the result of free choice (*actus humani*), those actus humani performed for some deliberate purpose. It is this purpose that gives an action its moral content and direction (*intentio*) intentio in relation to the goal.

Like Aristotle, Thomas defines virtue as an acquired habit, (a *habitus* see p. 179), because of which the will tends to act in accordance with reason. It is, in fact, reason that provides the highest principles for human actions:

habitus

> Reason is the guiding principle for human actions and the yardstick against which they are measured, it is the highest principle for them. . . . The role of our reason is, in actuality, to organize our actions in terms of our final destiny, 'which is the highest principle for all activity' according to the Philosopher.[65]

All laws must therefore be based on reason. The law can be defined as the dictates of reason for the good of society (*bonum commune*) and promulgated by its rulers. For this reason there must be as many laws as there are societies and therefore there also exists a supreme law for the whole of the world, the eternal law, promulgated by God. This eternal law is revealed in human nature, which has an innate tendency towards what is right and serves the final purpose. This tendency of reason is a participation in the divine reason and is called natural law (*lex naturalis*).

lex est dictamen practicae rationis

lex aeterna

lex naturalis

Reason is, in other words, of divine origin and as long as he can follow his reason a human being cannot go astray. 'All human laws are, insofar as they represent the correct application of reason, to the same extent expression of the eternal law.' Not even the final Christian revelation can add an iota to this eternal rational law. The contents of the ten commandments do not, in general, exceed the dictates of natural reason. Not even Jesus has added to them:

> That which belongs to faith exceeds the capacity of reason to perceive and therefore we can only acquire knowledge of it through revelation. When therefore grace was suffused in its entirety, additional articles of faith were given to us. In the exercise of virtue, however, we are guided by natural reason, which is a sort of rule for human behaviour, as has been said earlier. Therefore no new commandments need be given apart from the ethical norms of the Old Testament, which were dictated by reason.[66]

The Garden of Eden and the distortion of natural order

This seems to be an excessively optimistic ethical theory. Here, as in the ideas of Aristotle from which it is derived, one lacks the tension between the absolute demands of God and human inability to live up to them which is characteristic of Christianity. It would not appear to be a difficult task for any human being endowed with reason to determine goal after goal and follow the path of virtue with unerring certainty. Experience tells us, however, that reason seems to be inadequate and that the will is too weak. Nevertheless Thomas asserts that the will necessarily strives for the final good, the utmost goal, in exactly the same way that the intellect immediately and necessarily agrees with the supreme axioms as soon as it has perceived their truth. Why then is our environment so imperfect; the most obvious and tangible fact human beings are called on to recognize? The answer, according to Thomas, is that the tragedy of mankind is that we are not continually able to see our final goal directly. If we could, we would never act wrongly, any more than we could avoid agreeing intellectually with a logical axiom as soon as we have realized its truth.

The fact is that there are certain good things which are not necessarily related to the eternal bliss (*beatitudo*). It would be possible to be happy without them. The will does not therefore seek them out of necessity. There are also good things which are necessarily related to the eternal bliss and it is through these that mankind stays in contact with God, which is what bliss wholly consists of. However for as long as this necessary connection has not itself been proved by the certainty that contemplation of God endues us with, the will is not necessarily forced to remain fixed on God and the things which belong to Him. He who has seen God in His very being must of necessity adhere to God, just as at this moment we must of necessity desire to be happy.[67]

How can this faith in reason be combined with the story of the Garden of Eden and mankind's fall from grace, which suggests that the fundamental sin was mankind's boundless

211

Fig. 34.   Ever since Augustine the most commonly used theological image of earthly life was that of the 'road' (*via*) to the spiritual
'home' (*patria*). While a human being is 'on the road' (*in statu
viatoris*) the final destination, eternal bliss, is invisible. The only
guide is faith. For this reason it can often happen that errors are
made about both means and ends. The creation itself can become a
distraction and preoccupation with worldly cares can make of
them a final goal in themselves and not the means to a goal. This
confusion of values is a result of the fall from grace. If it were
possible for human beings to contemplate their final goal directly
in this world, they would, according to Thomas Aquinas, be
unable to sin, to act in contradiction to the natural order of things.
At every moment they would be guided by the first truth. The final
purpose of mankind is to contemplate God as He is, face to face, to
perceive His essence. For Thomas this was primarily an intellectual activity, for John Duns Scotus and later schoolmen it was
the final gratification of love and the will. This picture shows man
on the road with the heavenly goal appearing as a mirage.
Guillaume de Digulleville. *Boeck van der pelgrim*, printed in Delft
in 1498.

curiosity, the desire to know everything? What answer will a philsopher give, who himself could best be described as boundlessly and insatiably curious?

Mankind's first and fatal sin, wanting to eat of the fruit of 'the tree of knowledge for good or ill' was in no way the thirst for knowledge. In the very first sentence of the *Metaphysics* Aristotle says that by their very nature all human beings long for knowledge. This longing was therefore a natural urge implanted in Adam and Eve in the creation itself. Natural urges are part of God's design for mankind and they cannot be wrong or futile in themselves. The fall from grace lay in the pride or arrogance with which mankind itself wanted to lay down the limits of good and evil, of right and wrong. This would have been intervention in the God-given natural order; it was the desire to exercise God's supremacy over natural law.

Self-fulfilment in this world and the next

virtutes
theologicae
virtutes infusae

The concept of *habitus* taken from Aristotelian ethics was also useful in explaining the supernaturally acquired qualities that were needed in addition to natural ones if man was to reach his heavenly goal. These were the three 'theological virtues' which Paul the Apostle identified as faith, hope and charity, the 'infused virtues':

By virtue man is fulfilled so that he carries out the actions which lead to happiness. There is however, as has already been mentioned, a double happiness or bliss. The first is commensurate with human nature and can be achieved by means of the innate natural tendencies in human beings. The second is the bliss that surpasses human nature and this can only be achieved with the help of God's strength, through sharing in divinity which is why the second Epistle of Peter says that through Christ we are 'partakers in the divine nature'. As this bliss is not commensurate with human nature, makind's innate natural tendencies, by which human actions are governed to accord with human nature, cannot predispose human beings for this bliss. It is therefore necessary for human beings to be granted knowledge of some supranatural principles which can predispose them for this supranatural bliss in the same way that the natural principles predispose them for natural goals, without divine intervention. These principles are called the theological virtues, firstly because their object is God in that it is through them that our nature is directed to its purpose in God, secondly because they have been infused in us by God alone, and finally because they have been imparted to us solely by divine revelation in the Holy Scriptures.[68]

This is not very different from the way in which scholasticism in its early stages had used other Aristotelian terms for metaphysical concepts, such as the use of substance and accidence in connection with teachings about the Eucharist (see p. 147). This is how Thomas interprets the miracle of the transubstantiation of how accidentals can exist without a substance:

The only remaining basis of explanation is that the substance in this sacrament subsists without any support. Such things can happen through the power of God. As every effect is more the result of the primary cause than of secondary causes, God, who is the primary cause of both substance and accidentals, can by virtue of his infinite power maintain the continued existence of accidentals even when the substance, which is the secondary cause of the existence of the accidentals, has been taken away from them. In the same way he can produce the result of natural causes without the causes themselves as when the body of a man was conceived in the virgin's womb without human intervention.[69]

The distinction between form and matter is extremely useful in dealing with the sacraments. The matter of the sacraments is the material elements of which they consist such as water, bread, wine, oil, the laying on of hands, and so on. Their form consists of the words which are uttered at the same time and which turn these elements into a sacrament.

This synthesis of classical philosophy and Christian beliefs was elevated to the status of standard teaching in the Church as recently as 1879 by Pope Leo XIII. In the short term, however, Thomas failed to achieve his purpose with his writing. Three years after his death, several of his propositions were stigmatized by the Bishop of Paris, Estienne Tempier. Shortly afterwards several works were written to correct his teachings, especially those contained in the *Summa*. The aged Albertus Magnus was compelled to spring to his most eminent pupil's defence. Thomas's own order remained faithful, however, and in 1278 it declared Thomas's methods and findings official doctrine in the education of its own members.

The state, democracy and 'the rational distinction'

In his influential work *The City of God*, Augustine had coined the traditional view of the state and its powers of coercion as a necessary evil, a consequence of the Fall. Thomas turned this attitude inside out by claiming that the state corresponded to mankind's nature as a social animal (*animal politicum*) needing the services of its fellow beings. The state would have existed whether the Fall had taken place or not as the final safeguard of the common good (*bonum commune*), the crowning form of all natural associations. Aristotle's assertion that 'the majority should be sovereign' was reinterpreted by Thomas in a way that was to lead to an upheaval in ways of thinking:

The best form of government is a mixture of monarchy, meaning that one person should rule everybody, aristocracy, meaning that the majority should be governed by those who are most capable, and democracy, meaning that the people should elect their rulers and that the election of rulers is one of the rights of the people.[70]

Thomas saw one form of this method of government in the wanderings of the children of Israel in the desert. Moses and his legitimate successors governed the people but routine decisions and minor controversies were settled by seventy-two men elected for their competence by the people (Exodus 18).

Another typically Aristotelian principle that Thomas helped to make part of European thought was the idea that a good citizen was not necessarily the same as a good human being. It is possible to use a rational distinction to separate the moral and political dimensions in the government of societies and the lives of individuals. A rational distinction is a distinction in thought between things that in real life cannot be distinguished. For instance one and the same person can be thought of as having innumerable different social functions and can be seen as a citizen, a Christian, a decision-maker, an economic entity, a member of a family or

distinctio
rationalis

216

a representative of a culture and these functions, at least in theory, can be isolated from each other. It is however impossible to isolate these functions in any concrete person (there is, in other words, no possibility of making 'real distinctions'). This mental operation was to have unforeseen importance. In the early Middle Ages there had been no question of distinguishing between the conscientious tax-payer and the wife-beater in the same individual's behaviour. This now became possible and it was to lead to greater tolerance of people who held different opinions and to the co-existence of different groups of people in the same country. It was also ultimately to result in the loss of the view of man as a complete whole and the end of shared common values. Every silver lining has some cloud. distinctio realis

The new stimuli that Thomas's work gave rise to were to be developed during the fourteenth century and they were to have consequences that he himself could hardly have expected. A Dominican called John of Paris developed a rational distinction between Church and state as two different genera which, although they differed in essence, usually coincided in time, space and their individual members. In the Church as well as the state office-holders exercised their authority only by virtue of the consent of the people.

Marsilius of Padua, who was rector of the University of Paris and who died in 1342, developed these ideas to their logical conclusion. In his exhaustive survey of political ideas *The defender of the peace* (*Defensor pacis*) he maintained that the state was completely secular in essence and that any reference to the life to come was, from a political point of view, completely irrelevant. Politics, the organization of government and its execution were completely within the realms of reason. It was of no importance that human beings possessed both as social beings and as individuals higher goals outside the horizons of this world. That nature should ultimately be an expression of the designs of God cannot possibly be proved and is something that theologians can concern themselves with to their hearts' content, as long as they do not interfere in politics. The state consists of citizens and it does not matter whether they are Christians or not. All power is derived from the people; the law has binding force because and only insofar as it reflects the opinions of the people. Officials of the state are the agents of the will of the people. In the Church as well, all government should be exercised by general meetings of its members and in them nobody's voice should have greater weight however elevated his office might be.

In Thomas's system the state was part of a larger context. It guaranteed the temporal well-being of its citizens and in so doing made it possible for them to aspire to eternal joy. In Marsilius' theories this second stage has disappeared as an unverifiable and unimportant appendix.

The art of memory I: grammar, conduct and the essence of the true schoolboy

Medieval schools took advantage of a human faculty that is sadly wasted today. Until our teens it is possible for us to learn, whether forced to or not, units of language of almost any length, as long as they have some distinguishing characteristic such as regular rhythm, epigrammatic brevity, rhymes or the like. From antiquity dialogues and mnemonic verse (either in hexameter or in couplets) had been used in teaching and once they had been learnt in the classroom they could be recalled to provide all sorts of useful knowledge which, even if reference books were available, could not always be found easily. This technique can be compared with the ways in which people today remember how many days there are in each month, German prepositions or the number of colours in the rainbow and the order in which they are seen. In the Middle Ages it was a technique that was used more systematically than it is today and in every conceivable context. Donatus serves as the archetype of the educational dialogue. In the thirteenth century language teaching normally consisted of exercises from the educational poem *Doctrinale* by Alexander de Villa Dei, the university's basic textbook. Its hexameters summarized the declension of nouns, the comparative of adjectives, morphological irregularities, case endings, syllable length and some elements of style. Like Donatus, 'Alexander' became a household word. Its authoritative position is commemorated in an anecdote about the Emperor Sigismund who was corrected at the Council of Constance for his custom of declining the noun *schisma* as a first declension noun with a reference to Alexander. It was the same Alexander that finally obliged King Gustavus I Vasa of Sweden to renounce any aspirations he may have had to book learning. As a young man he left school swearing profanely after he had run a dagger 'through Alexander' and he vowed never to return. For the humanists the *Doctrinale* became the very embodiment of the 'Gothic' barbarity of the period that had preceded theirs, a swine in the service of Minerva, a collection of absurdities that made pupils even more stupid than they were from the beginning. What shocked their sensitive palates mainly was the choice of vocabulary, which was not always unobjectionable, and the blemishes in the use of metre. As help in memorization, supplemented of course by an extensive commentary, the Alexander displays an admirable economy of expression. To furnish this useful form with more elegant contents, it was rewritten at the end of the fifteenth century in accordance with more classical ideals.

In order to impart a richer vocabulary to schoolboys and students there were books like Johannes de Garlandia's *Opus synonymorum*, Matthaeus Vindobonensis' *Aequivoca*, and Johannes de Genua's *Catholicon*. The last-named work provides a rich sample of verbose and in most cases quite fantastic etymologies quite worthy of Isidore.

For beginners at the schools even works like the *Doctrinale*

Fig. 35. In their teaching the schoolmen used every method possible to give life to the theoretical subjects they taught. One rule in the art of remembering was that violent illustrations should be used to drive home abstract relationships. The didactic figure shown here meets every demand that could be made of it in that respect. It has nothing to do with anatomy, the art of warfare or the treatment of wounds. The text that accompanies it, a dialogue between a teacher and his pupil, deals with theoretical geometry:

— What is a body?
— Length combined with width and depth. If you imagine a surface that continues downwards, you have a body, which is measured by three lines which intersect each other at right angles at one point on the length, width and depth. The ends of these lines are referred to with the words up, down, in front of, behind, to the left and to the right. Imagine a spear which pierces the skull and comes out through the anus. This measures length. A second spear goes in through the chest and out through the back and this measures depth. A third spear goes in through one side and out through the other and this measures width.

Gregorius Reisch, *Margarita Philosophica* (first published 1496), printed in Basle by Sebastian Henricpetri in 1583.

were too advanced. The popular dialogue *Es tu scholaris?* combined as far as possible simple lessons in behaviour and in language with simple preparatory exercises in the use of the Aristotelian system of concepts:

— Are you a scholar?
— Yes.
— What is a scholar?
— Somebody who earnestly and diligently applies himself to the virtues.

— Where are you a scholar?
— Here, everywhere and in every seemly place.

— How many seemly places are there?
— Four: the church, the school, at home with my parents and in the company of orderly men.
— How many unseemly places are there?

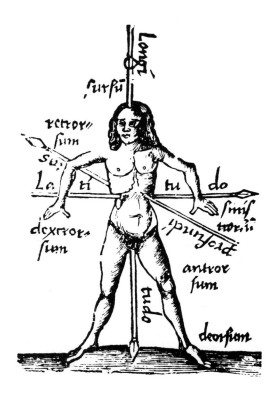

— They too are four in number: the dance-floor, the brothel, public roads and inns not frequented by orderly men. More places could be added to this list.
— Are you a scholar?
— Yes.
— What kind of Scholar are you?
— As God has created me.
— How many duties does a scholar have?
— Six.
— What are they?
— To get up early, dress immediately, comb my hair, wash my hands, pray to God and go willingly to school.

— Are you a scholar?
— Yes.
— What is the substance of a scholar?
— An animated physical substance susceptible of knowledge and virtue.

— Are you a human being?
— Yes.
— What is a human being?
— A corporal, physical, rational and mortal substance created by God to attain immortal life.

— What is God?
— The best and highest conceivable being who endows everything with its existence and life.[71]

Here pupils acquired a basic stock of necessary expressions and their importance was enhanced by the fact that in the schools it was strictly forbidden to utter even the simplest thing in any language other than Latin. They also acquired a set of definitions with the unique exhaustive conciseness that only scholasticism is capable of. A few simple words, learnt by heart and fixed in the memory for life, were enough to capture the most fleeting of essences, the thing in itself and its very being, its genus and *differentia specifica*.

The art of memory II: the abbot and the wild boar

It was the scholastic methods that gave rise to the medieval belief that all human activity consisted of 'arts' that could be learnt systematically. Textbooks were written on the art of preaching or the art of dying (*ars praedicandi* and *ars moriendi*).

Like everything else human memory could be developed with careful and systematic attention. This became a study in itself, the art of memory, *ars memorativa*. It was not created out of nothing, for classical rhetoric had laid great emphasis on training the ability to keep long and complicated dispositions for pleas in court and the like in the memory. Cicero and Quintilian, the leading theoreticians of Roman rhetoric, had supplied practical advice on this point. Martianus Capella, whose work was to be found in every medieval school, was also an authority. It is characteristic that Thomas Aquinas also became the purveyor of the wisdom of the ancients in this field as well. One paragraph in his *Summa theologica* provided the starting point for a new crop of tractates on the art of memory in theory and practice. While discussing classical rhetoric he classifies memory within the virtue of prudence (*prudentia*).

ars memorativa

On the second point it should be said that prudence depends upon natural gifts but is perfected through practice and the gift of grace. The same is true of the memory, as Tullius says in his Rhetoric. The memory is not perfected by nature but is based to a great extent on systematic training. There are four operations which improve human memory. The *first* is when we make use of pictures which resemble what we are trying to remember. They must not be too ordinary as it is the differences which entrance us and make the senses linger on something without wanting to leave it. It is for this reason that we remember our childhood experiences best. Similarities or pictures of this kind must be discovered because concepts and abstract ideas soon elude us if they are not fixed in the form of physical pictures. Human knowledge is best equipped to deal with the physical and tangible. Therefore memory is subordinated to the physical intellectual faculties. *The second* is that what is to be remembered must be arranged in a certain order in the imagination so that we can move easily from one part of it to the next. . . . *Thirdly,* great care and attention must be paid to what is to be remembered because the more firmly something is etched in our senses, the more difficult it is for it to escape our memory. . . . *The fourth point* is that we must meditate often about what is to be remembered. It is for this reason that the Philosopher says in his book On memory that 'it is meditation that saves the memory' because, as it says in the same book 'habit becomes second nature'. What we think about often is what we learn quickly so that we naturally make associations from one thing to the next.[72]

Fig. 36. A page from a textbook in the art of memory (*ars memorativa*) with pictures of twenty-five existing or fabulous animals. Using this table and three similar ones the author claimed that the reader would be able to learn to keep one hundred different things in his head in the correct order. Jacobus Publicus, *Ars oratoria*, printed by Erhart Ratdolt in Augusburg in 1490.

224

The important thing therefore is that one tries to imprint things in the memory in a certain order, preferably with the help of extreme pictures. A manual in this art was composed by Petrus Ravennas with the title *Fenix or the artificial memory*. His ingenious stratagems were reproduced in an abbreviated form in the very popular *Pearls of philosophy* (*Margarita philosophica*) by Gregorius Reisch, which was published in 1496 but remained in use until the seventeenth century (see Fig. 35).

With the help of a simple system it is possible to keep no less than one hundred pictures in the memory in a fixed order. The basis of this ability is the alphabet, in which I and J are regarded as the same letter, as are U and V. X, Y and Z are disregarded. This leaves twenty letters which, with certain readjustments (for example if *custos* is spelt *quustos*), can be the initial letters of words. Each letter is made to begin a series of five concrete nouns. These are chosen so that the first vowel (or the second if the initial letter happens to be a vowel as well) in the words in the series follow the order AEIOU. The first five words in the system are *abbas, aper, apis, astrologus* and *agnus*. These words mean abbot, wild boar, bee, astrologer and lamb in that order, and they are all phenomena that in some way or other have characteristics which enable them to be visualized easily. The point of the exercise is to use mental gymnastics that will associate what one is trying to remember with these pictures and the more far-fetched the relationships are, the more easily they are likely to be etched into the memory.

An example is taken from canon law to show how this works in practice. The clauses about ecclesiastical offices can be remembered if an abbot and a wild boar can be used to represent the rightful and the illegitimate holder of a lucrative office. Imagine, Reisch tells us, an abbot that we know who has not been officially appointed. He will serve to remind us that an office may not be held by anyone who has not been installed in it according to the rules of canon law. The wild boar can be used in a short narrative. Imagine that the boar has sought refuge in a cave. Outside a cunning wolf if prowling round and he shouts to the boar that he is the lawful occupier of the cave and that the boar must leave. The boar does not owe him an answer. Canon law says quite clearly and with no argument that anyone who makes any claim to the office of another by false pretences *ipso facto* renounces the right to exercise authority over other people.

The double-truth theory and intelligence as a source of enjoyment

The prohibition against Aristotle that had been laid on the arts faculty in Paris at the beginning of the thirteenth century had not applied to the theologians in the same city. They had therefore gained something of a lead in assimilating all this new material. By the middle of the century, however, the field was open to the philosophers as well and for many of the teachers Averroes, the Commentator, became the obligatory escort as they penetrated the Philosopher's works, which they wanted to drink in to the last drop without reference to Christian dogma or any other. The world was eternal, passive intellect was the same entity in all human beings, and the only immortality that could be envisaged was the immortality of man as a species, or in other words the continued existence of the species through reproduction. One could, if one wanted to, say that one thing was true in philosophy and another in theology (the double-truth theory).

Two teachers at the faculty of philosophy were identified as the sources of this pestilential infection and they were Siger of Brabant (who died in 1284) and a Danish scholar called Bo, or, in Latin, Boethius of Dacia (who died at the end of the thirteenth century). Although it is impossible to find any terrible statements in their written works, it should be remembered that there could well be a difference between what these philosophers said while they were teaching and the way in which this was understood and circulated by word of mouth by their listeners. Siger was attacked by no less a person than Thomas for advocating monopsychism, the belief that intellect was one and the same in all people, but Siger seems to have defended himself by saying that as a professor of philosophy he saw his task as mainly that of presenting and explaining the ideas of other philosophers and not of presenting any philosophy of his own. This is what Aristotle and Averroes must have meant, now go and draw your own conclusions.

There can be no doubt that Boethius was one of the most

brilliant figures of the thirteenth century and has hardly been equalled as master of clear presentation. In his essay 'On the highest good' (*De summo bono*) he composed a Song of Songs for intellectual life on the basis of a well-known Aristotelian theme. Mankind's supreme asset is the intellect. Supreme happiness must be the realization of this supreme asset, therefore using the intellect to the utmost must be the greatest happiness in life. Realizing the truth and deriving total satisfaction from this insight is the enviable privilege reserved for the philosopher:

Because insight into the truth is a pleasure. What is understood pleases people who understand it, and the more awesome and noble what is understood is and the more acute reason is when it comes to understanding it completely, then the greater this intellectual enjoyment is. Anyone who has once experienced this pleasure will despise all that cannot be compared with it. Fleshly pleasures are in reality slighter and poorer than this is, and people who prefer them are poorer than those who choose intellectual pleasure. Because the intellect bestows pleasure on the intelligent, the Philosopher asserts (in the eleventh book of the Metaphysics) that the first (divine) intellect exists in the highest voluptuousness.[73]

No form of life is therefore closer to nature than that of the philosopher, and no temptation is more irresistible than the temptation to direct one's gaze towards the extreme Cause, the origin and goal of everything, which is called God by both philosophers and saints.

Boethius of Dacia draws a clearer distinction than anyone else between theology and philosophy. In his essay 'On the eternity of the world' (*De aeternitate mundi*) the delicate question of how Aristotle can be wedded to the Judaeo-Christian belief in revelation becomes itself the starting point for a dissertation on principles. Boethius says that the natural philosopher is strictly obliged to limit himself to the facts and methods that his own discipline can provide and to work within the demands that they impose. With these as his only tools, the philosopher is not permitted to come to the conclusion that the world has had a beginning in time through the effect of a 'new' motion 'the alteration from non-existence to existence) that was produced at a specific moment in time. In the same way, as a *philosopher* he is not allowed either to come to the conclusion that a creation from nothing is possible, that there has even been a first human being, or that the dead will, while retaining their individual personality, arise from the grave on the Day of Judgement. Pronouncements on matters like these are outside the competence of the philosopher. It is wrong therefore to expect any such pronouncements from a philosopher. On the other hand he cannot deny such propositions by virtue of his scholarship, but he may not suggest that such propositions can be proved rationally. They are valid only because of the fact that they have been revealed (disclosed) by the divine Wisdom, the supreme cause, which underlies all subordinate natural causes. For it is possible for this cause to intervene directly and override natural causality. Boethius even goes as far as to say that these propositions ought to be *denied* by philsophy when it is claimed that they are possible for natural reasons.

Philosophy is therefore an autonomous branch of scholarship. It neither can nor may depend upon divine information or revelation and neither can it nor may it pay regard to miraculous exceptions, for in doing so it would cease to be philosophy. Boethius, however, also attacks those who say that a philosopher cannot at the same time be a believing Christian.

It can be seen that these ideas contain nothing that could have given rise to the 'double-truth theory', to the belief that one and the same person could by means of mental somersaults dispel contradictions and maintain that what is true in the area of faith can at the same time be false philosophy. Any attempt to popularize Boethius' teachings, however, would find it difficult to avoid having them hawked about in this form either in good faith or in order to tarnish the reputation of their originator.

Scepticism, delusion and the absence of free will

That this is what happened is evident. In 1277 Pope John XXI, who, using his personal name Petrus Hispanus, had written the famous compendium in logic, ordered an enquiry to put an end to the rumours circulating in Paris. Estienne Tempier, who was the bishop of the city, was not slow to obey this command. On his own responsibility he put together a list of no fewer than 219 propositions on varying subjects which, in his opinion, were in conflict with orthodox teachings and healthy philosophy. The list is a hotch-potch of opinions from Aristotle, Avicenna, Averroes, Thomas Aquinas, Boethius of Dacia and other lesser prophets and also contains opinions that go far beyond anything that any of these philosophers ever declared. At the same time Tempier seized the chance of condemning pamphlets with astrological, spiritualistic and pornographic contents, pamphlets praising free love and giving guidance for it, and those containing hints and tips on the art of summoning up the spirits of the dead so that they could give information about the future. The list of pernicious opinions contains those listed below, for instance, and according to Tempier, it was their contradictory meaning and not necessarily the contrary meaning (one should add: 'It is not the case that' before each proposition, see p. 63) that expressed the true teachings of the Church.

One should not believe in anything that is not evident or which cannot be derived from what is evident.

What is necessarily impossible cannot occur, not even through the intervention of God or some other agent. This is an error if the proposition is understood as using 'impossible' to imply 'impossible according to the laws of nature'.

God cannot produce the effect of a secondary cause without the participation of that cause.

The agent has no choice but is predetermined.

Nothing happens because of coincidence but everything happens of necessity: all future events which really will happen are enforced and those which will not happen were, from the very beginning, impossible: nothing is contingent if attention is paid to every single one of its causes.

The varying spiritual endowments and material conditions of different human beings can be observed in the variations of the heavenly bodies.

Intellect is one entity in all human beings and although it can depart from the individual body at death it cannot leave every body.

The results of human understanding are in themselves immortal and indestructible, but they cease to exist in the individual when his mental images are destroyed (because of sleep, syncope or death).

Our will is dependent on the heavenly bodies.

The will necessarily strives for that which our intellect has been convinced about and it cannot refrain from that which is dictated by reason.

Man's will is constrained by knowledge just as the will of animals is constrained by their urges.

All impulsive actions are enforced actions.

The highest good attainable by man is to be found in the intellectual virtues.   virtus intellectualis

Bliss is to be found within the limits of this life and not in the life to come.

The Christian religion is an impediment to education.

Theology bases its reasoning on fairy tales.

The creation is an impossibility, even though the Christian faith obliges us to maintain the opposite.

To say that there is a heaven and that it is immoveable is to be guilty of contradicting oneself.

To talk of accidentals with no supporter is to maintain something impossible and to contradict oneself.

Unnatural sin, in other words perverted sexuality, is admittedly against the nature of the species but not of the individual.

A coming resurrection should not be recognized by a philosopher, as it is impossible to make any rational enquiry about it.[74]

The last proposition incited Tempier to remark 'Error! Even a philosopher must make a prisoner of his intellect in the obedience of Christ', a reference to the second epistle to the Corinthians.

The effect of this catalogue varied a great deal. It was

never given legal force outside Paris. The proposition that Heaven is immoveable – and this means that the world is moveable and therefore not the fixed centre of the universe – was admitted indirectly by Tempier as a hypothesis which, although it could admittedly not be proved, could not be excluded as a possibility. The belief in Aristotle as an infallible source of truth in the field of physics was dealt a serious blow and in the long run this benefited experimental science. This was probably the most important consequence of the events of 1277.

Other points in the catalogue met different fates. Astrology which is condemned here categorically by an ecclesiastical authority as the very contradiction of Christian belief in providence and as a denial of free responsible will was, some centuries later, to be generally accepted and even practised by Popes. However in reacting so violently to any doctrine that everything should have been determined by inescapable fate (a concept that has its roots in Arabic Aristotelianism) Tempier heralded an important change in the climate that prevailed in theology. From this period on theologians were to place continual emphasis on the contingency of the Creation and the sovereign all-powerful freedom of the Creator.

'Sortes' and sophistry

The century after the death of Abélard saw a period of rediscovery, in the true meaning of that word, in the field of logic. The traditional (old) logic was supplemented with new material in the form of the teachings about *fallaciae* (fallacies) found in the *Sophistici Elenchi* and the syllogistic apparatus taken from the first *Analytics*. The major step forward was taken when this new stimulus was allowed to fertilize traditional grammar in the form in which it had been handed down by Priscian. This gave rise to strict analysis of the functions of the different types of sentences and the exact nature of the 'terms' that they contained. More than *termini* anything else *Elenchi* was a powerful driving force in this respect. Nobody who had with its assistance elaborated the many layers of meaning contained in language could find it easy to refrain from continuing the process and discovering whole new worlds of subordinate divarications. Particular study was made of the logical constants, in other words the terms that did not themselves refer to any independent phenomenon (the term that Priscian had used was 'syn- *syncategoremata* categoremes') such as 'every, no, some'. These can be described as the terms in a proposition that above all others support its truth or falsehood. They acquire their meaning completely from the terms that do refer to something (the categoremes 'the significants') or, to use modern termi- *categoremata* nology, the variables.

    Another new field which was developed for the first time along with these legacies from antiquity was the theory of suppositions. Its starting point was the observation that one and the same noun can, depending upon its context, 'stand for' (*supponere*) different sectors which cover the reality to which the noun in question possibly can refer. The noun 'man' stands for completely different conceptual or actual phenomena in sentences like ' "Man" is a monosyllable' or 'Man is mortal' and this is also true if it is qualified with terms like 'no, some, or all' or the like. It must be remembered that these intellectual gymnastics were taking place in Latin, a language that lacks for example the definite

fallacia

article and which allows such inexactitude as the use of one and the same word such as *homo* to refer both to one concrete human being and the written or conceptualized universal 'mankind'. It can easily be seen that this opened the way to an unlimited number of formulations of all kinds of sophisms, ambiguous propositions that were not always easy to see through. The logicians of the thirteenth century said that in these different contexts the term *homo* had different suppositions (*suppositio*).

The development of logic in the twelfth and thirteenth centuries was embodied in a compendium by Petrus Hispanus, later to be Pope John XXI, a Portuguese logician and medical scholar (died 1277), who had instituted the enquiry into conditions in the faculty of philosophy at the University of Paris (see p. 230). His short treatise *Summulae logicales* (which was the name it was circulated under although originally it seems to have been called *Tractatus*) contains not only the practical mnemonic *Barbara Celarent* (see p. 102) but also a diagram of the different suppositions:

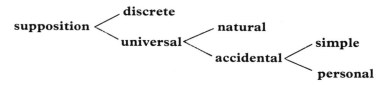

This diagram omits the crudest distinction which is the one between 'material' supposition (which is the kind that nowadays is marked by the use of quotation marks as in ' "Man" is a monosyllable') and other forms of supposition. In this context, discrete means denoting a certain individual ('Socrates is a man') and in this way individual determination is dealt with and all other suppositions are related to universals. Natural supposition arises when 'man' is taken to stand for all human beings who have ever lived, are living now, or will live ('Man is mortal'). Accidental supposition is however, limited for instance within the category of time ('Man mastered fire' or 'Man is facing universal destruction'). Simple suppositions consist of statements about the universals which cannot be applied to sub-categories (the sentence 'Man is motorized' assumes a supposition that is

234

sophismata

suppositio

Summulae
logicales
(Tractatus)

suppositio
materialis

s. naturalis

s. accidentalis

s. simplex

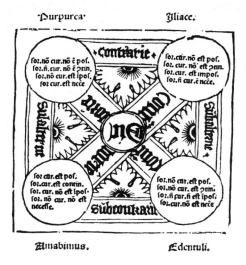

Fig. 37. This was called the square of opposition for modal propositions. A modal proposition, unlike a categorical proposition, contains the speaker's own judgement about the possibility, for instance, or the necessity of what is said. In the top left-hand corner is the type of sentence that says: 'It is necessarily the case that Sortes is running' (and the equivalent sentences: 'It is impossible that Sortes is not running', 'It is not necessarily the case that Sortes is not running' and 'It is not possible that Sortes is not running'). In the top right-hand corner is the type: 'It is necessarily the case that Sortes is not running' (and the equivalent sentences). In the bottom left-hand corner is the type: 'It is possible that Sortes is running' (and equivalent sentences). In the bottom right-hand corner is the type: 'It is not necessarily the case that Sortes is running' (and equivalent sentences). These types have the same contradictory, contrary, sub-contrary or sub-alternate relationships as those that can be found in the square of opposition for categorical propositions (Fig. 11). Petrus Hispanus, *Tractatus duodecim*, printed by Johannes Knob in Strasbourg in 1514.

quite different from the one employed in 'God was made man', in which 'man' stands for 'a member of the human race'). In personal suppositions, however, the statement is true both for the universal and for its sub-categories (compare for instance the sentence 'Man is facing universal destruction' if the first word is taken to refer to the whole of

s. personalis

235

mankind and also to each and every one of its individual members, including 'my wife'.)

This diagram has further ramifications and there are also other systems as well. The literature of *Sophismata* was to blossom into an extensive bouquet of logical riddles, paradoxes and systematically misleading formulations and it was not always that their deep structure, to use a term borrowed from modern linguistics, betrayed itself at first glance.

The syncategoreme *totus* 'the whole', can stand either for the whole of something in its entirety or sometimes also for each and every one of its component parts. In order to rebut the sophistry of one's opponent in a practice disputation it was necessary to know about this rule, or he could prove the thesis that 'The whole of Socrates (or Sortes as it was often written in order to save room and time) is less than Socrates'. This thesis could be proved in the following way:

Every single part of Socrates is less than Socrates. Therefore Socrates is, with reference to every part of himself, less than Socrates. Therefore the whole of Socrates is less than Socrates.[75]

If you had read your Petrus Hispanus you would be able to answer like this. Certain accidental features can be ascribed without distinction to both the whole and every individual part, as, for example, in 'The whole of Socrates is white, therefore Socrates is white.' It is, however, so that expressions like 'the whole of, most of, a rather small part of, or a small part of', which are true if used to describe parts of something, are not automatically true if they are extended to cover the whole. It is impossible therefore to say 'The hand is smaller than the body, the foot is smaller than the body, and so on, and therefore the whole of the body is smaller than the body.'

However clumsy this treatment of the subject may seem, it nevertheless marks the beginning of a major development towards the scientific research, in the modern meaning of the term, which took place in the fourteenth and fifteenth centuries into the 'properties of terms' that took account of a number of tacit assumptions underlying a speaker's utterances. Time was spent happily on examining paradoxes of

De proprietatibus terminorum

236

the type: 'What I am telling you is a lie' (*Insolubilia*).
Systematic rules were formulated for forcing your opponent
into a corner (*Obligationes, Obligatoria*). The validity of
implications of the type 'if . . . therefore' (*Consequentiae*)
were investigated and it was here that the most advanced
achievements of late scholasticism were made.

The modists and Occam's razor

Mention has been made several times of the challenge presented by the Aristotelian concept of science, that it must be able to prove that something is as it is because of necessary, universal and eternally valid causes. To apply this grammar was difficult. It is true that grammar formulates rules but when they are applied to actual languages it soon becomes obvious that exception must be added to exception (not to mention the irrational differences that exist between different languages). In thirteenth-century Paris the desire arose to come to terms with this problem. Some time around the year 1270 a special theory about language, called *modi significandi*, 'methods of signifying', began to take shape.

modi significandi

The basis of this new philosophy of language was the assumption that reality itself had a specific definite metaphysical structure, certain 'ways of being' (*modi essendi*) and that there were adequate counterparts for these *modi* in the *modi significandi* (ways of meaning) of language. The different language forms 'pain, pained, painful, painfully, ouch!' are related to one and the same phenomenon. Just as all these forms are related in some way because they refer, more or less, to the same meaningful nucleus, the stem 'pain-', there must in the structure of reality be some corresponding nucleus. Each of the forms then represents the metaphysical nucleus as well as some additional factor. The substantive represents the substance 'pain', the verb represents in addition the action of this substance, and so on. This relationship between reality and its expression in language exists from the very root (*radix*) itself and, even though different languages realize this relationship in different ways, there is an eternally valid and unchanging connection between 'ways of being' and 'ways of expressing'.

grammatica speculativa

modi essendi

In order to describe the process by which reality became thought and how thought (*modi cogitandi*) became expression, increasingly subtle concepts were devised. This gave rise to an undergrowth of terminology that at times became almost impassable and in time this added to the scepticism that the nominalists felt about the theory of metaphysics.

modi cogitandi

238

The methods of explanation used by the 'modists' became modistae
less and less convincing as they were elaborated more and
more. The demands made by Occam and his followers for
economy of thought ('always prefer the simplest explanation
possible' became known as Occam's razor cf. p. 246)
contributed to the disappearance of the genre. For their part
humanists attacked *modi significandi* vitriolically and
pointed out that it was possible to speak Latin eloquently
without having the slightest idea about these theories but
that, on the other hand, the modists themselves had used the
language barbarically.

Two incompatible approaches are at conflict here. The
aim of the modists was to employ all their ingenuity to its
utmost to solve the eternally elusive mystery of the true
nature of language and its relationship to the reality it refers
to. The aims of the humanist were more modest and
attainable in desiring to cultivate a fully rounded personality
by means of literary endeavour. In doing so they were to
portray *modi significandi* for posterity as the most detestable
deviation that arose from scholasticism.

Duns Scotus and the 'formalities'

John Duns Scotus (who was born *c.* 1226 at Duns in Scotland and died in Cologne in 1308) is by far the most inaccessible of the schoolmen. Not only did he use the system of concepts that had been established by scholasticism, but he also created new terms wherever he scented the opportunity of introducing a new and even more subtle distinction. It was not for nothing that he was called 'the subtle teacher' (*doctor subtilis*). Few thinkers in history can have equal right to lay claim to the epithet of 'perspicacious'. Fate, however, was to make sure that his followers, the Scotists, were to become scapegoats for his finely drawn abstractions. They were to be publicly assassinated by Rabelais and Erasmus of Rotterdam and, irony of irony, in English they were to give rise to the invective term 'dunce'.

doctor subtilis

But the master should not be judged by his disciples. Scotus launched a new era, one that is usually described in the textbooks on philosophy as the collapse of the scholastic synthesis, the new dawn or the first warning (whichever one chooses) which heralded the approach of nominalism and scepticism.

Scotus, like Thomas, based his thinking on Aristotelian ideas. The senses are the only path to knowledge of reality and everything that can be perceived by the senses is in itself comprehensible. There is no need, therefore, to rely as Augustine and Bonaventura did on the illumination of a divine light in the process of thinking. The soul is a *tabula rasa*, with no innate insights or ideas.

When it comes to *what* it is that we comprehend, however, the Scottish philosopher differs from Thomas and Aristotle. Thomas believed that it was the essence of things, what remained when all irrelevant individual characteristics in the reality observed had been filtered out (*abstractio*). We know what a rose is, quite independently of whether there is a rose in front of us and without thinking of this particular rose or that one.

abstractio

Scotus was not satisfied with this description of knowledge, which seems to proceed from a higher plane to a lower

240

one, from the concept of the rose to the rose in reality. He turned the process upside down. Knowledge is acquired first and foremost from what exists here and now in front of one, from this particular rose. He describes the act of knowledge as intuitive. It is an *intuitio*, a vision of the thing as it is within itself (*dicimur intueri rem sicut est in se*). The point of focus shifts therefore from the essence down to the individual object's 'thisness', which was the typically Scotist term used (*haecceitas*). It is not until Scotus that the Platonic fascination seems to lose its power and individual concrete objects became really actual and accessible. Scotus opened the way for an un-Aristotelian interest in individuals as more than elusive, temporary and uninteresting entities. In doing so, however, Scotus in no way reduced the reality of the universals. All of the individual items that our perception groups together in one single species are not linked by something only in our mental processes but primarily by their own innate and common nature (*communis natura*) which is the object of abstract knowledge.

'Thisness' is only one of many terms that shows the terminological inventiveness of Scotus and the Scotists. The driving force behind this was their 'realistic' view of the metaphysical composition of things. By *realism* in this context is meant, of course, the reality of concepts or, in other words, that we ascribe to the concepts that we use in abstract reasoning, an actual counterpart in reality. On this point Scotus goes further than Thomas had gone. Thomas had said that along with the real distinction (see p. 216) which separates two things that are objectively separated in reality (Peter and Paul), one can also speak of a rational distinction such as when I make a distinction between my partner Peter and my brother Peter even though in reality they are one and the same person. The distinction has at least a basis in reality (*fundamentum in re*) but there is no freely existing quality of 'partnership' or 'brotherhood' which is independent of my thought processes. Objects which in thought can have several different guises are in themselves (as is Peter) one and the same thing.

John Duns Scotus on the other hand would introduce the terms 'partnership' and 'brotherhood' eagerly and add that

intuitio

haecceitas

communis natura

fundamentum in re

241

they referred to two different forms that existed within Peter, two sets of characteristics that really exist in Peter independent of whether anyone is thinking of them or even knows about them. This division is the notorious Scotist 'formal distinction from the nature of things' (*distinctio formalis ex natura rei*). Scotus considered that everything acquires its nature as a result of being impressed by a great number of forms rather like stamps used to make coins. Each successive stamp increases the degree of individualization until the final one, the ultimate definition that cannot be shared by anything else, thisness. My brother Peter is therefore (from a metaphysical point of view) like an onion composed of different layers. The innermost core is his corporality, next to it comes his animality, then his rationality, then his humanity, and finally the outer layer which is his Peter-ness (cf. Porphyry's tree, p. 56ff.). These layers are not merely mental constructs but according to Scotus exist within Peter and are his formalities (*formalitates*) or 'metaphysical stages'.

distinctio formalis ex natura rei

pluralitas formarum

formalitates, gradus metaphysici

It is this that gave rise to the previously unheard of entities such as incommunicabilities, proportionalities, intellectualities and incompassibilities. Scotus' followers added to them and devised characteristics for things such as genereity, speceity, priority and aseity (this last meant the divine characteristics of being sufficient in itself, of being dependent only upon itself, *a se*) and a large number of others; some of them were to become part of the stock of international words in language used today. These neologisms were of course ridiculed by the humanists who failed to remember that prose of this kind was the language of research and not literature. Serious philosophy cannot, in the long run, survive without such terms.

242

The primacy of will over intellect

Scotus did not share Thomas's high opinions about the capacity of human reason to draw conclusions about the characteristics of God. In Scotus' opinion it was impossible for a philosopher to make pronouncements about whether God was omnipotent, just or merciful nor could he know as a philosopher if the soul was immortal or whether there were such things as eternal reward or punishment. These things belonged to the area of faith. He did, however, maintain that there was a philosophical proof of the existence of God. There must exist a first effective cause that is not itself caused, there must exist a supreme goal that is not itself the means to a higher goal, and there must exist some supreme being that depends only on itself. This is God, the only necessary primary source of everything else, which is not necessary. Scotus did not undertake, however, to prove any specific item of Christian faith.

The primary difference between Thomas and Scotus in the field of ethics is that Scotus attributes to the will (characteristically he made a terminological distinction between *voluntas*, will-power, and *volitio*, an act of will) primacy over the intellect as the highest of human faculties. The foremost characteristic of the will is its freedom. Whereas the intellect cannot avoid accepting a proposition as soon as its truth is perceived, the will is sovereign and can act in conflict with its insights. The will is also the driving force behind the noblest expression of humanity, love. By love Scotus means the love of what is good (all that is good and primarily the source of all goodness, God) for its own sake alone and with no subsidiary motives. Love and 'wisdom' are one and the same thing:

Wisdom (*sapientia*) is in fact love: it is the acquired disposition through which mankind gains a taste of the object that should be tasted for its own sake (*quo sapit habenti illud obiectum, quod est in se sapiendum*) . . . Wisdom is the means whereby the taste of God is the taste of good for me.[76]

Underlying all human aspiration will be found love, the

inclination to goodness for its own sake. This is the highest ethical ideal.

Here Scotus' theology is coloured by tones from Aristotle's language. In another important area, however, the *doctor subtilis* was to point his followers away from Aristotle. Thomas Aquinas had followed the Philosopher closely and had described the various commandments of ethics as the expression of a natural law. What is reasonable is good and what is good is reasonable. God created nature and reason as two faces of the same thing. Scotus saw things differently. He stressed the idea of the will of God as the highest norm in ethics. All that is good is good because God has so willed it and not otherwise. God is able to establish new rules of behaviour if He wants to and they can take any form He wants them to. This argument could be used by later philosophers like a magic formula. God's absolute sovereignty and independence could intervene in any course of events and this rendered all discussion about His being or the world's purposeless. Where a God of this kind disposes, mankind proposes in vain.

John Duns Scotus did not go as far as this himself. The world was still a unity for him, albeit less pellucid than it had been for the serene gaze of Thomas Aquinas. In his prayers Scotus is a Christian and a metaphysician. His philosophical conception of wholeness becomes a hymn in praise of the highest and eternal Being:

In Thee can be found neither quantity nor any other accidental. Therefore art Thou unchangeable in the matter of accidence just as I have said that Thou art unchangeable in Thy essence. Thou alone art perfect without further qualification ... the perfect being lacking no entity which can in any way supplement any other thing, Thou art the highest Being, alone eternal of all beings.[77]

Here Aristotle has been forced to kneel in reverence to the Christian God.

Occam: the universals as labels

William of Occam (who was born *c.* 1285 probably in Surrey in England and who died in 1349 in Munich) has been called by posterity *venerabilis inceptor*. This has often been mis-translated to mean 'the venerable innovator', but it has in fact a more prosaic meaning. The title of doctor was never conferred upon William as the result of a disagreement he had with his superiors. He had only given his *inceptio* (see p. 127). Innovator is, however, the least that can be said of him. He was ruthlessly consistent in demanding that the language used by philosophers should be purged of everything that was not absolutely necessary for its explanations. He took over where Scotus had left off in dealing with the individual and he shifted the focus of interest on to individuals to such an extent that he denied that the universals had any objective reality. Up to that point it had been generally accepted that the conceptual world was a reflection of the world of reality. Earlier philosophers had conceived of a genuine hierarchy from the highest genus down to individuals in which there were real boundary lines between the different levels (genus, species, sub-species, and so on) which were not just mental constructs. Occam, however, assumed that genus and species were different systems of labelling used to bring some order into the confusion of myriads of individuals. Only the individuals had any reality, while genus and species were based on psychological processes as we observe certain similarities between individuals and group them together on the basis of these likenesses. The concepts have no reality outside the brain. This theory, which should really be called conceptualism, is called *nominalism*.

Occam was convinced that a certain uniformity existed in nature but was not certain that this could be demonstrated. He did, however, deny categorically that there could be found any natural hierarchies of 'common natures' in Scotus' meaning corresponding to the classification system used by language. In doing so he also rejected the idea that it would be possible to discover reality by means of language. He reduced metaphysics to an exercise in logic, a method of

venerabilis inceptor

proving the functional truth of propositions. Traditional methods of metaphysical thought were criticized as naive. Interest shifted from things themselves (God, being, causal chains and the like) to the logical analysis of linguistic propositions about these things. In these conditions theology could not remain as lucid or as placid as it had been for a man like Thomas.

Everything that exists is an individual and but for these individuals there exists nothing. According to Occam it is therefore misguided to ask questions such as 'How is the essence of the species present in the individual?' He is equally firm in rejecting all 'formal' distinctions as unnecessary mental fabrications (Occam's razor – it is wrong to assume a greater number of entities than is necessary) that cannot be verified. Previously it had been supposed that the ten categories were a form of reinforcement in the fabric of reality, but Occam denied that anything but substance and quality had any real existence. Relationship, for example, is not something that 'exists' completely independent of two things and the person who thinks about how these two things pertain to each other. It is the abstraction of language that deludes us into dealing with the universals, categories and 'formalities' as if they in fact had any real existence outside the brain that conceives them.

'entia praeter necessitatem non sunt multiplicanda'

246

A capricious God and a frail universe

Occam's rejection of the inheritance of metaphysics does not imply that he also rejected the traditional faith of the Church which had previously been expressed in its terminology. He was not a reformer in this sense of the word. He had a strong feeling for the contingency of creation and its absolute dependence upon a God who was independent of all obligations and considerations. The old teachings that created things did not exist as the result of any necessary cause and that there was no necessary reason for them to be as they were was developed by Occam and driven to its logical conclusion. God, in His complete freedom, has willed creation to be as it is and to have the ethical norms that it has. God's freedom is such, however, that with one act of His will He could decree that hereafter murder, rape and hatred of God Himself are permissible or even praiseworthy. What is good is not good by virtue of some eternal and absolute goodness which even God has to comply with, it is good therefore that God has willed it so.

Just as God creates any created thing at all by will alone He can also make of His creation anything that pleases Him. If someone loves God and does all that can please Him, God can still destroy him without any motive because God is answerable to nobody's reckoning. If God has done something, it is right. Example: Christ committed no sin and yet he was punished with extreme cruelty, even unto death.[78]

The will of God is in Occam's thinking as in Scotus' the highest ethical norm.

God is represented here as a despotic tyrant. This is not really, however, Occam's opinion. The fact is that in God being, will and intellect are a unity, and He cannot will something which is in opposition to the goodness of His being. Admittedly God can, by virtue of His absolute power (*de potentia absoluta*), do everything that is logically possible (but cannot grasp a bald man by the forelock) but within the framework of the laws He has Himself ordained (*de potentia ordinata*) He cannot do anything that conflicts with His own

de potentia absoluta

de potentia ordinata

Fig. 38. The application of logic in prayer. The 'new piety' (*devotio moderna*) which dominated the spiritual life of Europe during the fifteenth century admittedly displayed strong scepticism about the ability of academic knowledge to satisfy man's deepest needs. The author of the *Imitation of Christ* quoted the words of Aristotle from the *Metaphysics*, 'all men long by nature for knowledge' but added 'but what is knowledge without the fear of God? Of what concern to us are all these genera and species?' The movement took some of its inspiration however from the scholastic methods of the universities. In a development parallel with the new emphasis on the individual contained in nominalism, *devotio moderna* paid almost exclusive attention to the life of Christ and its events in relationship to the individual human being and his life of devotion, neglecting other aspects of the articles of faith and the life of the Church. Prayer was seen as spiritual exercise which could be divided up into 'points' according to increasingly complex systems. Part of this programme consisted of a methodical examination of conscience. (Ignatius of Loyola, the leading figure in the counter-reformation, the founder of the Jesuit order and the author of *Exercitia spiritualia*, is a typical representative of those whose ideas were based on *devotio moderna*.) To assist meditation the author of *The fourfold path to contemplation of the sufferings of Jesus Christ* exploits the reflex universals *genus, species, differentia* and *accidents* (cf. Fig. 10) to explain how the sacrificial death of Jesus is of significance for the whole of the universe. Christ was betrayed, condemned and executed by human beings of every genus, his suffering was attested before elements of every genus (he was denied in front of fire, spat upon, hanged in the air and concealed in the earth); his suffering comprised every genus of agony which affected every *differentia* within the species of the senses. This suffering was rendered especially unbearable because of accidental circumstances, his noble temperament, that he was at the most sensitive age, his delicate sinews, the coarseness of the nails, the cruel stretching of the limbs, the long drawn-out hanging and the absence of consolation in any form. Every genus of benefit can be derived from this drama; the extinction of sin, the death of death, the restoration of man and the glorification of the Trinity. These references to the universals emphasized the universality of the story of the passion and served to help the memory to retain all its details. Preachers used to take delight in organizing their sermons according to similar systems, a technique that was also taken over by orthodox Lutheranism in the seventeenth century and echoes of it can still be heard in the traditional preaching of the west of Sweden. *Via contemplationis passionis Iesu Christi quadruplex*, printed by L. Hohenwang in Augsburg at the end of the fifteenth century.

INRI

Diſcipulo proprio
Cunctis apoſtolis
Pōtificibꝰ ſeri et pbi
Rege
Prelide
Turba
Militibꝰ

mi genere
ominum
Quia a

Venditus.
derelictus.
Traditus.
Iudicatus.
Flagellatus
Condēnatus
Crucifixus

Ad ignem
Aq ſaliue
In aere
Terra

mi genere
emētorum
Quia

Negatus.
Conſputus
Suſpenſus
Coopertus

Sudor.
Fletus.
Clamor.
Pauor.
Triſtis pro aiīs
Gemens pro ſuis

enaliſſima
mi gene
plotum
Quia

Sanguineus
Vberrimus
Validiſſimus
Horrendiſſimus
Peccatis nris
Penis infinitis

Viſus eius nimium
Fletus continuus
Auditus clamoribꝰ
Olfactus fetoribus
Tactus vulneribus
Guſtus aceto et felle

omni dra
nſuū qz

Caligauit
Extitit
Increbruit
Obſtupuit
Doluit
Inhorruit

Illuſus
Deriſus
Confuſus
Eductus
Adiūctus
Adductus

gnomioſiſſia
Omi gene
a fame qz

Colaphiſatione
Genuflexione
Expoliatione
Infami loco
Improbo ɔſortio
Enormi ſupplicio

Di gene Ceſus · Ligatus · Iudicatus
orm̄· Flagellatus coronatus irriſus
orū qa · Clauatus · ſuſpēſus · laceatus

Fuit

Coplexionis
Etatis
Neruorum
Clauorum
Extenſionis
Suſpenſionis
Conſolatiōis

Acerbiſſima
Omi genere
accidentium
Propter

Nobilitatem
Viuacitatem
Subtilitatem
Aſperitatem
Immanitatem
Continuitatem
Paucitatem

Peccatoꝝ nrōrū
Mortis noſtre
Humane ruine
Eterne trinitatis

vtiliſſima
Omi genere
proficuitatū
Quia ꝓpter

Deletionem
Deſtructionē
Reſtaurationē
Glorificationē

positive and rational will. The maker of laws is free to make what laws he will, but while a certain law remains in force even the lawmaker is obliged to follow its prescriptions. In this way Occam moved the focal point of ethics from objective nature to a personal God.

Occam did not challenge Scotus' proof of the existence of God. It is typical of him, however, to regard the main importance of the proof to lie in the continued maintenance of creation and not in the fact that it must have been set in motion by some prime cause. A new awareness of the fragility of the world and human existence is felt here. For Thomas the universe was a well-ordered harmony in which God is admittedly the cause of everything but normally works through causes other than Himself. In Occam's eyes it is God that is continually rescuing the world from imminent destruction.

According to Occam, it was also impossible to prove of God that He must be the only one. The highest conceivable being could in fact exist at the same time as another exactly similar preeminent being.

Occam's distaste for unproven and unnecessary modes of thought and his direction of attention to the individual had two important consequences. He encouraged interest in inductive reasonings based on observation and experiment. He also shifted the emphasis of theology away from objective universality, from the absolute validity of the sacraments, the Church and its offices, and on to the personal qualities of the individual, from intellect to will, from collective solidarity to personal destiny.

It was no coincidence that it was adherents of Occam who began to question Aristotelian physics. Nor is it a coincidence that a man like Martin Luther nurtured his ideas for reform while influenced by Occam's philosophical and theological teaching, a fact that he himself pointed out.

Via antiqua and via moderna

The period after Occam, in other words the period after the Black Death, which according to the latest estimates carried off as much as a third of the population of Europe, did not leave the Church or the universities unconcerned. From 1350 until the end of the Middle Ages is the era of the 'schools'. These were divided into two camps, usually labelled realists and nominalists, labels that have the disadvantage of being partly misleading but the advantage of having been accepted by the schools themselves. Plague, the Hundred Years' War, the Great Schism in the Church and a general feeling of approaching catastrophe did not provide a benevolent climate for the cultivation of great intellectual developments, or indeed any other kind either.

As always, it is important to distinguish carefully between the prophet himself and his school. The fourteenth century provided examples of nominalist philosophers who drew conclusions from the teachings of Occam that he himself would almost certainly not have approved of. Adam of Woodham (who died in 1358) denied even the possibility of proving the existence of God. Robert Holcot (who died in 1349) rejected the possibility of deducing the existence of any immaterial thing from the evidence of the senses. Teachings about the Trinity were, in the opinion of the same philosopher, in conflict with the logic of Aristotle, but this need not disturb any believer as it is possible to conceive of a logic of faith which ranks higher than the laws of identity or the laws of contradiction. Jean de Mirecourt (who died some time around 1350) maintained that the only absolutely true proposition that can be held was 'I exist'. Nicolas d'Autrecourt (who died around 1350) is the radical sceptic of the Middle Ages. He even rejected the idea that sense impressions would enable anything at all to be deduced. Even less was it possible to prove that there were any causal relationships between different phenomena. Of things invisible nothing can be said with certainty.

It is obvious that the more radical of these theses were still-born. They cut the ground from under their own feet.

251

Even though Occam had provided powerful incentives to question the authorities, Aristotle's position was hardly affected. On one point his teachings had to be modified however, and this was his assertion that an object that had been thrown (see p. 109) continued its motion because the medium (air or water) completed the function of the hand

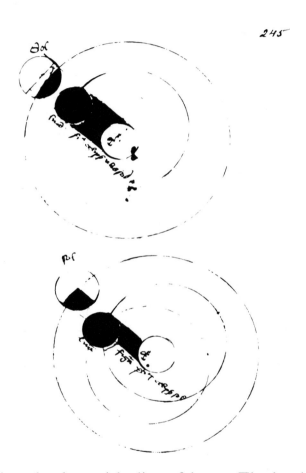

Fig. 39. A total and a partial eclipse of the sun. The drawing was made by a student from the island of Gotland in the Baltic called Olof Johansson (Olaus Johannis Gutho) some time around the year 1483. The Sun revolves around the Earth. Between them both revolves the Moon in an eccentric orbit and casts a shadow on the Earth. Uppsala university library, MS C 629, fol. 245.

and continued to press on the object until its power came to an end. This idea was abandoned by almost everybody. It was not difficult for men like Jean Buridan (who died around 1358) and Nicolas Oresme (who died in 1382) to demonstrate the absurdity of this theory. They proposed another model to explain what happened. The hand of the thrower transferred a 'thrust' (*impetus*, also called *impetus violentus* to underline the fact that the motion was not 'natural' but 'enforced') to the object, a force that is counteracted by resistance in the medium and the weight of the object and is therefore gradually neutralized. It was only the arch-conservative University of Cologne and the northernmost outpost of the academic world in Uppsala that refused to abandon the true Aristotelian teachings on this point. impetus violentus

Even the most orthodox Occamists, however, developed their own canon of *auctoritates*, statements made by ancient and more modern authors which were accepted generally without argument. (Or rather after they had been verified by a veritable armoury of arguments each expressed as a *quaestio*.) After 1425 'the modern way' was an unambiguous concept for those who had adopted nominalism. Their opponents grouped themselves in increasingly recognizable schools containing the protagonists of Albertus Magnus, Thomas Aquinas and John Duns Scotus. It was logical for this second group to call themselves 'the old way'. The nominalists accused their opponents, the realists, of maintaining that the goodness of God and the wisdom of God were two things and not one, while the nominalists believed that all that is in God is God. Here again we can see the rational and the formal distinction at work. The nominalists devoted a great deal of attention to the suppositions of terms (see p. 234) which, after all, determined the truth or falsity of a proposition. This was of no interest to the realists who used to claim: 'We concern ourselves with the thing, the terms are no concern of ours' ('*nos imus ad res, de terminis non curamus*'). The nominalists left Porphyry's *Isagoge* out, or, if indeed they did lecture on it, they interpreted its contents to refer to the *terms* genus, species, and so on and not to the *objects* genus and species, as the realists did. The nominalists refused to accept that the category of relationship was auctoritates via moderna via antiqua nominalistae – realistae 'nos imus ad res, de terminis non curamus' something that really existed. It was here that the realists made their stand by pointing out the perils to which this exposed the doctrine of the Trinity. Listening to a nominalist describe the relationship of the three divine persons to each other while at the same time he denied the category of relationship any reality was as crazy as asking for the opinion of a blind man on the nature of colour.

And so it went on. If the whole controversy can be reduced to one formula, it is this one. Do the universals exist as independent realities outside and independent of human thinking? Is there any necessary relationship between language and reality? Is the structure of language therefore constrained by reality?

This is the question that Porphyry left unanswered, the question that had provided Abélard with his first battle-honours. In the thirteenth century there had been no overwhelming interest for the matter. Thomas had been content to assert in vague terms that there is a universal 'before the thing' in the mind of God; 'in the thing' it has no reality in itself except in individuals, but 'after the thing' it becomes an abstract reality in our thinking. Scotus and his outspoken realism posed a challenge to Occam and those who felt as he did.

universale ante rem, in re, post rem

Naturally realism fitted hand in glove with the theories of the 'modists' (see p. 238). For the nominalist, however, science was in general something that dealt with propositions and their truth or falsity.

A striking example of how this nominalist interest in logic excluded all other interests is to be found in a syllabus from *via moderna* at the University of Erfurt. To acquire a baccalaureate degree there in the years around 1420 it was necessary to attend lectures and exercises dealing with the following sections:

Donat's *Ars minor*.
The second part of *Doctrinale* by Alexander de Villa Dei.
Thomas Maulevelt's The supposition of terms.
By the same author Confusions, Ampliations, Restrictions, Appellations, Alienations, Remotions (these were all different kinds of supposition) as well as his Syncategoremes.

254

By the same author Consequences, or alternatively John Sutton's
    Consequences.
Richard Billingham's Proof of propositions.
Hollandrinus' *Obligationes*.
Hollandrinus' *Insolubilia*.
Porphyry's *Isagoge*.
Aristotle's Categories, Perihermeneias, the first and second
    Analytics, Elenchi, Physics, On the soul.
John of Holywood's *Sphaera materialis*.[79]

Only the first two books and the last three deal with anything
but logic.

John Hus, the reformer in Prague at the beginning of the
fifteenth century, adopted extreme realism, and after he had
been condemned as a heretic and burnt at the stake,
nominalism served for a time as a guarantee of orthodoxy. It
contained, however, the seeds of theological schizophrenia,
as it denied the possibility of providing philosophical proof
for articles of faith such as the existence of God, the
immortality of the soul, transubstantiation, and similar
things. It abandoned mankind to a capricious God. It
tempted people to adopt a belief in the existence of a 'double
truth'.

The nominalists' theory of *impetus* was to have far-
reaching consequences for the Christian world-picture. If
the heavenly bodies moved as the result of some force that
had been imparted to them, it was no longer necessary
to envisage direct contact with the prime mover. The
Christian Aristotelian feeling that the universe was in
motion impelled by its love of God (see p. 110) was dealt a
death-blow. The schoolmen of the late Middle Ages did not
themselves draw any theological implications from the
theory of *impetus*, but even then the idea that love was the
dominant form of energy in the universe began to give way to
the soulessly mechanical view of the heavens that was to
prevail in later periods.

During the fifteenth century these two 'ways' co-existed
within the universities. They were, on the whole, accorded
the same value. Admittedly nominalism was banned in Paris
in 1474 but this prohibition was rescinded only seven years
later in 1481.

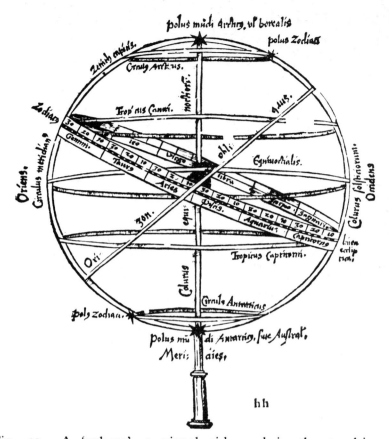

Fig. 40. A 'sphere', a visual aid used in the teaching of astronomy. It shows simply and clearly the axes and planes that were involved in the study of astronomy. At the centre can be seen the Earth. The broad vertical line is the Earth's axis, and the Equator is at right angles to it. The other horizontal circles are, from top to bottom, the Arctic Circle, the Tropic of Cancer, the Tropic of Capricorn and the Antarctic Circle. The broad belt is the Ecliptic and on it can be seen the names of the constellations that form the Zodiac. The narrower slanting belt represents the 'horizon' (*horizon obliquus*), the plane that coincides with the Equator for someone standing at either of the two poles. Here, on the other hand, the observer is thought of as standing to the left slightly under the Arctic Circle (at the 'zenith of the head', *zenith capitis*). The horizon is therefore what is known as the geocentric horizon, a plane that intersects the centre of the Earth at right angles to a vertical line drawn from the point of observation. Gregorius Reisch, *Margarita philosophica* (first published 1496), printed in Basle in 1583 by Sebastian Henricpetri.

256

The nominalists' interest in logic was also shown in the predilection for the *quaestio* rather than the *lectio*. The realists for their part were closer to the traditional authorities' ways of thinking and expressing ideas. The nominalists prepared the way for the humanists' concentration on the individual but it was the realists who had most in common with the philological respect for texts that characterized the approaching era.

As the year 1500 approached the battle between *via antiqua* and *via moderna* died down. It was difficult to discover new arguments and the old ones could no longer excite any passion. The question had lost its ideological force. From a religious point of view the choice of 'way' was regarded with indifference. There are signs that in some places scholars began to adopt a compromise between the two, a 'common way' (*via communis*).

via communis

A freshman's handbook about the 'ways'

A short handbook in Latin for freshmen by Paulus Niavis (*Latinum ydeoma pro novellis studentibus*), which was published at the end of the fifteenth century, contains some interesting information about the conflict of the 'ways'. In order to give new students a chance of mastering the jargon of the lecture halls and the refectories, two friends, Camillus and Bartoldus, talk at length about their attitude to teachers, fellow students, the fair sex and the vanity of the world. This is part of one conversation in which Bartoldus has just praised one master for his skill in dealing with his subject matter:

C : You sing that master's praise but he is a nominalist.

B : So what?

C : I am not going to go to any more of his lectures.

B : The more fool you to despise their teaching. It is not only the realists who have done a lot for the development of philosophy, the nominalists have also had a big part to play.

C : But they deal only with sophistry and feel that teaching the contents of texts is beneath them.

B : You treat the truth very casually. Among the nominalists you will find the most learned of men. Have you not heard that in some countries there are whole universities of nominalists, like Vienna or Erfurt, and as this one was once? You must admit that they were learned and good and that there are still people of that kind.

C : Oh yes, I know that and I can see what you mean, but their reputation is not very good. They spend all their time struggling with pamphlets on logic (*parva logicalia*) and exercises in sophistry.

B : Now you have got hold of the wrong end of the stick. They are famous for their analysis of propositions and their skill with syllogisms. You will not find any students of philosophy who are better masters of syllogisms or other types of argument than the nominalists.

C : And of real scholarship they know nothing.

B : What on earth do you mean by real scholarship?

C : Porphyry's Predicables and Aristotle's Categories. They know very little at all or nothing about these things.

B: Now you are going too far. It is shameful to claim that such famous men do not understand such things . . .

C: Please, Bartoldus, tell me what use the *via moderna* can be to anyone.

B: Willingly. But to begin with, you must realize that I do not have as high a regard for them as I have for the realists, but I feel that the teaching of neither school should be despised. Sharpen your ears and remember what I am going to say! The main advantage of *via moderna* is, in my opinion, that one learns about the characteristics of propositions. They are very advanced in that field. They are also good at oppositions, they know about types of propositions, *insolubilia* and *obligatoria*, inside out . . .

C: What you are saying is all very well. But the fact is that I have no desire to waste my life on sophistry and splitting hairs.

B: As you will.

Bartoldus had to take some pains to convince his friends of the excellence of the 'modern' masters. One could almost suspect that the author spends so much time on this subject in order to provide examples of all the finesses of logical terminology. On another occasion the two friends are on their way to a practice disputation:

B: Where are you going, Camillus?

C: To a disputation.

B: I will come with you. Wait a moment! I have a few small things that I must tell my master. I will be back soon.

C: Hurry up. There is not much time.

B: I will . . . Well, was that quick enough? I decided yesterday that I would go to the disputation today. The respondents are good, remarkably perceptive and they have odd opinions. They use different arguments from the ones we are used to and they do not give in easily. You are going to hear some remarkable things.

C: It is easy enough for them to make up arguments, but when the master launches his broadside they will be less sure of themselves.

B: They do not really have anything to say.

C: What else can one think? They will almost certainly be twenty-year-old masters. They have read thick volumes and works, and when they dispute they stick to authors they have

259

understood. But I do not see how they can provide any real opposition. They are beardless youths, after all.

C: Well, what do you think of this disputation?

B: The respondents did well. I would never have believed that they were so learned or well read.

C: Yes. Actually I liked it as well. But Master N is very pushy. He shouted at them like a madman.

B: But he does that to every respondent. It does not matter what they say. If they do not agree with him, he spits his venom at them, and if they do agree he says that they understand nothing.

C: It is an age-old ingrown habit. But what did you think of master N, who nearly took him in with his play on words?

B: Typical for a nominalist. They always introduce their quibbles. I do not like it.

C: But it is an elegant way if you can resolve the problem. He showed his teeth as a dialectician.

B: But who wants to spend the rest of his life with sophistry? There are other branches of knowledge and faculties that one can devote one's energies to.

C: That is my opinion as well. It is time for lunch. Goodbye.[80]

Epilogue

It is not very difficult to describe the university teaching of the late Middle Ages ironically and to emphasize its pedantic rigidity, its narrow-minded formalism and sterile speculation. The drawbacks of its uncritical acceptance of Aristotle, the geocentric picture of the universe and the like are immediately obvious. It should, however, be remembered that many of the answers have been revealed to us and we should not find fault with any period in the past over-confidently unless we are sure that generations to come will not be able to make the same criticism of us. In comparison with today, the period of scholasticism was, seen as an information system, a relatively closed world. A limited number of classical authors were available and the prospects of discovering more authors or texts were relatively limited. The texts that had been inherited were incorporated into a canon because of their intrinsic value, a canon of knowledge and wisdom that every individual with any claim to education should know, or of which he should at least know the main outlines.

When Aristotle was discovered, the first thing that was found to be impressive was the obvious rationality of his logic. Many sections of it had been formulated for the first time by Aristotle and his lifetime had been spent in refining and polishing it so that it would be convincing and clear. The whole subject appeared to be self-evidently conclusive. If his theories had to be accepted on one point where everybody could, after a certain amount of deliberation, check the validity of what was said and see that it was inarguable, it was natural that the whole Aristotelian store of wisdom should be regarded as a more or less infallible source of knowledge in the 'natural' sphere in the same way as the Bible was in the realm of 'grace'. His position is similar to that accorded to the standard works in scholarship today. Their information is accepted for as long as there is no reason to doubt their accuracy. They are relied upon without any checking of the reliability of their footnotes.

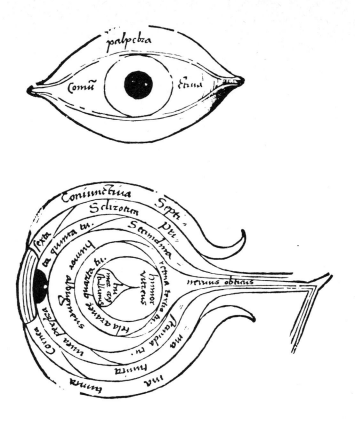

Fig. 41. The anatomy of the eye. Several of the terms used in this picture are still in use (*tunica coniunctiva, cornea, retina,* and *nervus opticus,* the optic nerve). At the end of the Middle Ages the accepted view of sight was that visible shapes were received as impressions in the eye like the tip of a pyramid of which they formed the base. The substance of sight (*spiritus visivus*) was transported from the brain to the eyes by means of the nerves and it was influenced by these sight impressions and returned to the brain irregularly. From the impulses that resulted from this the brain was able to form a clear picture. In this view the mental faculties of the brain resemble a form of wax which can receive any kind of impression at all. According to Gregorius Reisch it was obvious that rationality had some effect on the arrangement of visual impressions to form a clear image as although the observer is continually receiving innumerable impressions, only a few of them are remembered, the ones that had conscious attention paid to them. Gregorius Reisch, *Margarita Philosophica* (first published in 1496), printed in Basle in 1583 by Sebastian Henricpetri.

The techniques of scholasticism fascinated its practitioners precisely because of its limitations and its inexorable rule-system. The interminable conflicts between nominalists and realists (and within realism between Thomists, Scotists and Albertists) can best be compared with a game of chess. The pieces cannot be changed, the squares cannot be changed, the rules cannot be changed and yet the number of possible variations within these narrow limits is infinite and once the rules of the game and some basic theory have been learnt the game never becomes boring. The restrictions imposed by the rules are never in the least experienced as a dulling limitation of the possibilities of developing a free and personal strategy in the game. Both players voluntarily submit to the limitations of the game because these limitations serve a purpose, which is to define the situation and cleanse it from all irrelevant factors so that only acumen and attentiveness are rewarded.

Imagine two humanist scholars arriving in the room in which our scholastic chess players are still sitting, forgetful of both time and space. The newcomers point out that the chess players have been occupying a billiard table, clear away the chessmen and throw the chessboard into one corner of the room. The four people will probably begin to grapple with each other after this and both sides will be wounded. The whole thing will end with each of the protagonists going his own way. The chess players will try to reconstruct the chessboard with each of the pieces occupying the position it occupied before the game was rudely interrupted. They will not be very optimistic about the possibility of co-existence with individuals who believe that the game consists of dispatching as many pieces as possible into a hole in the table with the help of sticks of wood.

The billiard players, however, sit down to compose venomous pamphlets about the physical and mental decrepitude of chess players, their unfathomably vacant gaze, their blindness to the vibrant life around them, and their constricted jerky system of movement within a square, with unimaginative decorations (in black and white of all colours!). This is roughly how the schoolmen and the humanists saw each other. It would have been no use pointing out in the heat of the battle that both sides probably had something of value to give to the other.

Later periods – and I am definitely not referring to the Renaissance or the Reformation, which were direct attacks on the scholastic tradition in the name of what was regarded as an older and more authoritative tradition – were to lay proper emphasis on empiricism and observation and therefore to acquire a degree of self-awareness in relation to the older traditions.

The permanent contribution made by scholasticism does not lie mainly in its scientific discoveries or its medical conquests. It has bequeathed to us an obligation to respect the laws of thought and to guard against the suggestive power of language. We can learn not so much from the *materia* of scholasticism as from its *forma*.

Who would dare to subject his own favourite theories to a rigorous scholastic analysis? As someone pointed out, only minor prophets need fear to pass through that fire.

Texts

Aristotle: *Analytica Posteriora* 1:4 (73a28–34, 'James' translation'
Aristotle *Latinus* **LV, 1–4, 1968, p. 12)**

This paragraph can serve to illustrate the need for a thorough commentary on the text (in the form of lectio*). Aristotle's laconic and specialized prose has been translated into Latin with servile fidelity (cf. p. 92).*

De omni quidem igitur hoc dico quod utique sit non in quodam quidem, quodam autem non, neque aliquando quidem, aliquando vero non, ut de omni homine animal, si verum est dicere hominem, verum est animal, et si nunc alterum, et alterum, et si in
5 omni linea punctum, similiter est. Signum autem: et namque instantias sic proferimus sicut de omni interrogati, aut si in quodam non, aut si aliquando non.

I apply the term 'predicated of all' to whatever is *not* predicated of one instance but not of another, or predicated at one time but not
10 at another. E.g., if 'animal' is predicated of all 'man', if it is true to call X a man, it is also true to call him an animal; and if the former statement is true now, so is the latter. Similarly too if every line contains a point [this will be true of any line at any time]. There is evidence to corroborate this definition; for the objection which we
15 adduce against a proposition which involves 'predication of all' implies either an example to which or a time at which the predicate does not apply.
               (translated by E. S. Forster, Loeb Classical Library)

Petrus Hispanus (Pope John XXI, *Tractatus* (*Summulae logicales*)**, 1:13–15 (ed. L. M. de Rijk 1972, normalized spelling)**

Texts like this one on Categorical Propositions were everyday reading for students in the faculties of arts (cf. p. 63).

De triplici materia categoricarum. Propositionum triplex est materia, scilicet naturalis, contingens, et remota. Naturalis materia est in qua praedicatum est de esse subiecti vel proprium eius, ut *homo est animal,* et *homo est risibilis.* Contingens materia est in qua praedicatum potest adesse vel abesse subiecto, ut *homo est albus, homo non est albus.* Remota materia est illa in qua praedicatum non potest convenire cum subiecto, ut *homo est asinus.*

De aequipollentiis earum. Lex contrariarum talis est quod si una est vera, reliqua est falsa, et non econverso; possunt enim ambae simul esse falsae in contingenti materia, ut *omnis homo est albus, nullus homo est albus.* In naturali materia semper si una est vera, reliqua est falsa, et econverso, ut *omnis homo est animal, nullus homo est animal;* et in remota, ut *omnis homo est asinus, nullus homo est asinus,* et in contingenti, quando praedicatur accidens inseparabile, ut *omnis corvus est niger, nullus corvus est niger;* sed in accidente separabili ambae possunt simul esse falsae. Unde non semper in contingenti materia ambae sunt simul falsae. Lex subcontrariarum talis est quod si una est falsa, reliqua est vera, et non econverso; possunt enim ambae esse simul verae in contingenti materia. Unde lex subcontrariarum contrario modo se habet legi contrariarum. Lex contradictoriarum talis est quod si una est vera, reliqua est falsa, et econverso; in nulla enim materia possunt simul esse verae vel falsae. Lex subalternarum talis est quod si universalis est vera, particularis est vera, et non econverso; potest enim universalis esse falsa, sua particulari existente vera. Et si particularis est falsa, sua universalis est falsa, et non econverso.

De triplici conversione. Item. Propositionum participantium utroque termino ordine converso triplex est conversio, scilicet simplex, per accidens, et per contrapositionem. Simplex conversio est de subiecto facere praedicatum et econverso, manente eadem qualitate et quantitate. Et hoc modo convertitur universalis negativa et particularis affirmativa, ut *nullis homo est lapis – nullis lapis est homo; quidam homo est animal – quoddam animal est homo.* Conversio per accidens est de subiecto facere praedicatum et de praedicato subiectum, etiam manente eadem qualitate, sed mutata quantitate. Et sic convertitur universalis affirmativa in particularem affirmativam, ut *omnis homo est animal – quoddam animal est homo,* et universalis negativa in particularem negativam, ut *nullus homo est lapis – quidam lapis non est homo.*

Fig. 42. From *Expositio hymnorum secundum usum Sarum,* printed by R. Pynson in 1497.

40 Conversio per contrapositionem est facere de subiecto praedicatum et de praedicato subiectum, manente eadem qualitate et
quantitate, sed terminis finitis mutatis in terminos infinitos. Et
hoc modo convertitur universalis affirmativa et particularis negativa, ut *omnis homo est animal – omne non-animal est non-homo;*
45 *quidam homo non est lapis – quidam non-lapis non est non-homo.*

line 1   *categoricum* sc. *propositionum* categorical propositions
    3   *praedicatum,* the logical predicate, the statement
    3   *est de esse* is included in the definition of
    4   *animal* living being (Greek *zoon*)
    4   *risibilis* endowed with the ability to laugh, the charac-
        teristic (*proprium*) of human beings
    8   *aequipollentiis* equivalence
    8   *contriarum* sc. *propositionum* contrary propositions
   14   *accidens inseparabile* a characteristic which is not part of
        the essence of something but which is always present, e.g.
        the black colour of a raven
   18   *subcontrariarum* subcontrary propositions
   21   *contradictoriarum* contradictory propositions
   23   *subalternarum* subalternate propositions
   24   *universalis* universal propositions
   24   *particularis* particular propositions
   27   *propositionum participantium utroque termino* propo-
        sitions in which both terms are common
   29   *per accidens* accidental
   42   *terminus infinitus* an indefinite term which only says what
        something is *not* (e.g. 'non-member')

Thomas Aquinas, *Summa theologiae*, Prima secundae, quaestio 27, articulus 1: 'To what extent is the good sole cause of love' (Ottawa edition 1953)

Ad primum sic proceditur : videtur quod non solum bonum sit causa amoris.

    1. Bonum enim non est causa amoris, nisi quia amatur. Sed contingit etiam malum amari, secundum illud psalmi X (6) 'Qui
5 diligit iniquitatem, odit animam suam'; alioquin omnis amor esset bonus. Ergo non solum bonum est causa amoris.

    2. *Praeterea* Philosophus dicit in secundo Rhetoricae, quod 'eos qui mala sua dicunt amamus'. Ergo videtur quod malum sit causa amoris.

268

3. *Praeterea* Dionysius dicit (quarto capitulo De divinis nominibus), quod 'non solum bonum, sed etiam pulchrum est omnibus amabile'.

Sed contra est, quod Augustinus dicit (octavo De Trinitate): 'Non amatur certe nisi bonum solum'. Ergo bonum est causa amoris.

Respondeo dicendum, quod . . . amor ad appetitivam potentiam pertinet, quae est vis passiva. Unde objectum eius comparatur ad ipsam sicut causa motus vel actus ipsius. Oportet igitur ut illud sit proprie causa amoris, quod est amoris obiectum. Amoris autem proprium obiectum est bonum, quia . . . amor importat quandam connaturalitatem vel complacentiam amantis ad amatum; unicuique autem est bonum id quod est sibi connaturale et proportionatum. Unde relinquitur, quod bonum sit propria causa amoris.

Ad primum ergo dicendum, quod malum numquam amatur nisi sub ratione boni, scilicet inquantum est secundum quid bonum, et apprehenditur ut simpliciter bonum. Et sic aliquis amor est malus, inquantum tendit in id quod non est simpliciter verum bonum. Et per hunc modum homo diligit iniquitatem, inquantum per iniquitatem adipiscitur aliquod bonum, puta delectationem vel pecuniam vel aliquid huiusmodi.

Ad secundum dicendum, quod illi qui mala sua dicunt, non propter mala amantur, sed propter hoc quod dicunt mala; hoc enim quod est dicere mala sua, habet rationem boni, inquantum excludit fictionem seu simultaionem.

Ad tertium dicendum quod pulchrum est idem bono, sola ratione differens. Cum enim bonum sit quod omnia appetunt, de ratione boni est quod in eo quietetur appetitus; sed ad rationem pulchri pertinet quod in eius aspectu seu cognitione quietetur appetitus. Unde et illi sensus praecipue respiciunt pulchrum, qui maxime cognoscitivi sunt, scilicet visus et auditus rationi deservientes; dicimus enim pulchra visibilia et pulchros sonos. In sensibilibus autem aliorum sensuum non utimur nomine pulchritudinis; non enim dicimus pulchros sapores aut odores. Et sic patet, quod pulchrum addit supra bonum quendam ordinem ad vim cognoscitivam; ita quod bonum dicatur id quod simpliciter complacet appetitui; pulchrum autem dicatur id, cuius ipsa apprehensio placet.

line 16   *appetitiva potentia* the drives in their widest meaning
     17   *vis passiva*, a passive function which is activated by some influence from outside

17 *Unde . . . ipsius* 'Therefore these objects can be said to be in the same relationship to this function as the cause and object of motion (are related to the object in motion)'.

20 *importat* implies

21 *connaturalitatem vel complacentiam* natural agreement and attraction

22 *proportionatum* in the right proportions

26 *sub ratione boni* with regard to the good

26 *inquantum* insofar as

26 *secundum quid – simpliciter* under certain conditions – in itself

34 *habet rationem boni* has a good aspect

36 *sola ratione differens* the concepts only differ conceptually (the 'rational distinction')

37 '*Bonum est quod omnia appetunt*' is a definition of what is good in the first book of Aristotle's *Nichomachean Ethics*

37 *de ratione boni est* is contained in the definition of 'what is good'

39 *quietetur* is satisfied

41 *rationi deservientes* which serve reason

Auctoritates Aristotelis (a selection from *Les auctoritates Aristotelis*, ed. J. Hamesse 1974)

Auctoritates Aristotelis *is a collection of quotations taken mainly from Aristotle's writings and from Averroes, Boethius, Seneca, Apuleius, Plato's Timaeus dialogue and Porphyry. They were used in disputations in the late scholastic period as a permanent collection of axiomatic propositions with which it was possible to prove one's own theses. Each thesis could be shown to be the correct conclusion from premises stated in the* auctoritates. *The quotations in this florilegium come in the order in which they are to be found in the original texts and it is a fascinating mixture of observations from daily life,* bon mots, *metaphysical theories and pure tautologies. Some of these 'authorities' have become proverbs in modern languages ('Nothing comes of nothing', 'One swallow doesn't make a summer', 'Needs know no laws'), while others contain technical terms which because of the teaching in the universities have become part of our everyday speech* (vacuum, in infinitum, primus motor, animal politicum, hic et nunc, in fieri, '*second nature*', '*the lesser of two evils*').

Omnes homines naturaliter scire desiderant.

Signum scientis est posse docere.

Quattuor sunt causae, scilicet materialis, formalis, efficiens et finalis.

Finis scientiae speculativae veritas est, practicae vero opus.

Nulla ars particularis probat suum subiectum esse, sed supponit ipsum esse.

Singularium nec est scientia, neque definitio, quia quando recedunt a sensu, tunc non est certum aut manifestum utrum sint vel non sint.

Eadem est scientia contrariorum.

A primo principio dependet caelum et tota natura.

Contra negantem principia non est disputandum.

Ex nihilo nihil fit.

Ars imitatur naturam inquantum potest.

Natura agit propter finem.

Non est vacuum in natura.

Tempus est mensura motus rerum mobilium.

In moventibus et motis non est ire in infinitum, et ergo necesse est devenire ad primum motorem.

Deus et natura nihil faciunt frustra.

Oportet inquisitores veritatis non esse inimicos.

Natura desiderat semper quod melius est.

Melius est esse quam non esse.

Anima est principium quo primo et principaliter vivimus, intelligimus, sentimus et movemur secundum locum.

Anima est quodammodo omnia.

Necesse est quemcumque intelligentem phantasmata speculari.

Meditationes memoriam salvant.

Consuetudo est altera natura.

Natura dat unicuique quod sibi conveniens est.

Quicquid potest causa secunda, potest et causa prima, nobiliori et altiori tamen modo.

Quicquid recipitur ab alio, recipitur per modum rei accipeintis et non receptae.

Felicitas est perfectio animae secundum virtutem perfectam.

Sicut una hirundo non facit ver, nec una dies calida aestatem, sic nec una dies vel modicum tempus facit hominem felicem.

Ex actibus multum iteratis fit habitus.

Ignorantia excusat peccatum.

Quod primum est in intentione, hoc debet ultimum esse in exsecutione.

Nos sumus domini nostrarum operationum a principio usque ad finem.

45 In repentinis cognoscitur habitus.
Malum se ipsum destruit.
Requies et ludus in vita videntur esse necessaria.
Minus malum est magis eligibile maiori malo.
Non solum oportet verum dicere, sed et causam falsi assignare.
50 Delectationi intellectuali non est admixta tristitia.
Parentes amant filios suos ut aliquid existens sui.
Parentes plus amant filios quam e converso.
In actibus humanis minus creditur sermonibus quam operibus.
Delectatio tenet operantem in opere.
55 Speculatio ipsius veritatis est ipsa veritas.
Homo naturaliter est animal politicum et civile.
Silentium mulieri praestat ornatum.
Civitas non est una propter eosdem mores, sed propter eandem politiam.
60 Non est idem bonus homo et bonus civis.
Nulla ars considerat particulare, quia particularia sunt infinita et non scibilia.
Oblivio est signum parvipensionis.
Contraria iuxta se posita magis apparent.
65 Necessitas non habet legem.
Infinita, inquit Plato, relinquenda sunt ab arte, neque horum fieri posse disciplinam, id est scientiam, unde quia individua sunt infinita, de eis non potest esse scientia.
Accidens est quod adest vel abest praeter subiecti corruptionem.
70 Dubitare de singulis non est inutile.
De futuris contingentibus non est determinata veritas.
Propter nostrum affirmare vel negare nihil sequitur in re.
Singulare est hic et nunc, sed universale est ubique et semper.
Causa et effectus debent esse proportionata, unde eius, quod est in
75 fieri, debet esse causa in fieri, et eius, quod est in facto esse, debet esse causa in facto esse.
Non contingit res ipsas nobiscum ferre ad disputationem, sed in disputationibus nominibus pro rebus utimur.

line 3 *Quattuor causae*, cf. p. 118.
      6 *subiectum* subject
      6 *supponit* presumes
     15 *inquantum* insofar as
     19 *non est ire* it is impossible that motion takes place
     26 *secundum locum* in the room
     28 *phantasmata* concrete images
     31 *sibi* for that which is concerned

34   *Quicquid* . . . roughly: 'everything is received in accordance with the capacity of the receiver'
39   *habitus* cf. p. 179
59   *politiam* cf. p. 183
61   *particulare* the individual thing
63   *parvipensionis* disdain
67   *individua* the indivisible units, the individuals
69   *subiecti* the supporter's, in other words the substance's (cf. p. oo)
70   *dubitare* be doubtful about (cf. p. 82)
71   *De futuris contingentibus* cf. p. 63
74   *in fieri, in facto esse,* in the making, fully developed

Paulus Niavis: *A conversation about the syllabus at the University of Leipzig (Latinum ydeoma pro novellis studentibus,* **ed. G. Streckenbach in** *Mittellateinisches Jahrbuch* **7 (1972), pp. 198ff.: slightly abbreviated, normalized spelling)**

Paulus Niavis's (Paul Schneevogel) manual in Latin conversation was compiled around the year 1482 and provides us with valuable glimpses of the academic milieu at the University of Leipzig (cf. p. 258).

Quomodo discipuli de exercitiis lectionibusque loquantur.

Camillus: Mi Bartolde, scis tu, quot lectiones ad baccalauriatus gradum et exercitia complere opportuerit?
Bartoldus: Optime scio, nam lectiones sunt novem, exercitia sex.
5 *C:* Et quo pacto complentur, scisne?
B: Quidni? Nam tripartitae sunt et lectiones et exercitia. Itaque in tribus mutationibus quis integre complere poterit, id est in spatio anni cum dimidio; nempe in una mutatione tres lectiones duoque exercitia recipere ac audire necesse est, qui cito promoveri
10 voluerit.
C: Ego tecum una proficiscar, cum complete volueris, ad audiendum huiuscemodi libros. Sed audi: unum est, quod abs te scire volo! Nam ferunt, si in principio ac fine lectionum fuerimus, sat est pro completione, et si voluerimus medio tempore ter quaterve
15 intrabimus.
B: Cur hoc? Qualis illa completio esset?
C: Dicunt enim nihil nos percipere in lectionibus, praesertim in altioribus libris, utpote Physicorum et consimilibus; sed cum ad promotionem pervenerit, nobiscum dispensabitur.

20   *B:* Erras vehementer! Nam facultatis artium magistri ita in-
stituerunt, ut quemque, priusquam admittatur, affirmare oportet
iuramento, qualiter audiverit quotiensque neglexerit. Quondam
erat, ut permulti promovebantur, qui rarissime fuerunt in lectionibus; proinde magnam susceperunt pecuniam pro tali negleg-
25   entia. Sed notabant maiores nostri dissolutionem scholarium et
proficere vel nullos vel paucos. Statuerunt nunc, ut quis audiat
compleatque diligentissime.

    C: Atqui grave est, prope dixerim molestum, semper adesse;
timeo me non facturum.

30   *B:* Cupis promoveri? Non possis subterfugere.

    C: Dicam me affuisse.

    B: Et eris periurus. Verum enimvero robustae complexionis es;
non repente periurium in facie tua denotabitur.

    C: De hoc satis. Dic, a quibus audiemus?

35   *B:* Vidi intimatum hodie magistrum N. libros Elenchorum
propre valvam in auditorio hora sexta, ut arbitror, ante meridiem.
Septima vero audituri sumus in eodem libros Physicorum a
magistro Conrado, et post meridiem in libris De anima a magistro
N. lectio fiet in paedagogio.

40   *C:* Recte narras. Memoriae ista mandabo, ut, tu cum ire volueris,
paratus sim. Quid tum de exercitiis sentis?

    B: Magister meus parva logicalia disputabit in sua habitatione;
illic affuero; et Veterem artem magister Nicolaus; similiter me
applicabo.

45   *C:* Optime sentis. Ceterum quas audiemus resumptiones?

    B: Nondum deliberavi. At scrutinium quoddam et quidem
diligens habebo, quoniam plurimi sunt, quibus visum est
maiorem assequi scholares utilitatem in resumptionibus quam aut
in lectionibus aut exercitiis. Nam si quippiam magister
50   Vincentius resumeret, certe non neglegerem, est enim facundus.
Persuasivus quasi res ageretur mihi apparet, cum aliquid in
apertum ducit.

    C: Et eadem est mihi sententia de hac re. Nullum oculis meis
conspicatus sum magistrum, qui rem abditam maximeque oc-
55   cultam tam pulcre tamque lucide posset detegere et simplices tam
facile primum instruere. Te oratum facio, Bartolde, sic te
accingas, ne unquam negotium aliquod impedimento sit, quin
semper et frequentia quadam in eius simus resumptione.

line   I   *Exercitiis lectionibusque* (series of) exercises (practice
      disputations on selected *quaestiones*) and lectures
    3   *complere* 'sit out', meet the demands of attendance

7	*mutationibus* terms
9	*recipere* enrol oneself for
13	*sat est pro completione* one complies with the demands of attendance
19	*nobiscum dispensabitur* we shall be granted exemption
24	*susceperunt pecuniam* earned money (because of his bachelor's degree)
32	*complexionis* 'admixture of fluids', or, in other words, physiognomy (cf. p. 150)
35	*intimatum* . . . an announcement that master N was going to lecture
39	*paedagogio* one of the school buildings in Leipzig
42	*parva logicalia* pamphlets on logic (cf. p. 258)
42	*in sua habitatione* in his home (as a 'private college')
43	*Veterem artem* the 'old' logic (cf. p. 55)
43	*similiter me applicabo* I intend to be there as well
45	*resumptiones* revision courses

Petrus Tataretus, *Expositio super textu logices Aristotelis*, printed in Paris in 1500 (normalized spelling) Has Sortes as many fatherhoods as he has sons?

The master, Petrus Tataretus, was one of the objects of Rabelais' ruthless mockery and can serve as one of the most typical representatives of Scotism. He was active at the University of Paris around the year 1500. This quaestio *is related to the chapter on relationship in Aristotle's* Categories *and deals with the possible (one often formulated by the enemies of the Scotists) objection that to talk about the multiplicity of 'forms' in an individual substance demands in reality that one describe the substance as several elements. If Sortes (the abbreviated form of Socrates, which corresponds to John Doe) as a result of the fact that he has several sons really does bear several different 'forms' (his fatherhoods), is he not then in reality several fathers? Practice in the Scotist school at dealing with similar questions helped to make Latin into a flexible tool for abstract reasoning.*

Dubitatur tertio utrum Sortes habens plures filios habeat tot paternitates quot habet filios.

Et *arguitur primo* quod non, quia sequeretur, quod idem homo esset plures patres; sed consequens est falsum: igitur, etcetera. Consequentia probatur, quia sicut pater una paternitate dicitur pater, ita etiam et alia paternitate dicitur pater, et cum sint plures paternitates, sequitur quod dicetur plures patres.

Secundo sic: impossibile est plura accidentia solo numero differentia esse in eodem subiecto: ergo plures paternitates non
10 possunt esse in eodem.

Sed *in oppositum arguitur :* Quia correlativa sunt simul natura et posita se ponunt et perempta se perimunt, ergo destructo uno filio, ad quem pater refertur, destruetur una paternitas.

Sed ipse est pater respectu alterius filii : ergo in ipso erunt plures
15 paternitates.

Respondetur breviter ad dubium, quod tot sunt paternitates in Sorte quot habet filios, et sic albedo habet tot similitudines quot sunt albedines in mundo, et hoc non est inconveniens.

Ad rationes : ad *primam* dicitur, quod licet sint plures paternitates,
20 non tamen est plures patres. Et ponitur talis regula: ad multiplicationem concretorum non sufficit multiplicatio formarum, sed requiritur plurificatio suppositorum. Et quia Sortes non est plura supposita, ideo, licet habeat plures paternitates, non tamen dicitur plures patres, sicut licet Sortes habeat plures scientias, non tamen
25 propter hoc dicitur plures scientes. Ponitur adhuc alia regula, quod ad multiplicationem concretorum non requiritur multiplicatio formarum, sed sufficit multiplicatio suppositorum, ut si una albedo esset in pluribus rebus, illae res decerentur plura alba.

Ad *secundam* dicitur, quod verum est de accidentibus absolutis,
30 quae acquiruntur per verum motum et transmutationem, sicut est caliditas. Et si quis dicat: 'In aqua est caliditas, et tamen ibi sunt plures caliditates acquisitae per verum motum et transmutationem', dicitur quod omnes illae caliditates dicuntur facere unam totalem caliditatem, et non sunt ibi divisae. Et sic esse plura
35 accidentia absoluta eiusdem rationis in eodem subiecto non est inconveniens.

line 3   *arguitur* it can be objected

     4   *consequens* the consequence

     4   *igitur* therefore the questions must be answered in the negative

     5   *Consequentia* the logical implications, the logical consistency

     7   *dicetur :* the future simple is the normal tense used in formal deductions

     8   *plura accidentia solo numero differentia :* several accidentals of exactly the same kind which differ from each other only in being different 'individuals'

    10   *in eodem subiecto :* in the same 'supporter', in other words in the same substance

11 *in oppositum* in the opposite direction
11 *correlativa* things which are in mutual relationship to each other
12 *posita se ponunt et perempta se perimunt:* roughly: they presuppose the existence of each other (Aristotle, *Categories* 7, 7b 15ff.)
17 *albedo* whiteness (as an abstraction)
18 *albedines* the concrete realizations of whiteness, 'whitenesses'
19 *Ad rationes* against these objections
21 *concretorum* concrete objects
21 *formarum* metaphysical forms, the Scotist 'formalities'. Every individual accidental in a substance implies a new 'form'
22 *plurificatio* multiplication
22 *suppositorum* individual substances which are self-contained wholes, e.g. persons
24 *habeat plures scientias* knows several sciences (every individual science is a new 'form') (cf. p. 241)
25 *plures scientes* several scientists or scholars
29 *verum est* the objection is correct
29 *de accidentibus absolutis* concerning the absolute accidentals (but not the relative ones such as relationship, activity, passivity for instance, which unlike the absolute accidentals presuppose the mutual relationship of two things. Warmth, a quality, does not presuppose any relationship between two things)
30 *motum et transmutationem* alteration and transformation
35 *eiusdem rationis* of exactly the same nature (and only distinct because of the characteristics of being different 'individuals')

Martin Luther: *Disputation against scholastic theology* (**in selection; Weimar edition, 1, 1883, pp. 224–8**)

As dean of the faculty of theology Luther presided at a disputation in Wittenburg on 4 September 1517. The respondent was called Franz Günther. As was the practice, the presiding scholar had composed the theses. The title conclusiones *suggests that these theses were the conclusions drawn from syllogisms and they were proved in the disputation by formulating the premises that led to them. The task of the opponent was to demonstrate faults in the formulation of the premises or in the forms of the syllogisms. The ninety-seven theses here aroused little attention, unlike the ninety-five theses about indulgences which Luther was to make public two months later.*

Ad subscriptas conclusiones respondebit magister Franciscus Guntherus Nordhusensis pro biblia, praesidente reverendo patre Martino Luthero Augustiniano, sacrae theologiae Vuittenbergensi decano, loco et tempore statuendis.

5   5. Falsitas est quod appetitus liber potest in utrumque oppositorum, immo nec liber sed captivus est. Contra communem.
   31. Vanissimo commento dicitur: praedestinatus potest damnari in sensu diviso sed non in composito. Contra scholasticos.
   35. Non est verum quod ignorantia invincibilis a toto excusat.
10   Contra omnes scholasticos.
   39. Non sumus domini actuum nostrorum a principio usque in finem, sed servi. Contra Philosophum.
   40. Non efficimur iusti operando, sed iusti facti operamur iusta. Contra Philosophum.
15 41. Tota fere Aristotelis Ethica pessima est et gratiae inimica. Contra scholasticos.
   43. Error est dicere: sine Aristotele non fit theologus. Contra dictum commune.
   46. Frustra fingitur logica fidei, suppositio immediata extra
20   terminum et numerum. Contra recentes dialecticos.
   47. Nulla forma syllogistica tenet in terminis divinis. Contra cardinalem.
   49. Si forma syllogistica tenet in divinis, articulus trinitatis erit scitus et non creditus.
25 50. Breviter totus Aristoteles ad theologiam es tenebrae ad lucem. Contra scholasticos.
   52. Bonum erat ecclesiae si theologis natus non fuisset Porphyrius cum suis universalibus.
   53. Usitatiores definitiones Aristotelis videntur petere
30   principium.
In his nihil dicere volumus nec dixisse nos credimus quod non sit catholicae ecclesiae et ecclesiasticis doctoribus consentaneum.
1517.

line 2 *pro biblia* for the degree (of Bachelor) in theology
     3 *Augustiniano* member of the order of Augustinian Hermits (Austin Friars)

5   *potest in utrumque oppositorum* can choose either of the two opposites at all. An Aristotelian definition of the freedom of the will

6   *Contra communem* sc. *opinionem*

8   *in sensu diviso, in sensu composito* if the subject refers to another time than the predicate or, in the second case, to the same time. 'Someone who was once predestined (to eternal bliss) can be damned' or 'Someone who is predestined can, while he is predestined, be damned' (cf. p. 97)

9   *ignorantia invincibilis* ignorance about a rule or a fact even though one attempted as far as was normal to find out about the laws prevailing and circumstances as they were. According to an Aristotelian maxim, which was taken over by scholastic moral theology, such ignorance freed the individual from all responsibility (cf. p. 271)

11   *domini actuum* cf. p. 209 and 271

13   *efficimur iusti iusta operando* we acquire the *habitus* of righteousness by carrying out righteous actions

19   *suppositio immediata* a 'supposition' beyond that of normal language in concerning terms and number with reference to the Trinity (cf. p. 251)

21   *tenet* holds

21   *terminis divinis* the persons of the Trinity

22   *cardinalem*, sc. *Caietanum* Cardinal Thomas de Vio Caietanus, a commentator on Thomas Aquinas' *Summa theologica*

23   *articulus* article of faith

29   *petere principium* start from that which is to be demonstrated, begging the question (cf. p. 97)

Juan Luis Vives: *Against the so-called logicians (Adversus pseudodialecticos,* **printed in 1520)**

Juan Luis Vives, 1492–1540, a Spanish humanist and teacher, attacked scholasticism violently and pointed out the areas of learning it had ignored: knowledge of society, moral philosophy, history, and the classical languages in their 'pristine purity'. He attacks here his fellow-countryman Petrus Hispanus for his 'barbaric' Latin and because he introduced novelties which the classical philosophers did not deal with, and for the general lack of 'social relevance' in scholastic attitudes. Apart from one or two exceptions, the humanists showed no understanding of the schoolmen's formal exercises in thinking and the need for a specialized language in which they could be expressed.

Quis, quaeso, auctoritatem hanc dedit Petro Hispano, ut novas ferret leges in lingua, quam ne de facie quidem norat, cuius etiam si nonnulla vocabula pronuntiabat, vim tamen cuiusquam verbi non magis scivit, quam ille, de quo modo loquebar, Scyta vim
5 sermonis Hispani, cuius nec verbum vel scriptum legit vel prolatum a quoquam audivit? Quod ego sane hominis non dico fuisse vitium, sed illorum temporum. Modestiam tamen ipsius, ut aliorum permultorum, requiro, qui sua placita, sua plus quam pueriliter somniata, volebant ilico pro lege esse in lingua ipsis
10 ignotissima. Ac voluissem iuxta vetus praeceptum, ut sese novissent nec pelliculam excessissent suam, ne in eos protinus iactatum esset illud ex trivio, quod iam fit passim, 'Ne sutor ultra crepidam'. Verum ego a Petro isto Hispano, quamlibet nostrati, seu ab eo qui nobis hanc tam elegantem dialecticam peperit – nam
15 sunt qui putent haec primum in Britannia aut Hibernia orta, deinde Parisiis alita atque aucta – ab illo igitur, quisquis tandem fuit, pervelim audire, cur cum ipse suppositiones et expositiones illarum enuntiationum, atque horum similia, quae traduntur in parum logicalibus, numquam a Boethio acceperit, Aristoteles ipse
20 non praecipiat, tam impudenter illa confinxerit et praescripserit sensus profatorum contra rationem omnem sermonis latini?
In alium quendam orbem perductos eos esse credas, ita usum vitae et communem sensum ignorant. Ita impeditos, ita implicitos eos videas, sive quid agant, sive loquantur, ut illos non esse
25 homines iures. Adeo sicut sermo, ita et mores et actus omnes ab homine abhorrent, ut nihil illis cum ceteris hominibus commune praeter formam iudices. Hinc quoque fit, ut negotiis gerendis, legationibus obeundis, administrandis rebus aut publicis aut privatis, tractandis populorum animis ineptissimi sint, non plus in
30 eiusmodi rebus valeant, quam homines fenei. Neque enim iis sese artibus tradunt, quibus haec omnia percipiuntur, quae et animum et vitam humanam instituunt, cuiusmodi est philosophia moralis, quae mores mentemque ornat; historia, quae mater est rerum cognitionis et usus, id est prudentiae; oratoria, quae vitam
35 sensumque communem docet et moderatur; politica facultas et oeconomica, quibus civitatum rerumque familiarium status et regimen constat. Iam satis superque quingentos fere per annos multa mala mentibus hominum invexerunt. Tempus est, ut simul cum lingua latina, id est cum suo seminario, reliquae quoque artes

280

40 tam diu sopitae excitentur. Haec opinionum commenta, ut inquit
Cicero, delebit dies, naturae iudicia confirmabit. Non semper cum
hominibus male agetur. Tempus ipsum prava convellet, recta
veraque secum inferet. Itaque non egent haec tam inania multis
magnisque oppugnatoribus ut pereant: ipsa, ut sunt ficta, ut
45 adumbrata, ut nihil habent solidi, nihil firmi, ita paulatim per se
decident dissolventurque, et memoria rerum istarum simul ac in
scholis homines sapere melius coeperint, tota prorsus conticescet
ac interibit.

line 12   *illud ex trivio* well-known proverb from the *trivium* (*Ne
sutor* . . . Pliny the elder, *Naturalis historia*, 35, 85)
    17   *suppositiones et expositiones* suppositions (cf. p. 234) and
theories about the deeper structure of propositions
    18   *in parum logicalibus* an ironic reference to the genre called
parva logicalia (cf. p. 258)
    21   *profatorum* axioms
    30   *quam homines fenei* than any dunce at all
    41   *Cicero* De natura deorum 2, 5

Comentaria Iaco/ bi de Marquilles super vsaticis barchiñ.

Notes and References

It has not been possible to cite evidence for every piece of information or the provenance of every quotation. Those interested are referred to the following works, all of which are more or less readily available:

R. R. Bolgar, *The Classical Heritage and its Beneficiaries* 1954 (1973).

A. B. Cobban, *The Medieval Universities: their Development and Organization* 1975.

F. C. Copleston, *A History of Medieval Philosophy* (includes a bibliography) 1972.

E. Grant, *Physical Science in the Middle Ages* 1970.

C. H. Haskins, *The Renaissance of the Twelfth Century* 1927 (1976).

G. Leff, *Medieval Thought: St Augustine to Ockham* 1958 (1970).

G. E. R. Lloyd, *Aristotle: The Growth and Structure of his Thought* 1968 (1973).

A. A. Luce, *Logic* (Teach Yourself Books) 1958 (1976).

M. Müller and A. Halder, *Kleines Philosophisches Wörterbuch* (Herderbücherei vol. 398), 5th ed., 1976.

W. Ullman, *Medieval Political Thought* 1965 (1975).

1. Augustine, *De doctrina christiana* 2, 60, in Corpus christianorum XXXII: IV, 1 (Turnhout 1962).
2. Isidore of Seville, *Etymologiarum, Libri XX*, ed. W. M. Lindsay (Oxford 1911), 1.
3. Cassiodorus, *Institutiones* 1, 30, ed. R. A. B. Mynors (Oxford 1937).
4. Alcuin, *Epistolae* 170, in *Monumenta Germaniae historica* Epist. IV: 2, p. 279.

Fig. 43.   From James of Maquilles, *A Commentary on the Usages of Barcelona.*

5. Donatus, *Ars grammatica*, in *Grammatici latini*, ed. H. Keil (Leipzig 1864), 4, p. 355.
6. Ibid., p. 401ff.
7. Alcuin, *De dialectica* (*Patrologia Latina* 101, 952–3, hereafter referred to as *PL*).
8. Isaac de Stella, *Sermones*, 51 (*PL* 194, 1862).
9. *Glossa ordinaria* on Gospel according to St Matthew 7:6 (Holy Bible with *glossa ordinaria*, vol. 5, col. 146, Antwerp 1617).
10. Hrabanus Maurus, *Enarrationes in epistolas Pauli* 15, 4 (*PL* 112, 331) (extracts from the Epistle of St Paul to the Galatians 4:22–6).
11. Virgil *Eclogues* 4, 5–7.
12. Hrabanus Maurus, *De clericorum institutione* 3, 18 (*PL* 107, 396).
13. Conrad of Hirsau, *Dialogus super auctores*, ed. R. B. C. Huygens, Collection Latomus 17 (1955), pp. 52–3.
14. Adam of Bremen, *Gesta Hammaburgensis ecclesiae pontificum* 3, 5, in *Monumenta Germania historica*, Scriptores 7, p. 337.
15. Bernard of Clairvaux, *Sermones super Cantica canticorum* 1, 6, 11, in *S. Bernhardi opera*, 1 (Rome 1957).
16. Smaragdus, *Diadema monachorum* 3 (*PL* 102, 597–8).
17. Hugo of St Victor, *Eruditio didascalica* (*PL* 176, 742d).
18. John of Salisbury, *Metalogicon* 3, 4, ed. C. C. J. Webb (London 1932), p. 136.
19. Ibid. 1, 24 (pp. 55, 57).
20. Ibid. 1, 23 (pp. 52–3).
21. Pseudo-Soranus, *Quaestiones medicinales*, in V. Rose *Anecdota Graeca et Graecolatina* 2 (Berlin 1870), p. 245.
22. Ibid., pp. 255–74.
23. Pierre Abélard, *Historia calamitatum*, in H. Rüthing, *Die mittelalterliche Universität* (Göttingen 1973), p. 10.
24. Porphyry, *Isagoge, translatio Boethii*, ed. L. Minio-Paluello, *Aristoteles Latinus I, 6–7 Categoriarum supplementa* (1966), p. 5.
25. *Digesta* 1, 1, 1–10 in Mommsen-Krueger (ed.), *Corpus iuris civilis* 1 (Berlin 1922), p. 29.
26. *Stemmatis Bulgarici epitome*, quaestio *LXI*, in H. Kantorowicz, *Studies in the Glossators of the Roman Law* (1938), p. 251.
27. Ibid., *quaestio XXXII*, p. 248.
28. G. Otte, *Dialektik und Jurisprudenz. Untersuchungen zur Methode der Glossatoren* (1971), p. 105.

284

29. Ibid., p. 107.
30. Ibid., p. 147.
31. Ibid., p. 205.
32. Bernold of Constance, *De Sacramentis excommunicatorum* (*PL* 148, 1214).
33. Gratian, *Decreti prima pars, distinctio I, C. I–II*, ed Richter-Friedberg, I, col. 1.
34. Lanfranc, *In omnes Pauli epistolas commentari* (*PL* 150, 207–12).
35. Anselm of Canterbury, *Monologium*, prologue to chapter 4, in *Collana di testi filosofici* I:1 (Padua 1951), pp. 1–2, 10–11.
36. Pierre Abélard, *Sic et Non* (*PL* 178, 1349).
37. Bernard of Clairvaux, *Epistolae* (*PL* 182, 355).
38. Ibid. 353.
39. Conrad of Hirsau, *Dialogus super auctores*, op. cit., p. 19.
40. Hugo of St Victor, *Eruditio didascalica* (*PL* 176, 769d).
41. Peter Lombard, *Libri quattuor Sententiarum III*, 24, 3, ed. Ad Claras Aquas (1916), 2, pp. 663–4.
42. Dante, *Il Paradiso* X, 103–108, trans. Dorothy L. Sayers and Barbara Reynolds (Penguin 1962), p. 138.
43. John of Salisbury, *Metalogicon* 4, 6, ed. C. C. J. Webb (London 1932), pp. 170–1.
44. Author's summary.
45. Author's summary.
46. Author's summary.
47. John of Salisbury, *Metalogicon* 2, 7, ed. C. C. J. Webb (London 1932), pp. 72–3.
48. Rüthing, op. cit., p. 19.
49. H. Koeppler, 'Frederick Barbarossa and the Schools of Bologna', in *The English Historical Review* 54 (1939), p. 607.
50. Peter Lombard, *Libri quattuor Sententiarum IV*, 12, 1, ed. Ad Claras Aquas (1916), 2, p. 808.
51. Gentilis de Fulgineo, *Quaestio de actuatione medicinarum* (Perugia 1339), printed and published with Avicenna's *Canon* (*Fen quarta primi*) (Venice 1503).
52. Bonaventura, *Breviloqium*, prologues 3, 2, in *Opera omnia* (Quaracchi 1882–1902), vol. 5, p. 205.
53. Idem, *De scientia Christi* 4, in ibid., p. 23b.
54. Idem, *In Hexaemeron* 4, in ibid., p. 349.
55. Albertus Magnus, *De animalibus*, in *Opera omnia*, ed. A. Borgnet (Paris 1890), vol. 12, p. 500.
56. Thomas Aquinas, *Quaestiones quodlibetales* 4, 18.
57. Roger Bacon, *Fratris Rogeri Baconi Compendium studii*

theologiae, ed. H. Rashdall (British Society of Franciscan Studies, Aberdeen 1911), 3, p. 34.

58. Thomas Aquinas, *Summa theologiae* I, q. 1, a. 2.
59. Ibid., I, q. 13, a. 5c.
60. Ibid. I, q. 1, a. 8.
61. Ibid. I, q. 46, a. 1c.
62. Ibid. I, q. 2, a. 3c.
63. Ibid. I, q. 75, a. 6c.
64. Ibid. I, q. 78, a. 4c.
65. Ibid. I–II, q. 90, a. 1c.
66. Ibid. I–II, q. 108, a. 2 ad 1.
67. Ibid. I, q. 82, a. 2c.
68. Ibid. I–II, q. 62, a. 1c.
69. Ibid. III, q. 77, a. 1c.
70. Ibid. I–II, q. 105, a. 1c.
71. *Es tu scolaris?* in J. J. Baebler, *Beiträge zu einer Geschichte der lateinischen Grammatik im Mittelalter* (1885), pp. 189–92.
72. Thomas Aquinas, *Summa theologiae* II–II, q. 49, a. 1 ad 2.
73. Boethius of Dacia, *De summo bono* in *Corpus philosophorum Danicorum medii aevi* VI. II, p. 370.
74. P. Mandonnet, *Siger de Brabant et l'averroïsme latin* (Louvain, 1908), 2, pp. 176–91.
75. Petrus Hispanus, *Tractatus*, ed. L. de Rijk (1972), p. 277.
76. John Duns Scotus, *Reportata Parisiensia* III, q. 1, n. 11.
77. Idem, *De primo principio*, cap. 4.
78. William Occam, *Quaestiones in quartum Sententiarum*, q. 9.
79. L. Thorndike, *University Records and Life in the Middle Ages* (1944), pp. 296–7.
80. Paulus Niavis, *Latinum ydeoma pro novellis studentibus*, ed. G. Streckenbach, *Mittelateinisches Jahrbuch* 7 (1972), pp. 187ff.

Fig. 44.   From a calendar for the year 1478.

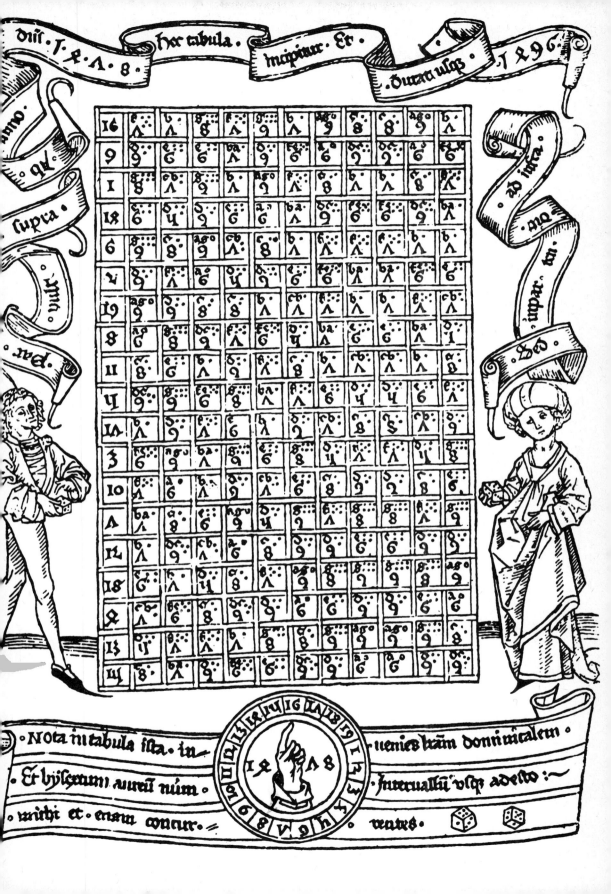

European universities until the year 1500. The dates indicate the
year in which a charter was granted (dates in brackets indicate the
first mention of the university in a written source)

288

Chronology

392	Christianity becomes the official religion of the Roman Empire
420	St Jerome, translator of the Bible, 'Father of the Church'
430	St Augustine, theologian, philosopher, 'Father of the Church'
476	The last Roman Emperor is deposed by the barbarians
524	Boethius, translator and commentator on the 'old' logic, dies
547	St Benedict of Nursia, father of western monasticism, dies
c. 580	Cassiodorus compiles the knowledge of antiquity
636	St Isidore of Seville writes *Etymologies*
715	The Arabs masters of Spain
735	The Venerable Bede, exegetist, philologist, historian, astronomer, dies
796	Alcuin, the architect of the Carolingian educational reform, dies
768–814	Charlemagne's reign. Organization of the school system and the establishment of fixed syllabuses
1037	Avicenna, physician and philosopher, dies
1087	Constantine the African, translated medical literature from Greek and Arabic, dies
1121	Abélard's *Sic et Non*
1121–1158	The 'new' logic becomes available in Latin
c. 1125	Irnerius, the father of scientific jurisprudence, dies
1140	Gratian's *Decree*
1145	Al-Khwarizmi's *Algebra* is translated into Latin
c. 1150	Petrus Lombardus' *Sentences*
1158	Frederick Barbarossa grants a charter to the University of Bologna
1167	Birth of Oxford as a *studium generale*
1195	Averroes, 'the Commentator', dies

1200	Philippe II Augustus grants a charter to the University of Paris
1204	The Fourth Crusade. Greek manuscripts become available
1208	St Dominic founds the Order of Preachers (the Dominicans)
1209	The first Franciscans appear
1220	*Universitas medicorum* in Montpellier granted a charter
1224	University in Naples
1227	University in Salamanca
1229	University in Toulouse
1231	Papal Bull *Parens scientiarum* consolidates the position of the University of Paris
1233	Papal recognition of Cambridge
c. 1235	Petrus Hispanus writes the compendium in logic called *Tractatus*
1230–1250	Averroes becomes available in a Latin translation
1240	Robert Grosseteste translates the *Nichomachean Ethics* into Latin
c. 1240	John of Holywood writes the textbook in astronomy *Sphaera*
1245–1246	Albertus Magnus teaches in Paris
c. 1250	The manufacture of paper begins in Italy
1252–1259	Thomas Aquinas teaches in Paris
1260	William de Moerbeke translates Aristotle's *Politics* into Latin
1265	Thomas Aquinas begins *Summa theologica*
c.1270	The whole of Aristotle available in direct translations from Greek
1274	Bonaventura and Thomas Aquinas die
1277	219 ˙ philosophical propositions condemned by Bishop Tempier in Paris
1308	John Duns Scotus dies
1323	Thomas Aquinas canonized
1337	Occamism condemned in Paris
1347	University in Prague
1349	William of Occam dies
1364	University in Cracow
1365	University in Vienna
1385	University in Heidelberg
1388	University in Cologne
1409	The German nation from Prague settle in Leipzig

1419	University in Rostock
1424	The first professor of Greek in Bologna
1425	University in Louvain
1431	Pope Eugene IV introduces study of the humanities at the University of Rome
1450	Gutenberg opens his printing house in Mainz
1453	Constantinople falls to the Turks. New manuscripts in Greek arrive in western Europe
1456	University in Greifswald
1465	Fust and Schöffer print Cicero's *De officiis* in Mainz
1466	First professor of Greek in Paris
1470	The first book printed in Paris
1476	The first book printed in Greek in Milan
1477	University in Uppsala
1478	University in Copenhagen
1506	Reuchlin publishes a textbook in Hebrew
1516	Erasmus has the New Testament printed in Greek
1517	Luther's theses against scholastic theology and against indulgences
1540	Steuco summarizes the philosophy of antiquity in *Philosophia perennis*
1543	Copernicus' *De revolutionibus orbium caelestium* implies the collapse of the Aristotelian conception of the universe
1879	Leo XIII declares Thomas Aquinas the normative philosopher of Catholicism (the sanctioning of neo-Thomism)
1931	Albertus Magnus canonized
1974	To celebrate the 500th anniversary of Thomas Aquinas a monumental concordance is compiled with the help of computers

a
Auicéne perhypateticid
¶ Incipit Logica
¶ Comparatio autez
op singulare ab

b
nis hoc aliqo
cipiemus a cóitatibus

c
¶ Incipit probemkum
priuscp causam:
entiam cum sua
faceremus aut non

o
le esse. Sed nobis
lignoz ex suo
spódeat p illa.
ab extrinseco:

e
nis qui est oppositus
aut nó alicubi
op accidat disperfio.
sua totalitate eé

f
¶ Incipit liber
etiam magis
remotú: siue

A
¶ Incipit opus
accipiatur in itellectu
cum propriú de
quo nihil est

B
z occidentaliú
gnauimus ei multas
tentiam: z ramos
facilitatem

L
op ptingit in spú
bilium. z facies
illusiones in
res itelligibilioj

D
destruendum: z
habet esse effectus.
cidere ex aliqua
¶ Capitulum. VIII.

E
intestinú: qd pcedit
marina lati cozporis
fi vt in plurib?
vná canem aliquádo

g
pter hoc oz inungi
la cá cóis erit:
omyomeron z
fuerit impeditus:

h
tiganalie: z figura
op sunt tres musculi:
nó: z ppe epiglotim
spm: parú declinatq

D
ex parte domestica.
bo vident similes:
quibus magis
didimalia. Sed in

I
principia noticiam
volumus auté
z ipsa quodámodo
¶ Incipit liber

K
nosti in logicis
differentias vel
vt remaneat
per aliquid

L
per se destructione
Color igit iste
stet ab eo oib?
cantur multis modis

M
qd cótinet sub
in ea bis nasus
nó est nisi circuli
ignis est occasio

N
videlicet vt vel
mis essentialib?
primú. Nó itelligit
desiderat oio

O
nobilioze multis
tm: ita vt sit ei eé
ipediés aias
forma que possens

P
Patitur res melius
Accipitrum decez
Domo vbi sperma

¶ Finis

¶ Aduerte lector: impssor: siue bibliopol
lege serenissimi atcp excelsi dominú ex spe
li priuilegio cautum est ac definitus: ne c
liceat hec Auicenne opera imprimere:
imprimi facere: nec alibi impressa vender
hac vrbe: nec in aliquibus terris vel l
eiusdem serenissimi dominú. Sub pena v
gratia continetur: que notata est in offici
minozum aduocatozum.

Fig. 45. From *The Philosophical Works of Avicenna*, printed in Venice in 1508.

Index

abbreviations 114f
Abélard, Pierre 53ff, 76, 81ff, 87f, 92, 125, 137, 233
abstraction 197, 240
accidens 57f, 60
accidents (categ.) 61, 64, 90, 118, 147, 168, 214f, 231, 236, 244
actus hominis – actus humanus 209
actus purus 119, 200
Adam of Bremen 35
aequivocatio 97,
agent 198
actuality – potentiality **108**, 112f, 118, 156f, 168, 198, 200, 202
active intellect 112f, 121f, 207
Aix 12
Albertism 99, 164, 236
Albertus Magnus 27, 101, **174ff**, 185, 201, 204, 215
Alexander de Villa Dei 219, 254
Al-Fārābī 121
Algorismus 9
alchemy 131
Al-Khwarizmi 9
Alcuin 12, 15f, 22f
allegory 28f, 31f, 36, 189ff
Almagest 120
Amalric of Bène 131, 133
Ambrose 24, 89, 193
anagogic 28, 30, 36, 189
analogia entis 192
Analytica Posteriora 92f, 99, 103f, 121, 170, 255
Analytica Priora 99ff, 233, 255
anatomy 48, 136, 146, 151, 152, 153, 154f, 262
angels 164f, 181
animal politicum 183, 216
Anselm of Canterbury 27, 78ff, 201
Anselm of Laon 28, 54

Arabs 48, 93, 121f, 150f
arabic numbers 9
arbor consanguineitatis 73
arbor Porphyriana 56f
Aristotle 7f, 17, 55, 92f, **95ff**, 130, 163, 166, 176, 185, 187, 196, 201, 204, 209, 211, 227, 230, 232, 240, 243f, 251f, 255, 258, 265
Aristotle, prohibition against 130, 133f, 227
Aristotelianism 93, 117, 121f, 145, 150, 198f
arithmetic 9, 18
ars dictaminis 21, 132
ars memorativa 48, 160, 220, 223ff
ars moriendi 223
ars praedicandi 223
arts faculties 130, 137f, 227
artes liberales 7, 13, 15ff, 21ff, 126, 130
astrolabe 170
astrology 110, 230ff
astronomy 18, 111, 120, 170, 256
auctores 31ff
auctoritas auctoritates 77, 145, **193ff**, 253, 270ff
Augustine 4, 7, 24, 31, 74, 87, 89, 166, 176, 187, 194, 196, 203, 209, 212, 216, 240
Augustus 33
Autrecourt, Nicolas d' 251
Averroes 122, 150, 183, 204, 227, 230
Avicenna 121f, 150f, 157, 204, 230
axiom 103, 145, 181, 211

baccalaureus 127, 143, 156, 254
Bacon, Roger 172f, 186
Barbara Celarent 100, 102, 218, 234
beatitudo 211
Bede, the Venerable 9, 12, 13
being, (*ens*) **117f**, 159, 244

Benedict of Nursia 13, 161
Bernard of Chartres 41ff
Bernard of Clairvaux 36f, 83f, 166
Bernold of Constance 74ff, 76, 81
Bible interpretation 24ff, 166, 191f
biblia pauperum 190f
bliss (*felicitas*) 179, 181, 198, 209
bloodletting man 46
Bobbio 13
bodily fluids 151, 154
Boethius 7ff, 17, 22, 55, 92, 95
(pseudo)-Boethius 101
Boethius of Dacia 227ff, 230
Bologna 67ff, 76f, 138ff, 151, 153
Bonaventura 27, 163ff, 185, 196, 240
bonum commune 210, 216
brain 154f, 206f
Bulgarus 68f
Buridan, Jean 253f

Canon, Avicenna's 146, 150f
canones 49
canon law 73ff, 137, 138, 143, 225
cardinal virtues 181
Carolingian miniscule 15
Cassiodorus 7, 13, 15
categorical propositions 62f, 235, 265f
categories (*praedicamenta*) 61, 70, 108f,
    110, 118, 145f, 157, 246, 253
causes, Aristotelian 85, 118, 151f, 198,
    199, 202
chancellor 49f, 129, 137, 143f
Charlemagne 12, 22, 49
Charles VI 153
Chartres 40ff, 42ff, 49, 52
chronology 170
Church, doctors of, see *doctores
    ecclesiae*
Cicero 17, 223
circular argument, see *petitio principii*
Cîtaux 49
Clementinae 77
Cluny 49

Codex 67ff, 143
Cologne 174, 253
commentum 114
communis natura 241
communism 172, 183
computus ecclesiasticus 9
conclusio 99, 101, 277
Concordantes discordantium canonium
    76f
Consequentiae 237, 255
contradiction (*principio contradictionis*)
    118, 251
Corpus iuris canonici 77
Corpus iuris civilis 68
Courçon, Robert 130f, 132, 133f
creation 133, 164, 199f, 201f, 228, 231

Dante 90, 91, 108, 110
David of Dinant 131, 133
De aeternitate mundi 228
De anima **110f, 112f**, 237, 255
De consolatione philsophiae 7
De nuptiis Mercurii et Philologiae 17
De summo bono 228
Decree 76
decretals 77
Decretum 76f
deduction 103f, 163
Defensor pacis 217
definition 64, 95, 103, 196
democracy 172, 183, 202f, 216f
determinatio 143, 148, 175, 186
devotio moderna 232f, 248
diagnosis 157
dialectics 18
Dialogus super auctores 32f
differentia specifica 56f, 58f, 60, 61, 64,
    66, 93, 95, 207, 221
Digestum 67ff, 69ff, 138, 143
(Pseudo-)Dionysius Areopagita 26ff,
    185, 203
disputatio de quolibet 148

disputation 95, 148, 150, 186, 236f, 259f, 277ff
distinctio formalis ex natura rei 242f, 246, 253
distinctio rationalis – realis 184, 253
distinction 89, 96, 97, 188
doctor 123, 127, 138, 143
doctor communis (angelicus) 185
doctor mirabilis 172
doctor seraphicus 163
doctor subtilis 240
doctor universales 174
doctores ecclesiae 24
Doctrinale 205f, 219f, 237, 254
Dominicans 159, 161, 174f, 215
Donet 3, 17, 19f, 131, 219, 254
double truth 122, 227ff, 251, 255

efficient cause – final cause (*causa efficiens – finalis*) 118
elements, the four 110, 151
Empyrium 111, 164
ens, see being
enuntiatio 62
Erasmus of Rotterdam 240
Erfurt 237, 240, 254, 258
Es tu scholaris? 221f
eschatology, see anagogic
essence **64**, 196, 227
essens – existens 122, 189, 199
Ethica 131, 132, 172, 178, **179ff**, 184, 209
Etymologiae 10f, 76
Euclides 17
exemplarism 166, 187, 199
Extravagantes 77
eye 243, 262

faculties 133, 137, 144, 147, 150, 153
fallacia consequentis 98
fallaciae 233
felicitas (intellectualis), see bliss
fides quarens intellectum 79

fides – ratio 181, 184, 193, 196
figures, syllogistic 100, 102
firmament 109, 111, 156, 164
flatus vocis 60
florilegia 38
form – matter **118**, 121, 168, 215
formalitates 242, 246
Franciscans 159, 169
Frederick Barbarossa 138
fundamentum in re 56, 241
futura contingentia 63, 273

Galen 44, 151, 158
Garden of Eden 211ff
Gaunilo 80
Gentilis de Fulgineo 156
genus 56f, 59, 64, 95, 202, 217, 221f
geometry 17, 18, 105, 220
glossa interlinearis 54
glossa ordinaria 28, 54
glossators 67ff
glosses 31, 114
good, the (*bonum*) 179, 183
grace – nature 43, 194, 196ff
grammar 17, 18, 238f
grammatica speculativa 238
Gratian 76f, 87, 91, 138
Greek 24, 172
Gregory the Great 24, 29, 156f, 164
Grosseteste, Robert 172, 178
Guido of Arezzo 21
Gustavus I Vasa 219

habitus 179, 209f, 214, 273, 279
haecceitas 241
Hebrew 24, 172
Henry II 170
Hippocrates 45, 48, 151
historia 30
Historia calamitatum 54
history 35, 104
Holcot, Robert 251
Hollandrinus 255

Hrabanus Maurus 32
Hrotswit 35
Hugo of Orleans 28
Hugo of St Victor 40
Hus, John 255
hypothesis 103

Ignatius de Loyola 248
illumination theory 168, 196, 240
immortality 112f, 121f, 227, 231, 255
impediments to marriage 73
impetus (violentus) 253f, 255
inceptio 127, 245
individua 56f, 59
induction 95, 103f, 180, 250
Innocent 111, 129
insolubilia 101, 237, 255, 259
Institutiones 67ff
intellects 121f, 165
intellectus agens – possibilis, see *active*
  and *passive intellects*
intention 85, 209
intentiones primae – secundae 57
intuition 241
Irnerius 67ff, 91, 137
Isagoge 7, 55, 253, 258
Isidore of Seville 9f, 76, 85
ius ubique docendi 136

Jacobus 70
James of Venice 92
Jarrow 13
Jerome 24, 194
Johannes Peyligk 154
John XXI, see *Petrus Hispanus*
John Duns Scotus 101, 125, 240ff, 245,
  253
John of Erfurt 111
John of Garlandia 220
John of Genua 220
John of Holywood 9, 170
John of Paris 217
John of Salisbury 42ff, 92, 106

jurisdiction, academic 135
justice 67, 180
Justinian 65, 67ff, 138

knowledge, theory of 159, 163, 168, 196,
  238, 240ff, 245, 253
Koran 121f

Lanfranc 78
Latin 3, 55, 125, 219f, 233, 239
lectio 86, 114, 143, 148, 150, 257
lectio divina 13
Legenda aurea 33
Leipzig 206
Leo XIII 215
lex aeterna – lex naturalis 210
Liber extra 77
Liber sextus 77
liberal arts, see *artes liberales*
licentia docendii 127
littera 85, 114
loci 70f, 78, 95f, 101, 145
logica nova 92, 106, 130
love 110, 212, 243
Luther, Martin 250, 277ff

magister 127, 137
Margarita philosophica 225 (and figures
  passim)
Marsilius of Padua 217
Martianus Capella 9, 17ff, 223
maior – minor 99
materia prima 198
materialism 133
matricula 128, 143
Matthaeus Vindobonensis 220
Maulevelt, Thomas 254
Mauricius 131
maxims 68, 96
medicine 44ff, 137, 141, 146, **150ff**
meditation 38, 43
memorization 18, 219ff

memory 113, 119, 155, 205, 206, 219ff, 223ff
mendicant orders 159ff, 169
Metaphysica **117ff**, 121, 131, 132, 213, 228
metaphysics 17, 104, **117ff**, 193f, 197, 198
middle way 179
Mirecourt, Jean de 251
mnemonic rhymes 219f
modal propositions 235
modi, syllogistic 100f
modi significandi 238f, 254
modists 238f, 254
motion 108f, 110f
music, 18, 21

Naples 185
nations 139, 140
natural law 67, 180, 183, 210, 217
negative theology 189
neo-Platonism 121, 185, 203
new logic, see *logica nova*
Niavis, Paulus 258ff, 273ff
nominalism 57, 60, 238f, 240, 245f, 248, 251–257, 258ff
Novellae 67

Obligationes (Obligatoria) 237, 255, 259
Occam, William 57, 101, 159, 238, 245f, 251
Occam's razor 239, 246
Occamism 101, 251ff
Olaus, Johannis Gutho 252
old logic, see *vetus ars*
ontological proof of God's existence 79f, 201
opposition, square of 62f, 235
Oresme, Nicolas 253
Organon 95ff
Oxford 134, 170ff

Pantheism 133
Parens scientiarum 135

Paris 40, 53, 106, **125ff**, 138, 159, 161, 170, 174, 227ff, 232ff, 256, 275f
Parmenides 101
parva logicalia 101, 258, 281
passive intellect 112f, 121f, 204, 207, 227
Paul 28, 34, 159, 214
per accidens 268
Perihermeneias 55, 62f, 255
petitio principii 96
Peter Lombard 17, 87ff
Petrus Hispanus 101, 102, 230, 235, 236, 265ff, 279ff
Petrus Ravenna 225
Philippe II Augustus 128
philosophia prima 197
philosophy 163, 166f, 188, 193f, 196f, 228f, 293
Physica 106f, 118, 161, 188, 237
physics 108f, 112
physicus – medicus 156
Placentinus 69
Plato 7, 15, 40, 167, 176, 181, 183
pluralitas formarum 242
politia 183
Politica 178, 183f
positive law 180
post hoc, propter hoc 98
potentia absoluta – potentia ordinata 247
praedicamenta, see *categories*
predicables 56f, 59f, 232
premises 99, 101
primum mobile 111, 164
primus motor 108, 110f, 121, 198f, 202
Priscian 17, 130f, 233
privilegium fori 128
problem 95, 101
promotion 125, 127, 139
propositions 62f, 235, 259
proprietates terminorum 236
proprium 56, 60
prototype 88
Ptolemy 17, 120
Pythagoras 9, 17

quadrivium 15ff, 105
quaestio 87f, 145, 156, **185ff**, 257, 268ff, 275ff
quaestio disputata 148
quidditas 64
quinta essentia 110
Quintilian 223
quodlibet 148

Rabelais, François 240, 275
ratio – auctoritas 145
realism 57, 60, 241, 251ff
rector 137, 141, 143
reflex universals, see predicables
Reisch, Gregorius 225 (and figures passim)
reportatio 86
res – signum 87
responsibility 180, 232
revelation 164, 177, 182, 188, 194
rhetoric 17, 18, 19, 36f, 131, 132
Roman law 67ff, 127, 137, 138, 143

sacrament 87f, 9ʋ, 147f, 191, 214f
Salerno 47, 141, 151, 153
Sallust 35
scepticism 240, 251
scholasticus 49f, 125, 129
Scotism 101, 240ff, 254
Seneca 17
senses 113, 154, 196, **204ff**
sensus communis 113, 154, 206
sensus compositus – sensus divisus 97, 279
sensus interiores 154, 204ff
Sentences 87ff, 126, 185
sibyl 33
Sic et Non 81f
Siger of Brabant 227
Sigismund 219
simpliciter – secundum quid 270
solmization 21
Sophistici Elenchi 95ff, 233, 255
sophistry 217, 219f, 233, 236

sores, man of 46f
Sortes 57, 233ff
soul **112f**, 176f, 204
species 56f, 59, 64, 95f
speculation 119, 166, 181, 184
sphere (instrument) 170f, 256
spheres 110, 111, 121, 164f
state 183, 216f
statutes 129, 135, 137
students union 139f
studium generale 135
sublunary world 110f
substance **61**, 64, 90, 118, 147, 168, 214f, 222, 238
substantial – accidental form 198
Summa theologica 174, 185, 249ff, 268ff
summae 132
Summulae logicales (Tractatus) 102, 234, 265ff
supposition 234f, 253f
surgery 153
Sutton, John 255
syllogisms 70, 72, 97ff, **99ff**
syncategoremes – categoremes 233, 254

tabula rasa 194, 206f, 223, 240
temperament, theory of 151, 154
Tempier, Estienne 134, 215, 230ff
Terence 32, 35
terminology 55, 125, 241f
terms, logical 233ff, 253f
Thabit 153
theodicy problem 122, 202f
theological virtues 214
theology 9, 24ff, 163f, 168, 186, **187ff**, 228f, 243f, 246
theorica – practica 156
Thomas Aquinas 27, 57, 91, 101, 174, 178, **185–218**, 223f, 230, 240f, 243f, 253, 268ff
Thomism 101, 174, 198f, 253
Toledo 93, 150
topic 70, 78, 95f, 131, 132, 201

Toulouse 134, 135
transcendental attributes 118, 159
translations 7f, 48, 92f, 125, 178
transubstantiation 90, 147, 214f, 255
trivium 15ff, 42
tropology 28, 30, 36, 189
types 191

unctio 36, 169
universale ante rem, in re, post rem 254
universalia 53, 56ff, 245ff, 254
universitas 129, 135, 139
university 125ff
Uppsala 111, 114, 253
uti – frui 87, 176

venerabilis inceptor 245
ventricles of the brain 148f, 154f, 192f,
    194, 206f
vetus ars 55, 64, 95, 130, 233
via – patria 211

via antiqua – via moderna 251ff, 258ff
via communis 257
Victor, St 40
Vienna 258
Virgil 32, 33
virtue (*virtus*) 169ff, 179ff, 215, 231
virtus intellectualis – moralis 179ff, 231
virtutes cardinales, see cardinal virtues
vita activa – contemplativa 184
Vivarium 7
Vives, Juan Luis 279ff
voluntarism 226f, 230f, 243f, 247f

will 180, 209ff, 231, 243ff, 247f
William of Champeaux 53, 126
William of Moerbeke 178, 185
wisdom (*sapientia*) 119, 166f, 181, 188,
    243
Woodham, Adam 251

Zodiac man 46